50

 JORDAN SCHNITZER
MUSEUM OF ART WSU

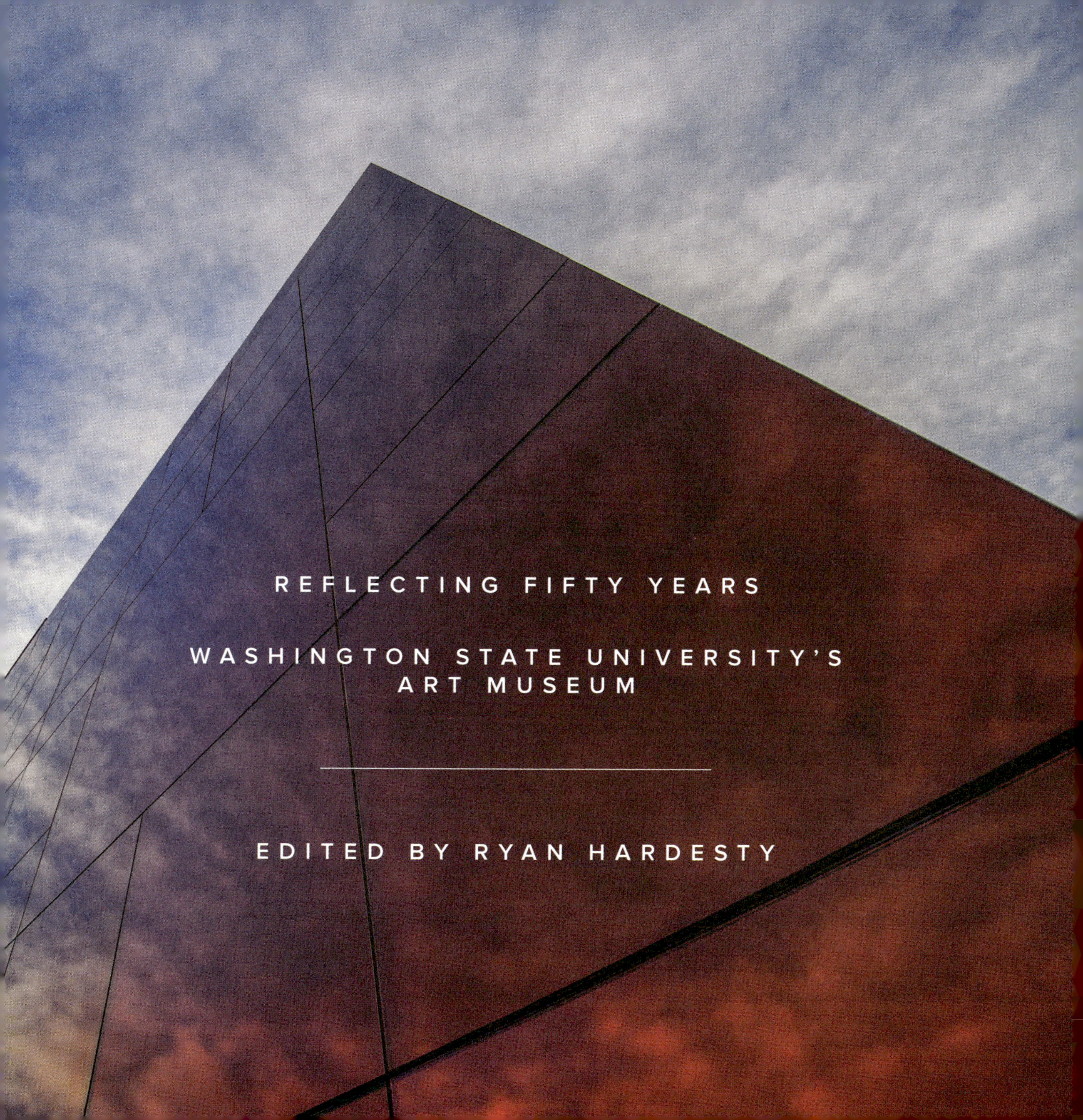

REFLECTING FIFTY YEARS

WASHINGTON STATE UNIVERSITY'S
ART MUSEUM

_____

EDITED BY RYAN HARDESTY

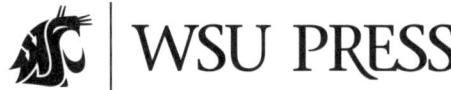

WSU PRESS

JORDAN SCHNITZER
MUSEUM OF ART WSU

Washington State University Press
PO Box 645910
Pullman, Washington 99164-5910
Phone: 800-354-7360
Email: wsupress@wsu.edu
Website: wsupress.wsu.edu

Jordan Schnitzer Museum of Art WSU
PO Box 647301
Pullman, Washington 99164-7301
Website: museum.wsu.edu

Library of Congress Cataloging-in-Publication Data is available.

Cover design by Patrick Brommer
Graphic design by Tracy Randall
IMAGE CREDIT (previous spread) Bob Hubner, WSU Photo Services
IMAGE CREDIT (following page) @NicLehoux

The Washington State University Pullman campus is located on the homelands of the Niimíipuu (Nez Perce) Tribe and the Palus people. We acknowledge their presence here since time immemorial and recognize their continuing connection to the land, to the water, and to their ancestors. The Jordan Schnitzer Museum of Art WSU and WSU Press are committed to fostering a deeper understanding of the contributions of the Native peoples of the Pacific Northwest.

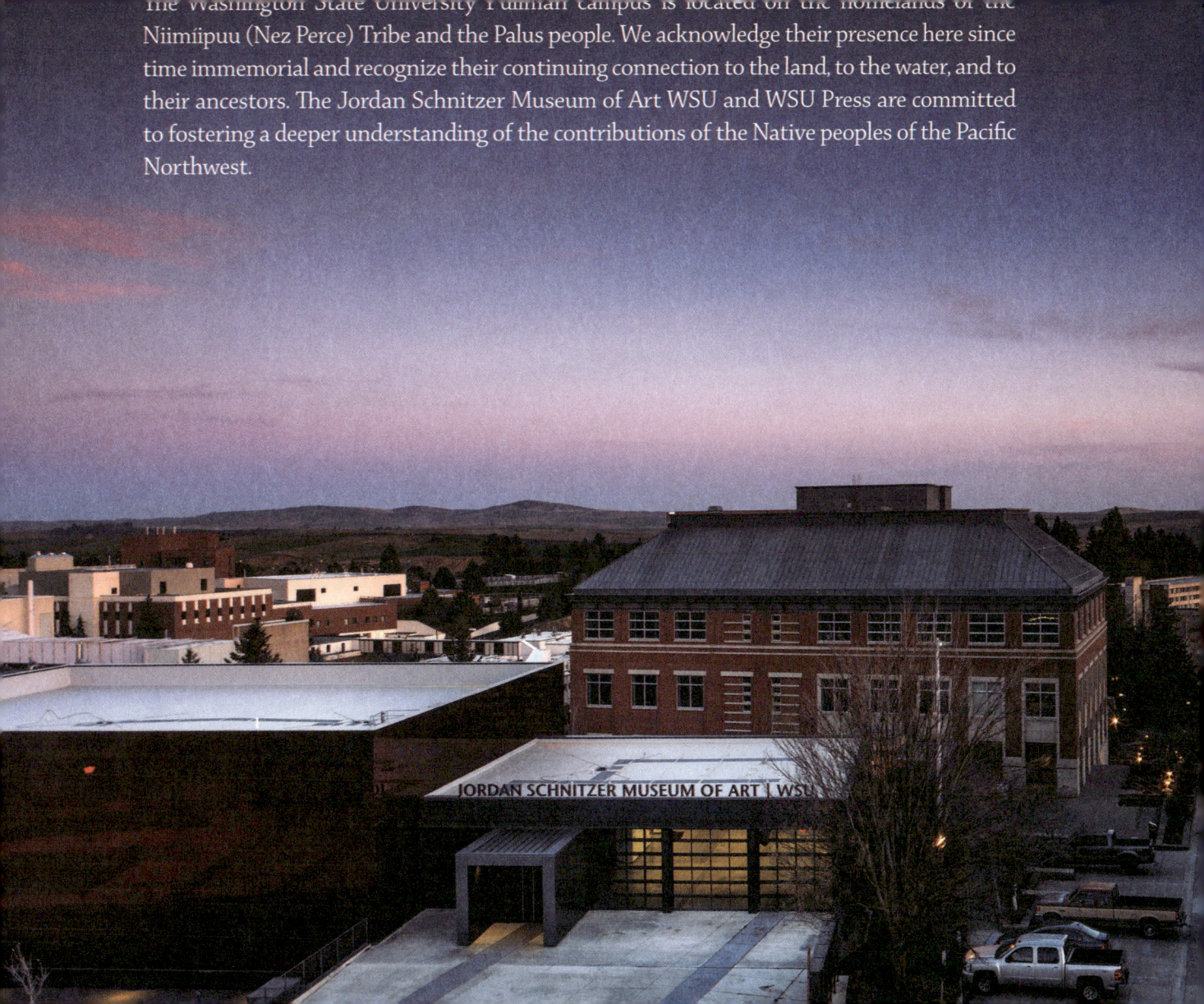

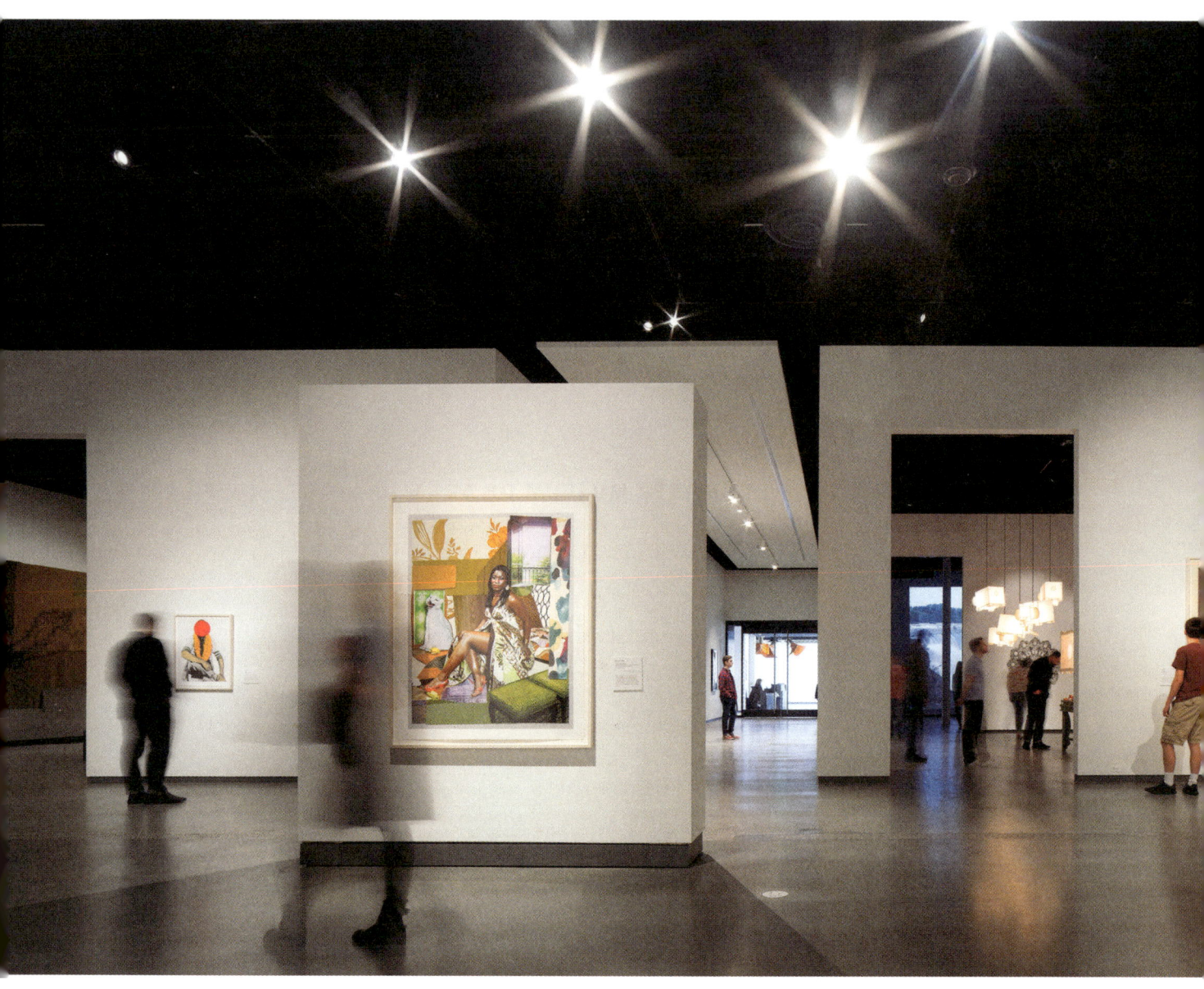

Person(a): Portraiture from the Collections of Jordan D. Schnitzer and His Family Foundation, 2018
Photo: @NicLehoux

CONTENTS

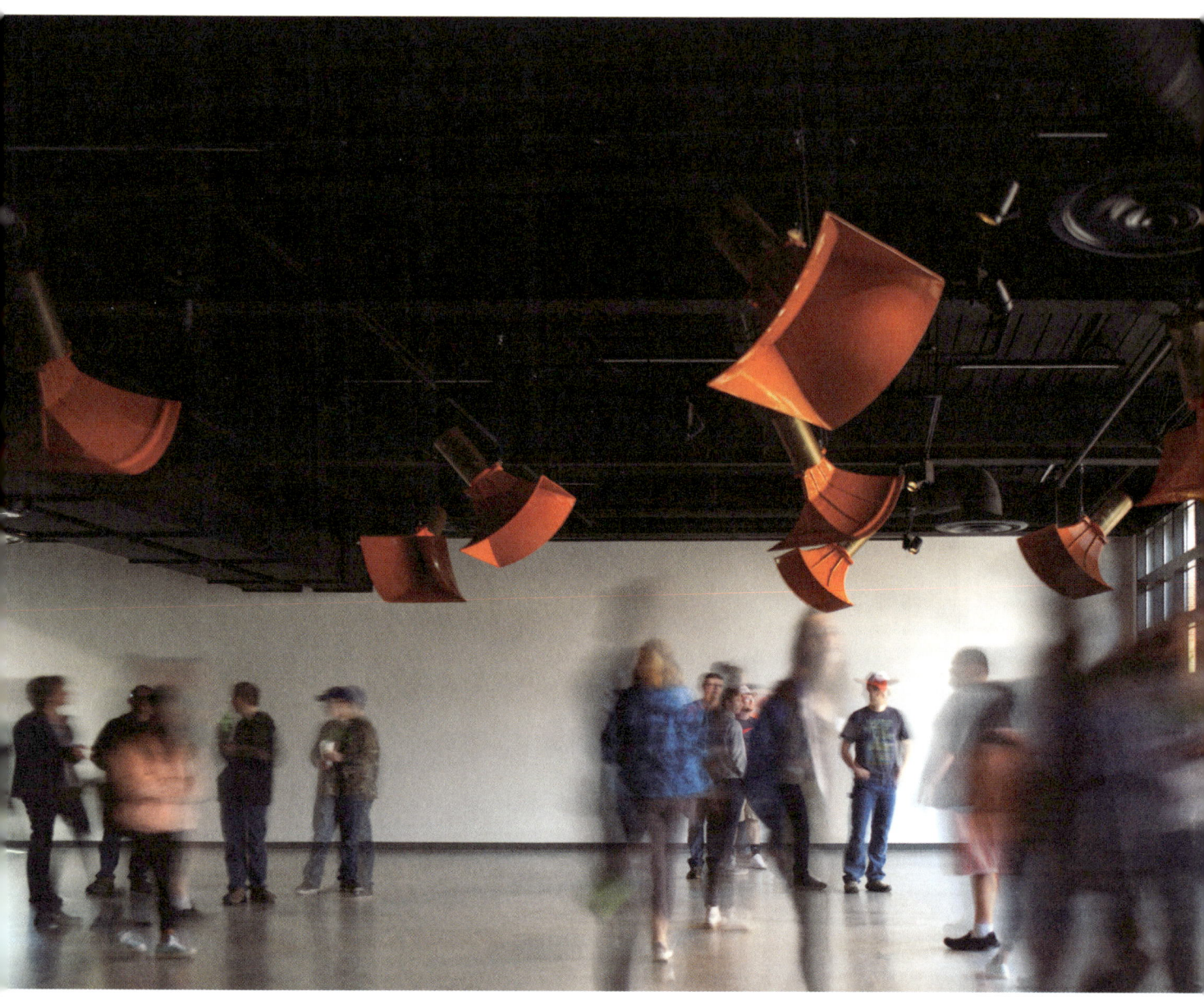

Trimpin's *Ambiente432* was commissioned for the 2018 inauguration of the Jordan Schnitzer Museum of Art WSU
Photo: @NicLehoux

INTRODUCTION

REFLECTING FIFTY YEARS:
CELEBRATING WASHINGTON STATE UNIVERSITY'S ART MUSEUM

Ryan Hardesty, Executive Director

Museums are revered spaces for many. They hold both unknowable mysteries and timely reckonings, culture made visible by our most innovative and creative. Museums teach patience and curiosity and reward in inspiration and even revelation. Along the way, they encourage comfort within ambiguity—a critical ingredient that moves us toward more expansive ways of thinking and being. When we describe this museum, we often do so as an alternative classroom—a dynamic space to learn together where we view the world through the lens of art and artists.

Museums have certainly been the most valued spaces in my life and I am honored to be leading this museum with our brilliant team into its 50th year. With any project steeped in historical review, you are made more aware of those who came before, their successive eras, never-ending work, accomplishments, occasional missteps, and more than anything, efforts to build something of lasting meaning and utility.

Where would we be had inaugural director Harvey West not petitioned the university for the establishment of the first-ever art museum on the campus of Washington State University? His proposal eventually resulted in a presidential-level committee that worked regularly, and on July 31, 1974, submitted their findings as to the merit of a campus art museum. Subsequent counsel was sought from across the spectrum of the university—central administration, deans, department chairs, and faculty. After much deliberation, President Glenn Terrell in September 1974 established the "Washington State University Museum of Art."

Or without curator and director Bruce Guenther's moxie to create an exhibition and lecture program throughout the remainder of the 1970s in Pullman, Washington, that could rival any other? He metaphorically planted a flag in the Palouse soil as a place for the cultural zeitgeist, where students and community would learn from the nation's most relevant artists and scholars, including Robert Smithson, Judy Chicago, Robert Motherwell, and Mark Di Suvero. What an auspicious beginning for a

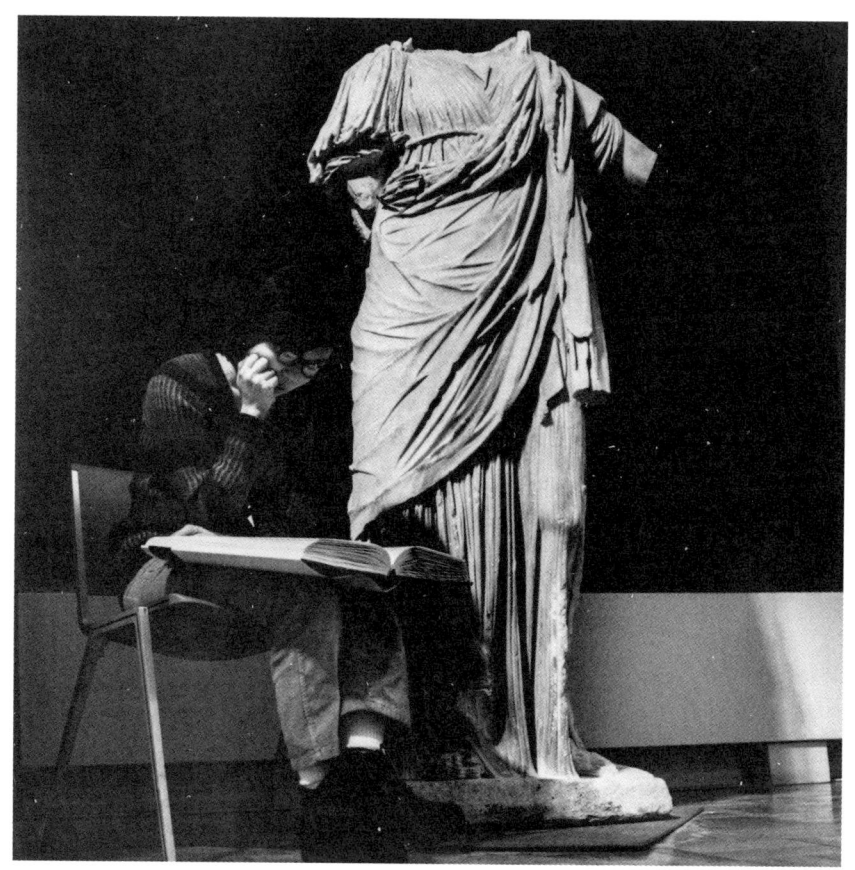

Rae Iwamoto reads next to a statue that is part of an exhibition from the Getty Collection, December 13, 1972. Objects from the Getty were featured at WSU for multiple exhibitions over a span of years

Photo: WSU Libraries' Manuscripts, Archives, and Special Collections

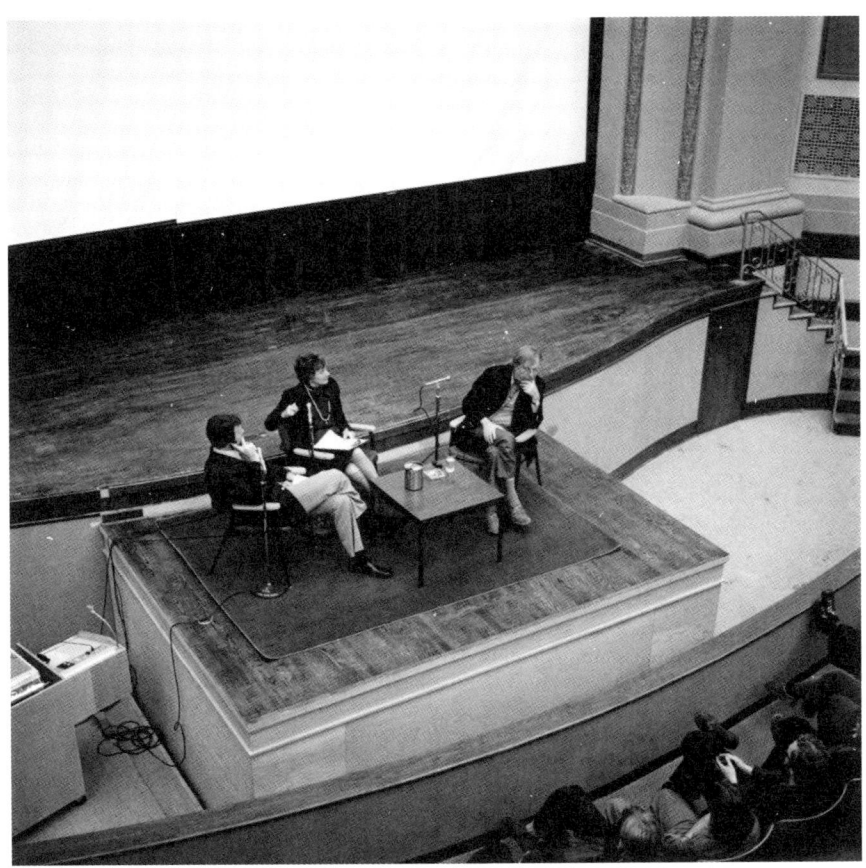

Museum of Art director Harvey West (left) leads a discussion with art collector Virginia Wright (center) and artist Robert Motherwell (right) in Bryan Hall on November 8, 1975, at the two-day symposium on American printmaking. The event took place during the featured exhibition *American Printmaking 1960–1975: A Major Survey Exhibition of Directions in American Printmaking*

Photo: WSU Libraries' Manuscripts, Archives, and Special Collections

fledgling museum emerging in the most unlikely of places. During director Patricia Watkinson's long tenure throughout the 1980s and 1990s, great care was given to cultivating—perhaps nurturing is the better term—an immense family of devoted museum friends. What we call community engagement these days was in fact something closer to an "it takes a village" approach to standing up a museum program to thrive. From this support network—community and university faculty who fell in love with the museum's charge—emerged what may be considered the museum's bedrock: a host of people, funds, and endowments that we rely upon to this day.

When Chris Bruce, a highly respected museum professional from Seattle, arrived in Pullman to assume his role as director of the museum in 2003, it sent a wave of excitement across the regional arts community—something decidedly artistic was brewing in a land more commonly associated with Cougar athletics and agricultural sciences. I certainly felt it from my museum post in Spokane. In tandem with presenting and publishing heady curatorial projects, he went about testing the waters to build a new museum facility that would make the arts unmistakably visible. The campaign that would ultimately result in the opening of the Jordan Schnitzer Museum of Art at WSU in

April 2018 was both strategic and a nearly decade-and-a-half effort. It brought together university leadership and project managers alongside steering committees, architects, and designers, as well as hundreds of supporters, and of course, the transformational patronage of Jordan D. Schnitzer, for whom the new facility is named. Once you encounter architect Jim Olson's now iconic exterior, aka the "Crimson Cube," there is no mistaking that this is a place for innovation and creativity. Within the interior, a sequence of perfectly-scaled galleries carry the names of those—Smith, Bruce, Floyd, Borth, Creighton, Harmon, and Wright—who made the vision a reality.

If you need more validation as to the museum's newfound visibility and integration into the academic experience, WSU men's basketball coach David Riley was recently asked why he wanted the job. He responded, "...think about it. It's Washington State. You look around [the campus], these facilities, the school. It's an amazing institution. There's a dang art museum right next to the athletic facilities. It's a university."

My own place in all of this began with a phone call in the summer of 2013. On the other end of the line was then director Chris Bruce, making me aware of a new art museum on Washington State University's horizon. They had fought for and

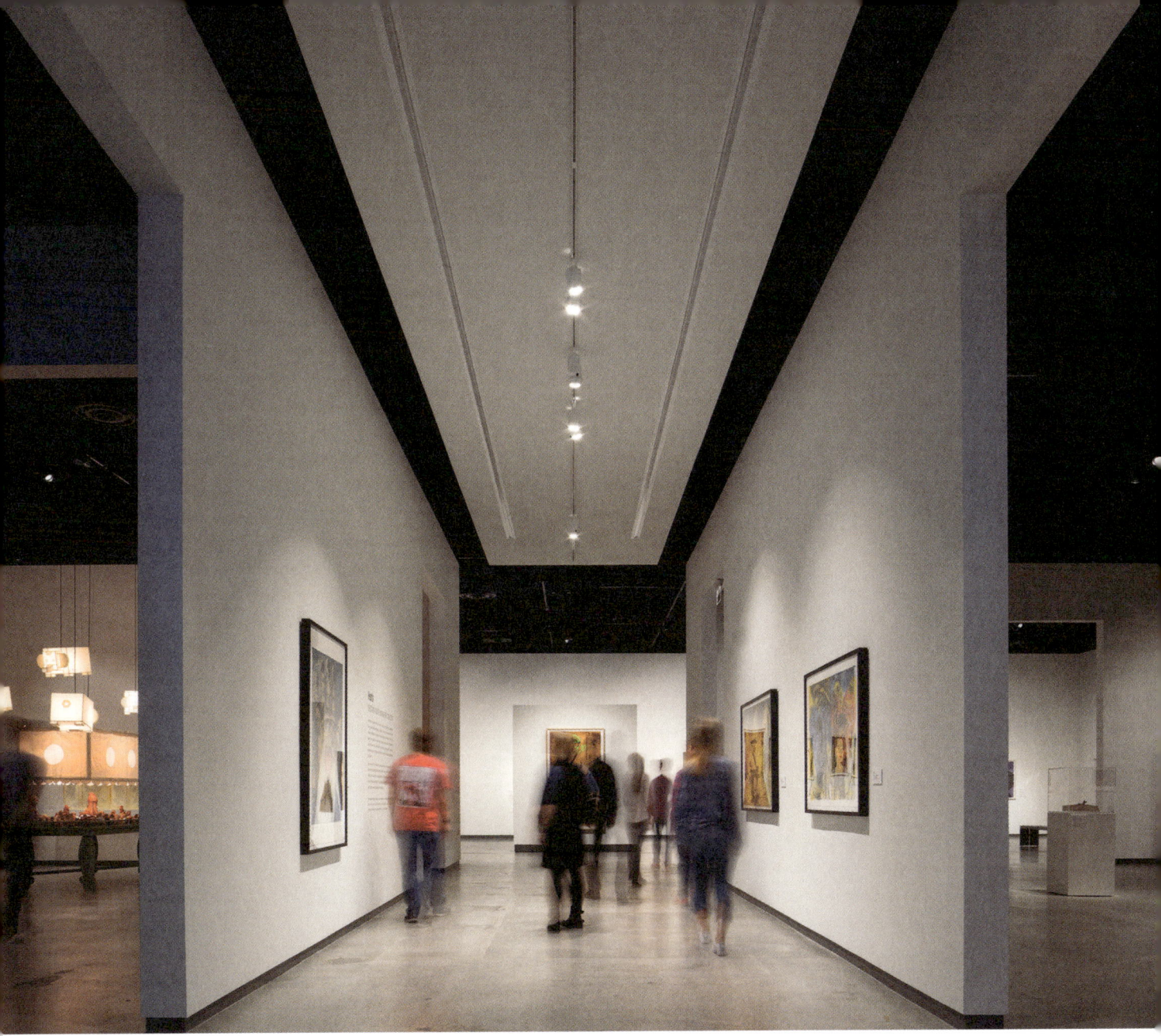

Inaugural exhibitions at the JSMA WSU featuring
Hearts: Selections from the Jim Dine Print Collection in the central Smith Gallery, 2018

Photo: @NicLehoux

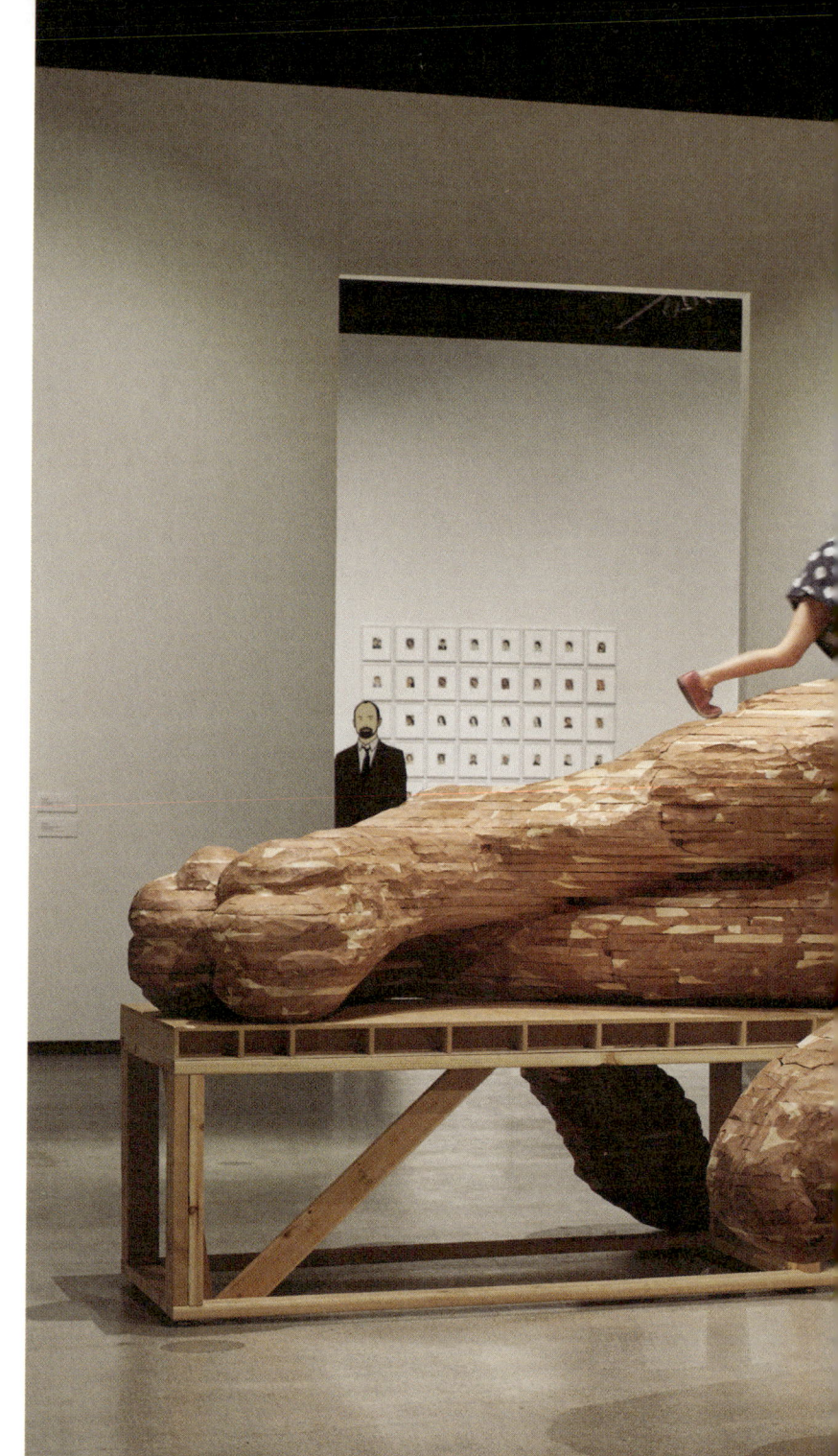

The exhibition
*Marie Watt: Companion Species
(Underbelly)* as seen in 2018

Photo: Benjamin Benschneider / OTTO

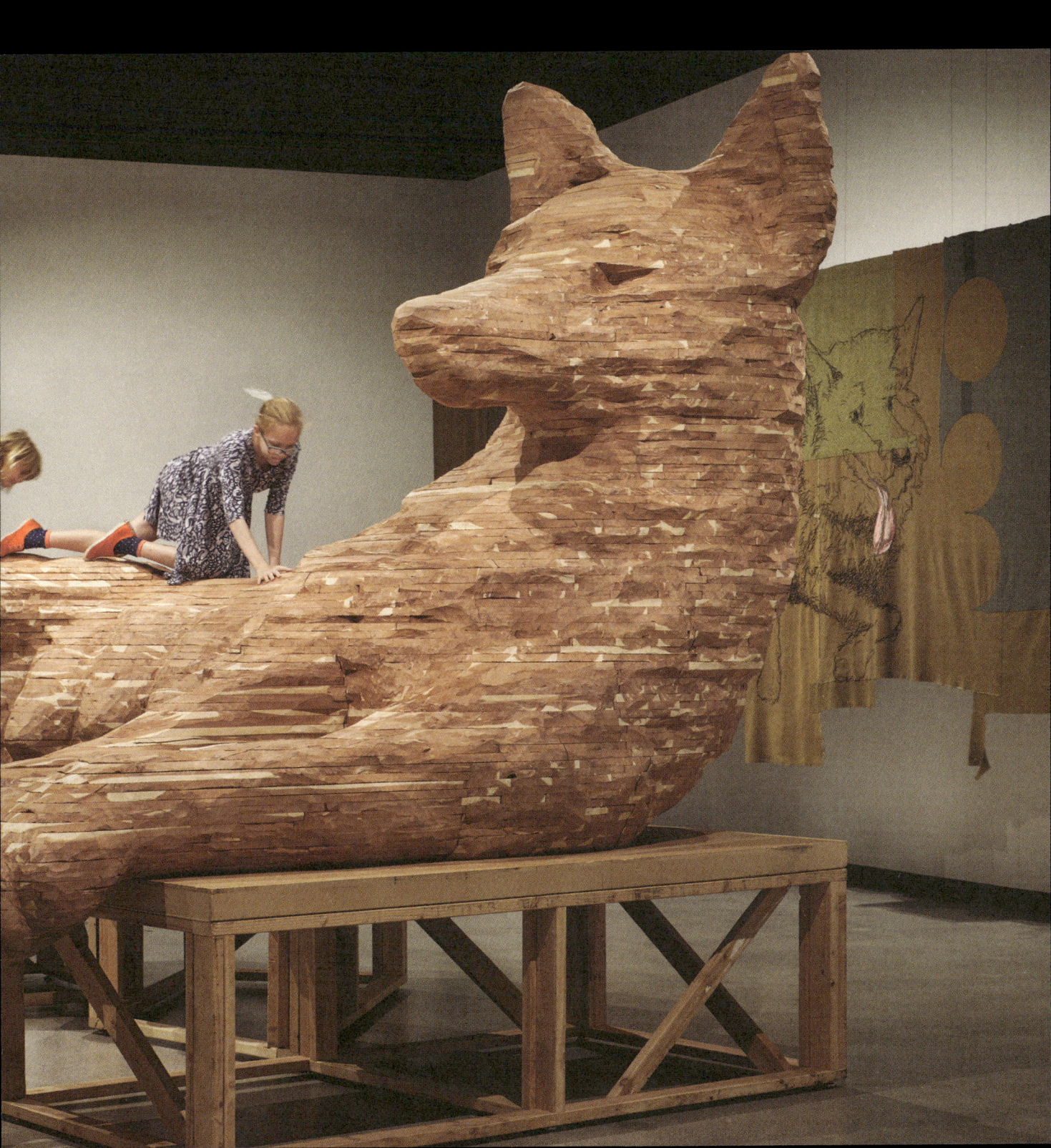

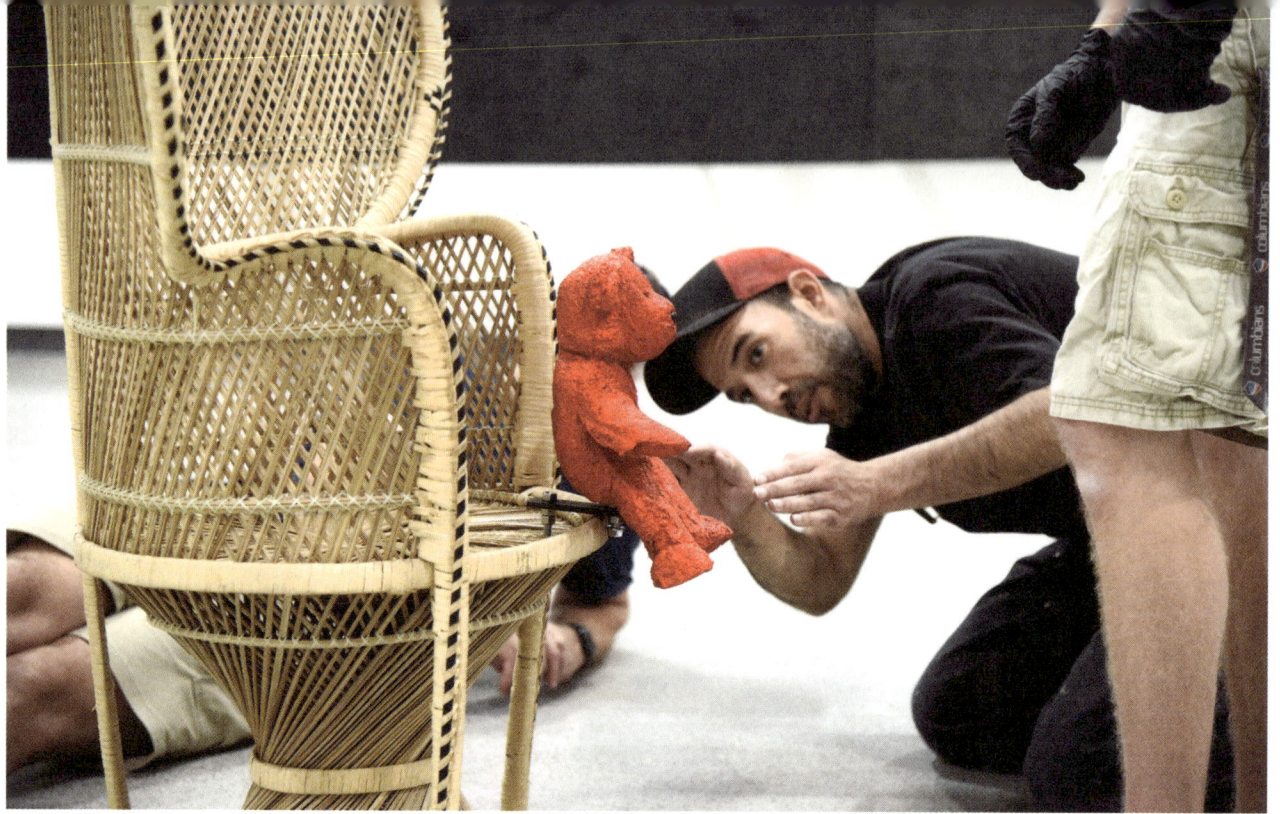

The artist installing *Juventino Aranda: Esperé Mucho Tiempo Pa Ver* on August 12, 2022
Photo: Kristin Becker

secured a site at the heart of campus; funding was coming into place. After deliberations with my family, we made the move to Pullman in the summer of 2014, and I joined the most dedicated team, ultimately led by interim director and longtime associate director Anna-Maria Shannon, who brought the new museum to fruition after Chris's retirement in 2016.

Since the new facility's inauguration, we have ridden a wave of curatorial projects balancing a long-held belief that our students, faculty, and community—whether from Washington State, Washington, DC, or the world—deserve an exhibition program that is national, even international, in scope. At the same time, we work within the context of a land-grant institution

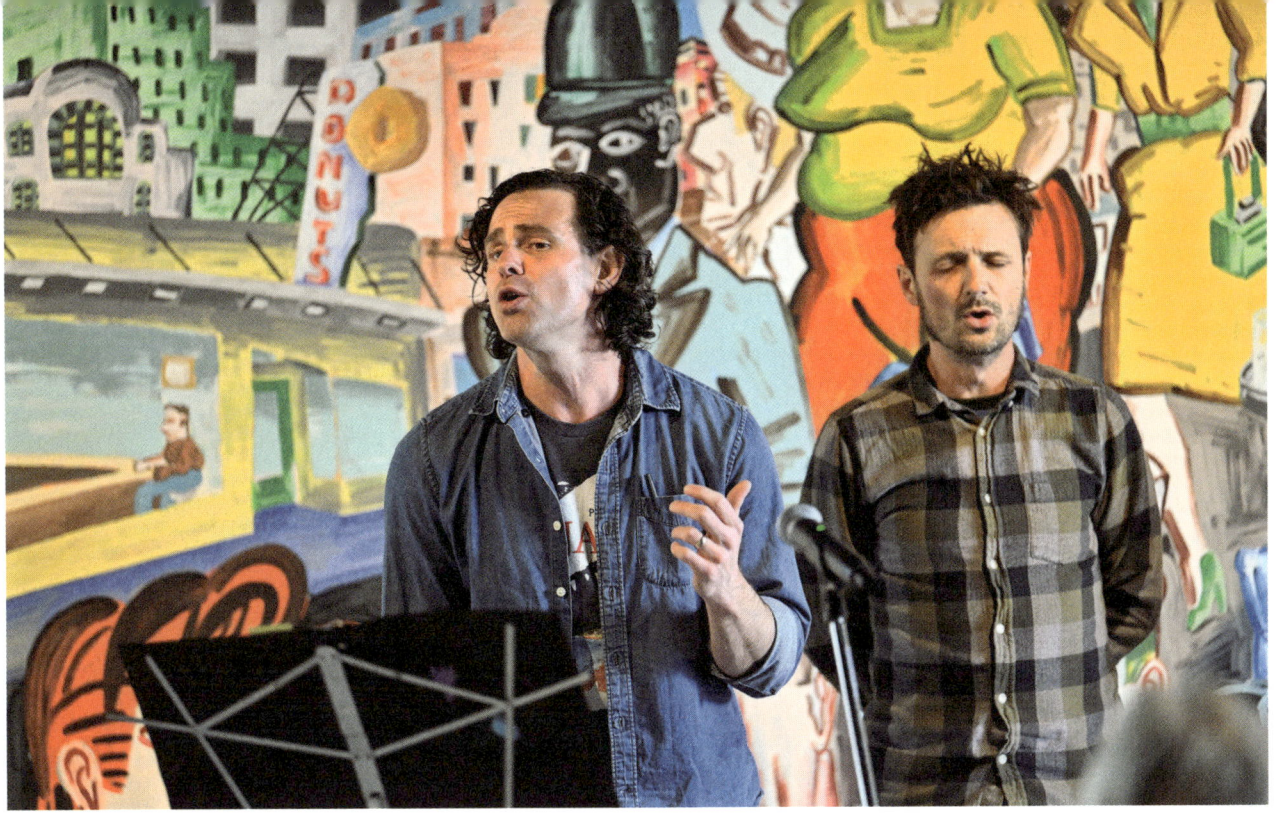

Indie Folk: Sounds from the Northwest concert with a cappella group Bigger Boat singing sea shanties and maritime songs, April 2022

Photo: WSU Photo Services

dedicated to serving local communities and helping tell their stories.

To this end, the last six years have seen aspirational exhibitions and programs that have aimed to fundamentally express and improve the experience of our shared humanity. Significant artists from across the Pacific Northwest, such as Marie Watt, Jeffry Mitchell, and Trimpin, as well as Juventino Aranda and Keiko Hara, have been presented alongside projects examining the works of Polly Apfelbaum, Louise Bourgeois, Sky Hopinka, Alison Saar, Wangechi Mutu, and so many others. This year, our museum organized and put forward a sweeping survey of the multi-faceted work of Jeffrey Gibson. I can't help but smile when thinking of the thousands of visitors in

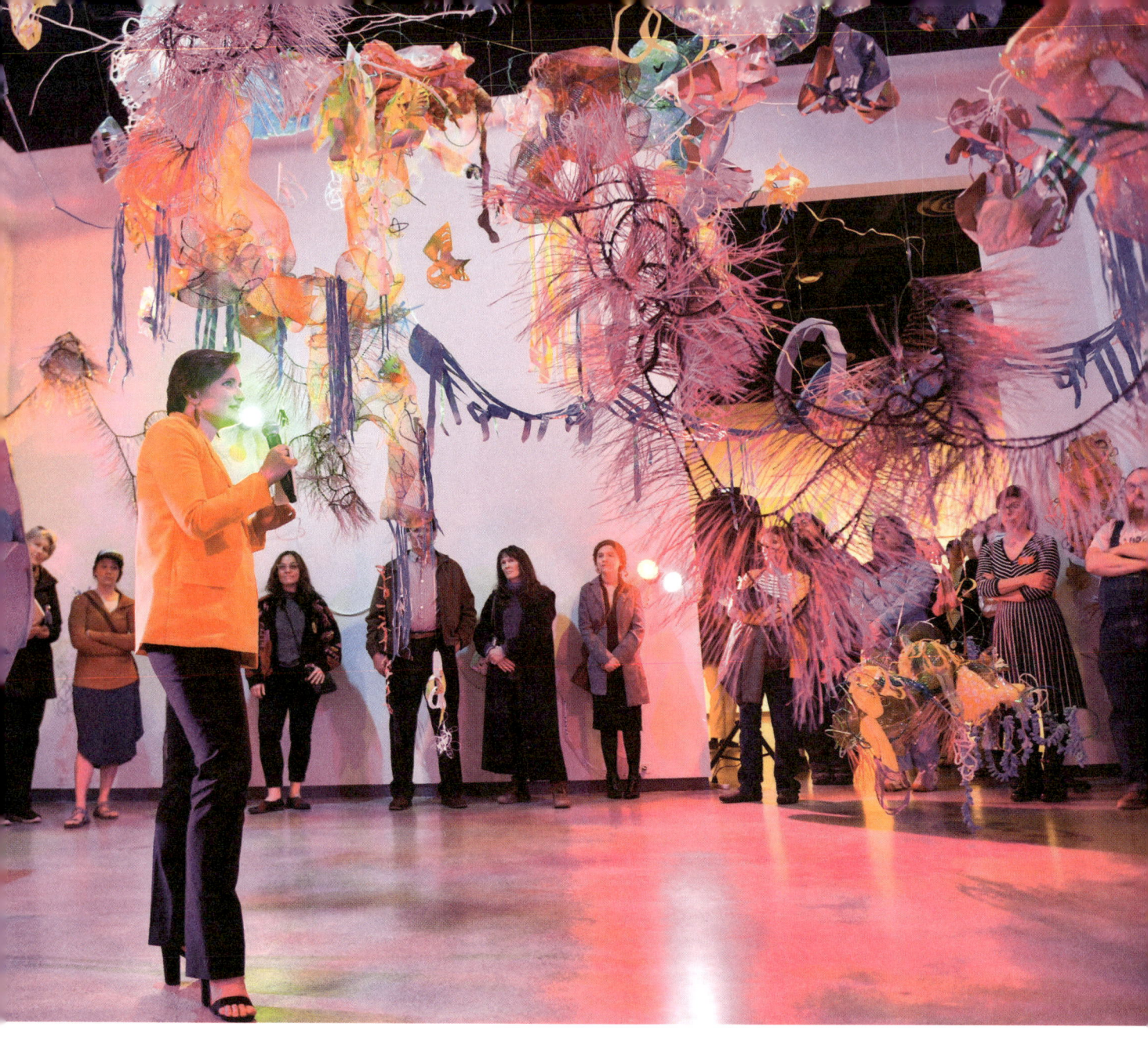

Siri Stensberg's artist talk during
the *MFA Thesis Exhibition* on April 1, 2022

Photo: WSU Photo Services

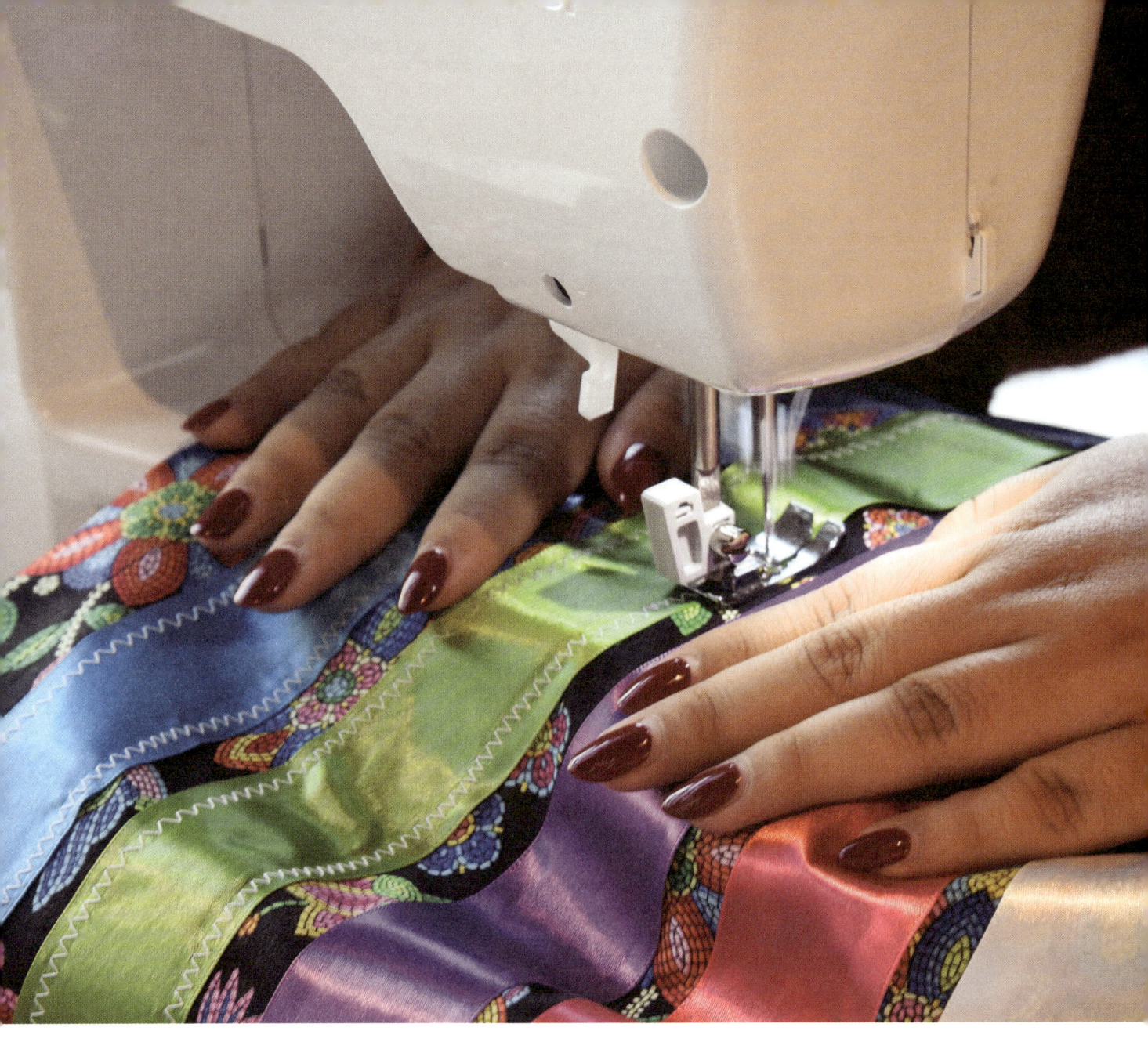

A ribbon skirt and shirt workshop on October 12, 2023
was led by WSU's Native American Student Center

Photo: Kristin Becker

Pullman who experienced his uplifting vision for Indigenous empowerment just months before he was to represent the United States of America at the prestigious 2024 Venice Biennale.

The origin of the term "curator" comes from the Latin root "curare," which means "to care for" or "to take care of." Over the past five decades, hundreds and hundreds of individuals have been instrumental in caring for WSU's art museum. We extend our deepest appreciation to all past museum staff and museum friends, whose ceaseless efforts have been integral to the museum's journey. Their efforts have opened doors to innumerable visitors who have found inspiration within our galleries.

In similar fashion, this publication required a considerable community effort, and my list of acknowledgements is frankly too lengthy to publish in full. However, it is important to state it would never have been possible without the dedication and collaboration of colleagues, supporters, and friends—all of whom played their respective roles in bringing this commemoration to life.

I wish to thank each of our essay writers—Patricia Grieve Watkinson, Chris Bruce, and Sean Elwood—who enthusiastically accepted my invitation to chronicle the history of the art museum and its growing collections. I have been fortunate to count these three individuals as cherished mentors and some of the museum's greatest torchbearers. The "many voices" section of the publication presents nearly thirty reflections from a selection of those who have engaged with the museum across time—artists, gallery owners, WSU leadership and faculty, supporters and community members, as well as museum staff—and we are exceedingly honored to share their words here.

I work with an immensely dedicated museum team and this publication required their steadfast involvement from start to finish. In particular, Kira MacPherson, the museum's director of development, led the effort to digitize over 4000 archived posters, photographs, and slides with our partners at WSU's Manuscripts, Archives & Special Collections. The fruits of this labor may be enjoyed within this volume as well as online at the museum's 50th anniversary website created by Kira and marketing manager Debby Stinson, who also played an indispensable role as editor for the book's text and images, ensuring the accuracy and clarity of our content. Kristin Becker, the museum's curator of education & programs, and Ann Saberi, collection manager, were both essential in their efforts to engage our contributors, proof text, and prepare images from the collection. Karey Strong, associate director, not only kept us all in line but made sure things ran smoothly while we worked on this very special project.

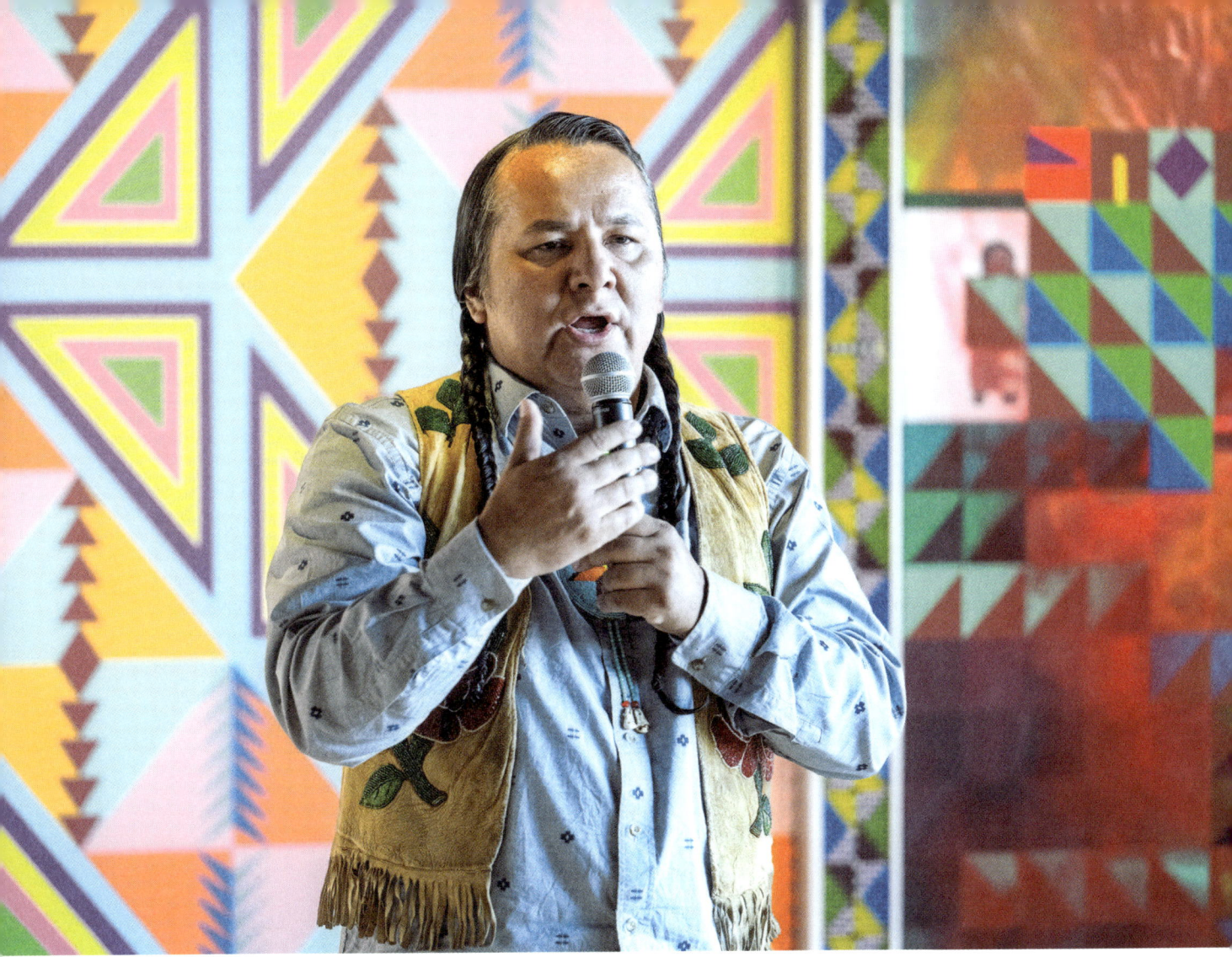

Nakia Williamson-Cloud speaking during the opening program for *Jeffrey Gibson: They Teach Love, From the Collections of Jordan D. Schnitzer and His Family Foundation* on September 19, 2023

Photo: Dal Perry

To the staff at WSU Press—genuine appreciation goes to Linda Bathgate for shepherding the project with skill and enthusiasm as we brought this book to press. Melissa Smith facilitated the design and printing stages, and Tracy Randall's graphic design brought balance to this anniversary publication.

Finally, a very special set of recognitions is reserved for our publication's donors. We begin with past WSU president Sam Smith and Pat Smith, herself an avid museum supporter and former docent, who graciously underwrote the publication through a substantial gift. Additional and valued support came from Keith Peoples, J. Scott Patnode, and members of the museum's Advisory Council.

One of our museum friends recently observed, "Great universities deserve great art museums." I couldn't agree more. Our belief has always been that the museum is perfectly positioned to enhance the campus experience, to expand dialogue and cultural understanding, and just as importantly, to provide a space for reflection, beauty, challenge, and creative renewal. Through our staff, volunteers, community members, donors, and visitors, we will continue to fulfill our mission of inspiring, engaging, and educating through the power of art for decades to come.

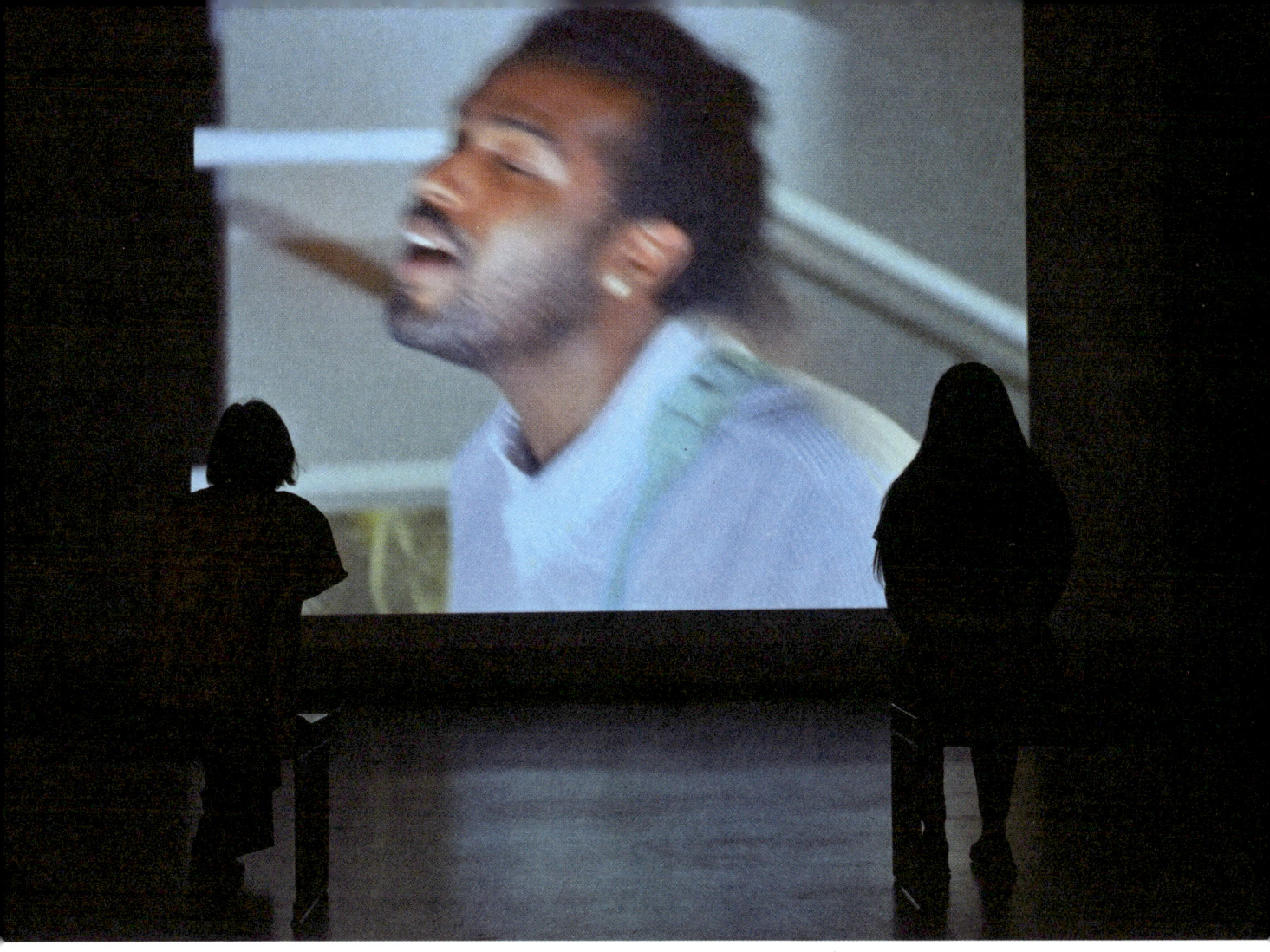

Visitors with Sky Hopinka's film *Lore* on June 14, 2022
Photo: WSU Photo Services

INSTITUTIONAL HISTORY

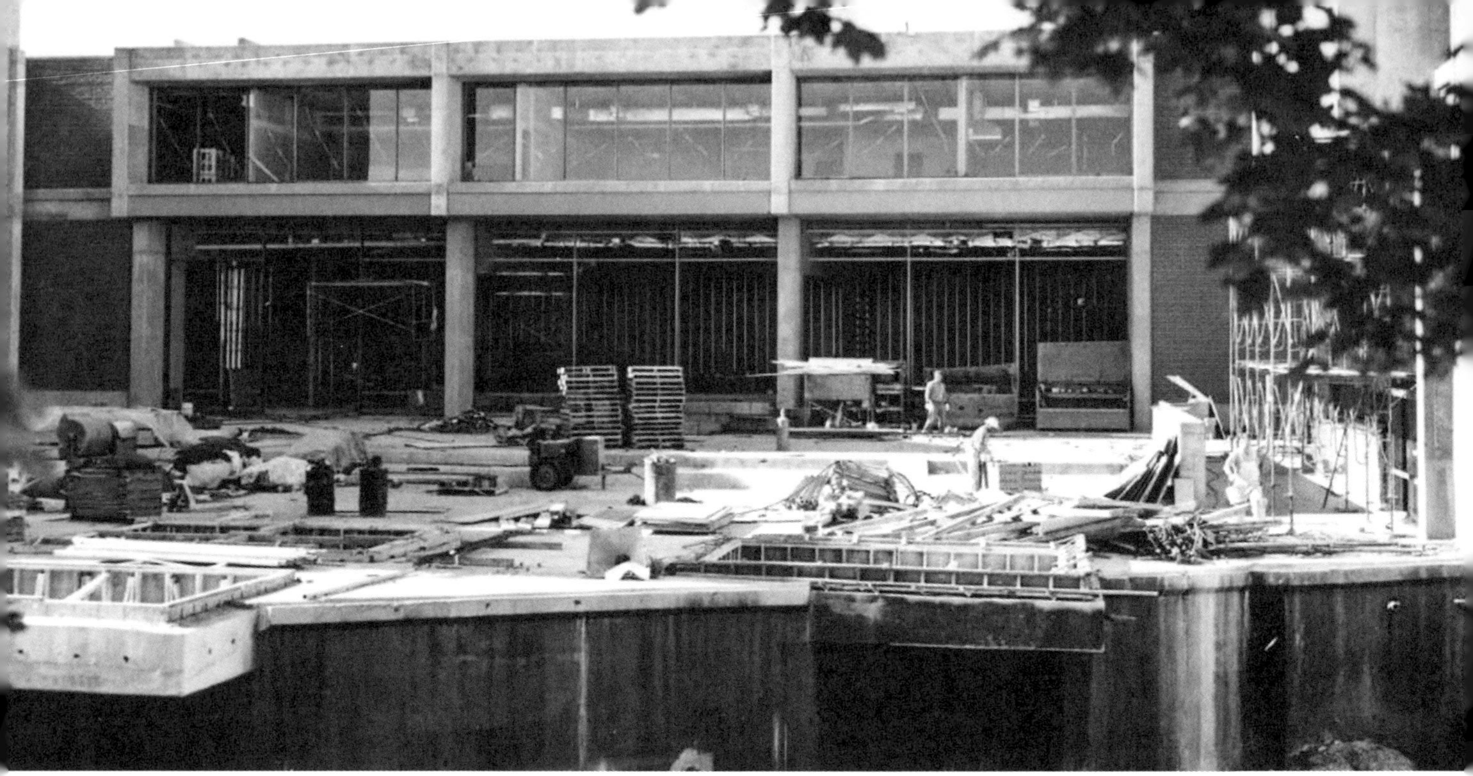

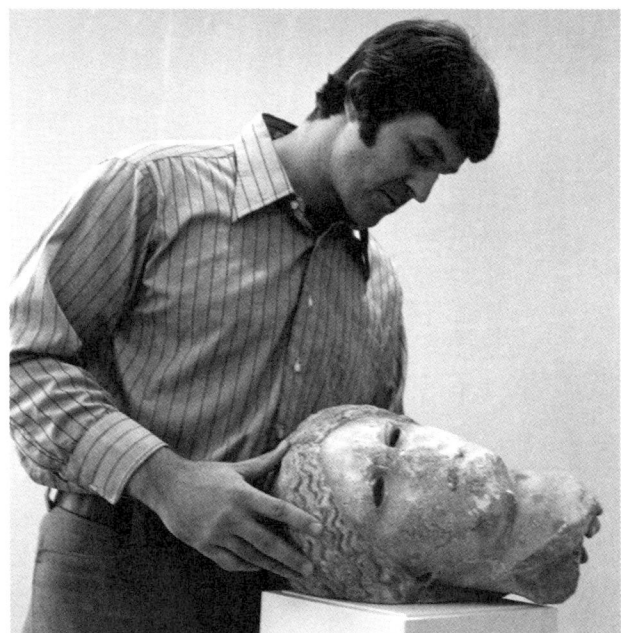

Construction of the Fine Arts Center, 1970–1972, the original home of the Museum of Art/WSU

Photo: WSU Libraries' Manuscripts, Archives, and Special Collections

Harvey West examines an ancient stone bust atop a pedestal in the fine arts gallery, 1972

Photo: WSU Libraries' Manuscripts, Archives, and Special Collections

VERSO:
THE OTHER SIDE OF THE FRAME

Patricia Grieve Watkinson

How do you start a museum?

Hopefully, with a good deal of care and forethought. After all, you're creating "a permanent institution in the service of society."[1] If you're an art collector, you might build an art museum to share your collection with the world, to engage and educate the public, and to leave a legacy. The Henry Art Gallery at the University of Washington, the Frick, the Getty, the Tate—all began this way. In Pullman, in 1916, President Ernest O. Holland began collecting art on behalf of Washington State College. But it wasn't until over 50 years later that the idea of an art museum to house his collection was born. It was the brainchild of Harvey West, an assistant professor of painting in the university's fine arts department. After years squeezed into a cramped, old building, in 1972 the fine arts faculty had moved into a spacious, award-winning building with studios, offices, and galleries.[2] West saw this as an opportune moment to propose the concept of an art museum that would contain the university's works of art, curate art exhibitions and travel them to other venues, and, above all, play a new role in the education of students. The museum would be housed in the new fine arts building. West's concept had the support of just one of his

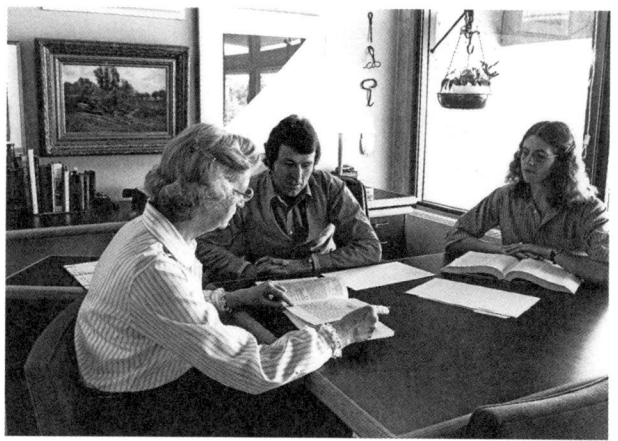

June Harbour (left), Harvey West (center), and Julie Thompson (right) in the museum offices, 1970s

Photo: Jordan Schnitzer Museum of Art WSU Archives

fellow art faculty members: his other colleagues, not surprisingly, had their own ideas of how their long-awaited building might be used in the service of art education. The university's administration, however, found favor with West's idea... and so the Museum of Art/WSU, now the Jordan Schnitzer Museum of Art WSU, began.

President Holland held strong beliefs about the arts at a land-grant institution:

What place should a knowledge and appreciation of music and art have in the life of American men and women? Those subjects are taught...on the assumption that they are part of the social heritage of rich and poor alike, and make for human happiness and appreciation...[3]

Welcome to Pullman

I arrived in Pullman from Britain in November 1972, a young "faculty wife" with zero knowledge of an American land-grant institution, although I certainly saw the land itself—the treeless, rolling hills of the Palouse stretching into the distance in all directions. Nothing could have been a farther cry from the London art galleries where I'd been working. I sought out every offering in the scant arts in this tiny town and clearly remember attending a Le Corbusier film in an art series that Harvey West was presenting. In 1974, optimistically, I applied for the brand-new position of curator at the art museum; I was beaten out by Bruce Guenther. Later, I worked alongside him and learned much about exhibition installation, Pacific Northwest art, and the incredible energy that museum work takes, both mental and physical. Later still, I spent over two memorable and rewarding decades at the museum—ultimately as director (1984–98)—motivated by a contemporary understanding

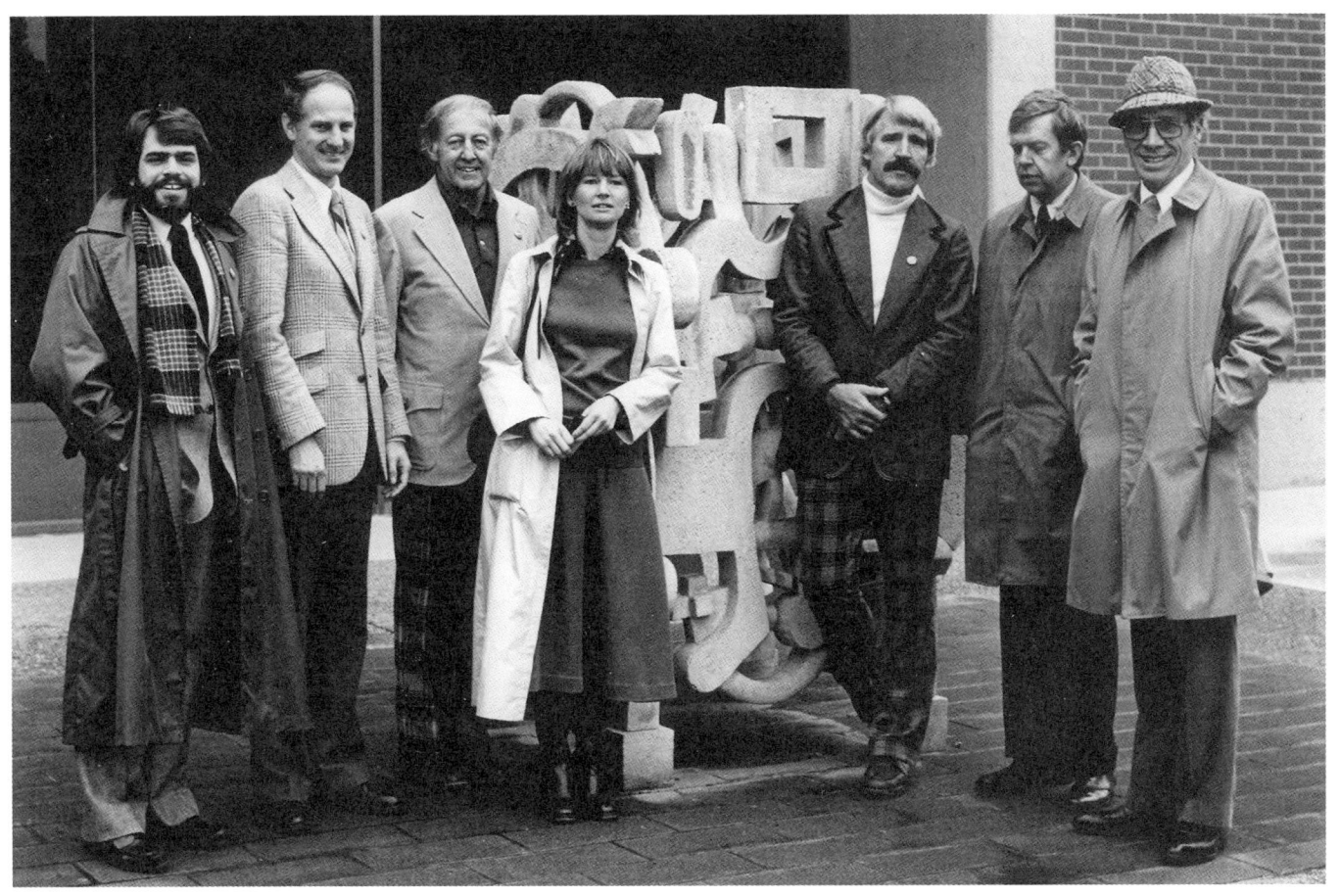

The Friends of the Museum's dedication of a Harold Balazs sculpture in 1979

Left to right: Bruce Guenther, acting director; Ken Spitzer, Friends president; Keith Monaghan, WSU fine art faculty; Patricia Watkinson, acting curator; Harold Balazs, sculptor; Bill Nugent, dean of the College of Liberal Arts; Glen Terrell, WSU president

Photo: Jordan Schnitzer Museum of Art WSU Archives

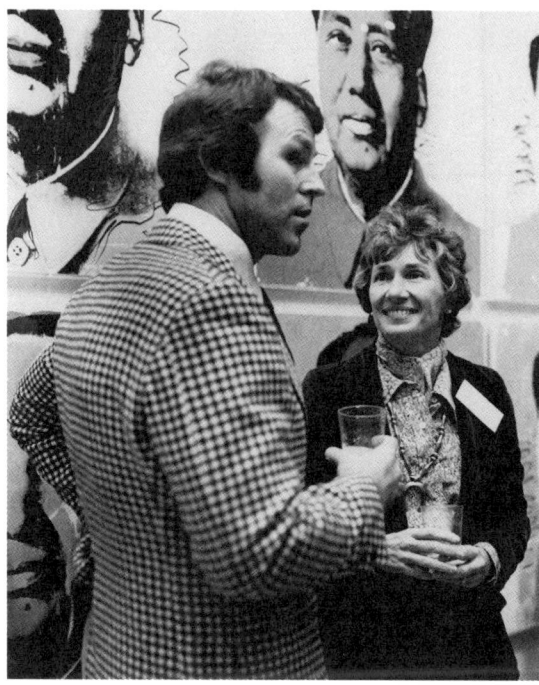

Harvey West (left) and Virginia Wright (right) converse at the symposium for the exhibition *American Printmaking 1960–1975: A Major Survey Exhibition of Directions in American Printmaking*, November 7, 1975

Photo: WSU Libraries' Manuscripts, Archives, and Special Collections

of President Holland's words and guided by a desire to help bring the world of art to Pullman.

> When you look back, and forgetfully wonder
> What you were like in your work and your play,
> Then, it may be, there will often come o'er you,
> Glimpses of notes like the catch of a song...[4]

This essay is drawn from my years at the museum—an involvement that continues, in different ways, to the present day.[5] It is neither a history nor a memoir, both fallible, but an attempt to show that the museum has achieved its fiftieth anniversary—and will undoubtedly achieve its hundredth—not as a monolithic institution that has smoothly navigated the years, but as a living entity that has drawn its life force from the dedication and love of many. They are students and faculty, museum staff and community volunteers, donors and docents, artists, and scholars.

To serve students

Let's not kid ourselves: the hardest part of serving students is getting them to cross the museum's threshold! Unlike attending class, a museum visit normally doesn't contribute to the all-important student credit hours of the university system. Plus, for many students, even arts students, a museum is *terra incognita*. The new museum building with its assertive campus location may soften

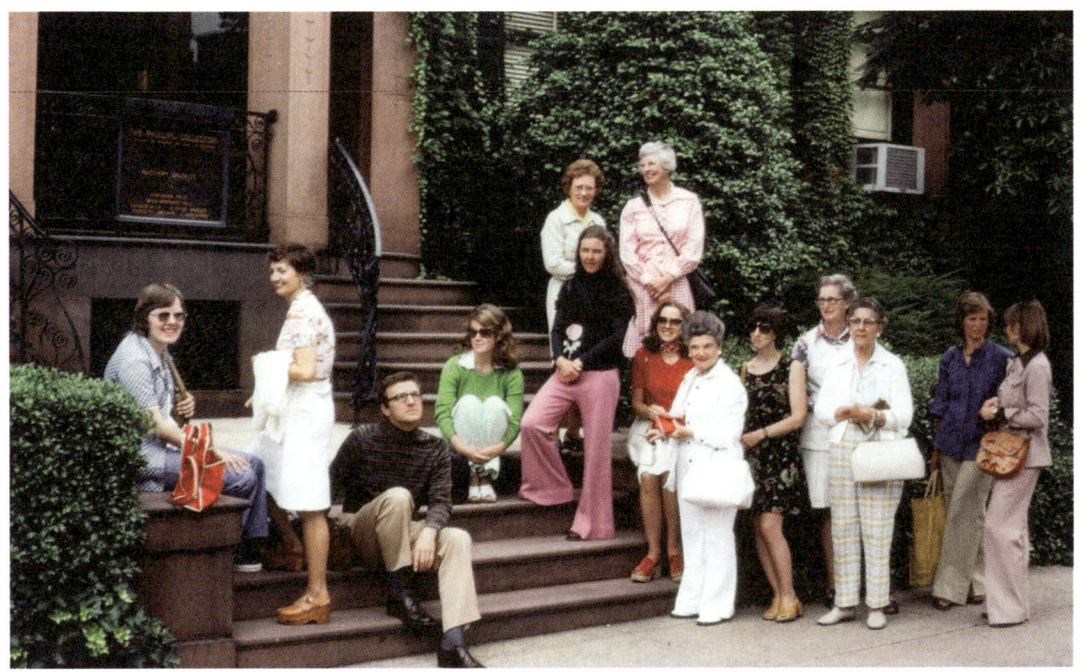

resistance, but one successful idea has been to partner with enthusiastic faculty who understand that looking at and thinking about art can develop independent thinking and alternative ways of seeing.

Anthropology, English, Education, Fine Arts, Theater, Architecture, and Honors were (and still are) some of the many disciplines involved, even if their earlier faculty are long gone. Remember the WSU initiative *Writing across the Curriculum*? It was an opportunity for our exhibitions to serve as raw material for creative writing. Insightful essays were often shared with the artists concerned, to the delight of artist and author. Foreign language classes also used exhibitions as a "laboratory" for students to try out their new vocabulary: art is generous in offering flexibility in interpretation, making room for many levels of spoken ability.

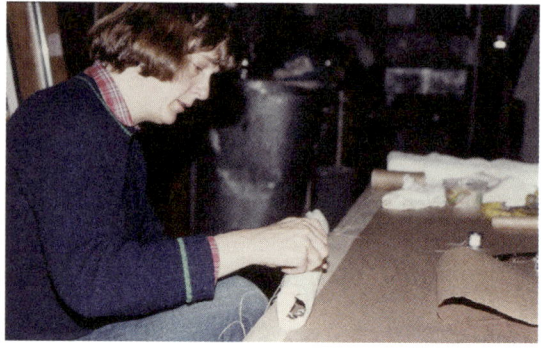

A volunteer preparing materials for an exhibition, 1980s
Photo: Jordan Schnitzer Museum of Art WSU Archives

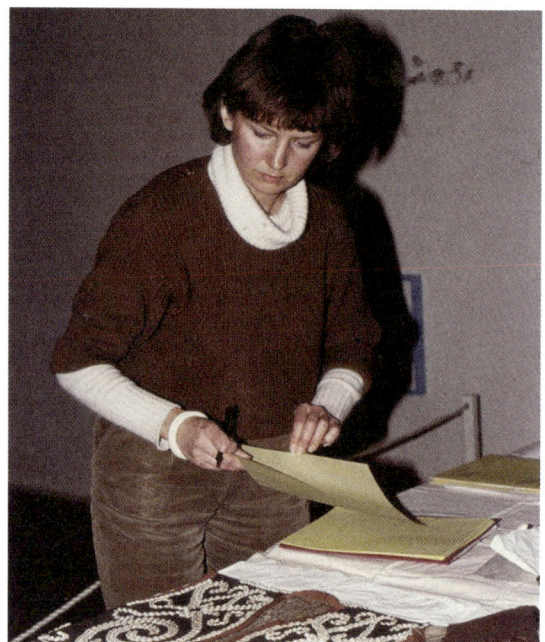

Patricia Watkinson prepares a textile vest for the exhibition *Fabric Traditions of Indonesia*, exhibited November 6–December 16, 1984

Photo: Jordan Schnitzer Museum of Art WSU Archives

But students have been much more than visitors. From the beginning, the museum has offered a museum procedures class: students learned to install exhibitions and research artists. Much later, they helped with website design and created YouTube videos. It's gratifying to know those who have gone on to become museum professionals. In the early days, as now, work-study students from every discipline imaginable were employed as security guards (now "visitor ambassadors"). Then, in the all-too-short gap between exhibitions, they would change hats completely and become exhibition installers—requiring a totally different set of skills. Some shone: a young man who paid his tuition by playing pool not surprisingly had the most exacting eye for hanging art! For others, it was literally the first time they'd held a hammer or navigated a spirit level.

With a little help from my Friends

Ingenuity and self-reliance have been—of necessity—the museum's watchwords. A tiny staff and a slim budget from university state funds have been at least one constant of the museum's fifty years. And even those funds have waxed and waned, more than once requiring the museum to reduce staff hours and close its doors for part of the year.

Enter the Friends of the Museum of Art! Started in 1977, with little experience, much optimism, and some bottles of sherry, the Friends' original steering committee numbered fourteen enthusiasts. The organization grew close to 500 members through the following decades. Indeed, Friends in many cases became personal friends. They were a reliable and eager audience, invaluable volunteers, trip organizers, docents, overnight hosts for visiting artists and speakers, wise counselors, and savvy advocates for the museum in the quicksands of university life. Above all, their annual memberships and fundraising activities supplied the wherewithal for key exhibitions and programs. Friends received postcard announcements and colorful posters—this was, of course, before email, websites, and all things digital. Among Friends' events, the February *Sweet Art* gala remains one of the most remembered—its sideshows of fortune telling and body painting (by a fine arts faculty member), the art auction, and the cake judging (Most Romantic, Most Artistic, Most Delicious!). The cakes, made by Friends, were then auctioned for ridiculously high prices, shared, and consumed immediately...all to benefit the museum.

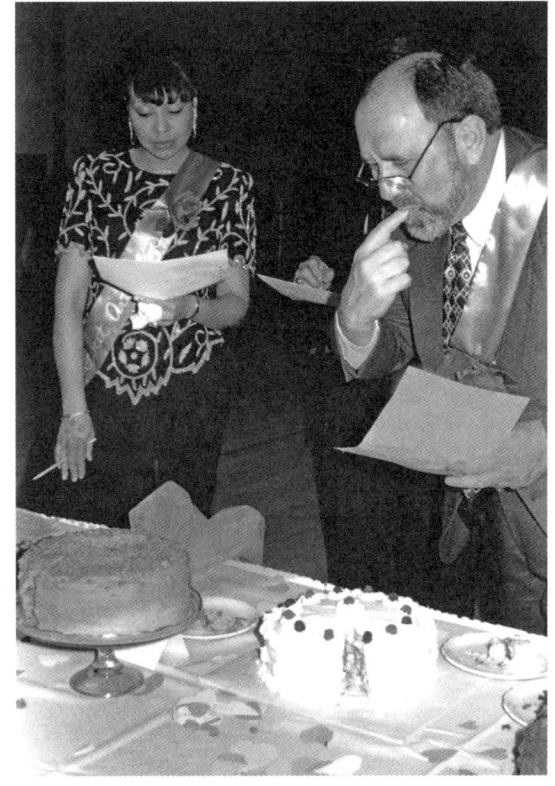

Dessert judges Deborah Love (left) and Ken Cassavant (right) take a critical review of the desserts of the Sweet Art auction, which raised funds for the museum, 1979

Photo: Jordan Schnitzer Museum of Art WSU Archives

Rumor has it that the Friends, with its own 501(c)(3) charter and local bank account, was actually one of the first official support groups at the university...after Athletics and Alumni. However, as the university's fundraising arm, the WSU Foundation (established in 1979) grew stronger, the Friends were looked at as operating outside the fold. Eventually relinquishing their financial independence, the Friends went on to play a role in WSU's first-ever capital campaign (1993–96), when several members established endowments for the museum. Now, three decades later, it's heartwarming to hear the current museum staff express gratitude for these earlier donors whose endowments help

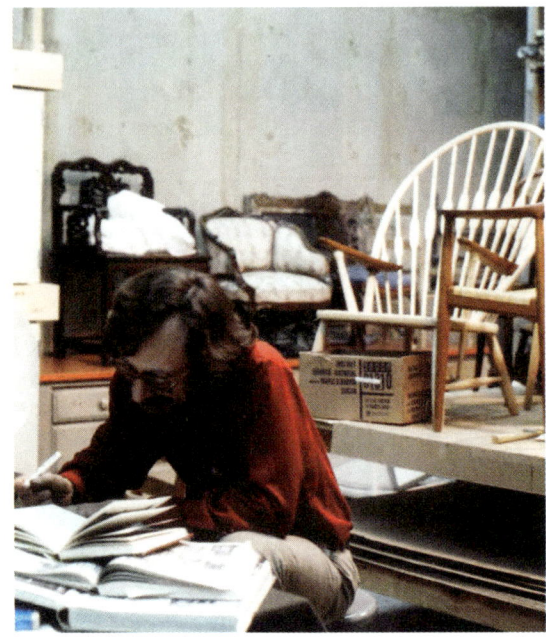

keep today's museum afloat. However, the biggest "thank-you" always goes to the Friends board that, in 1987, had the foresight to start an endowment, the Museum of Art Friend's Fund—now a main source of museum operating support.

Fundraising—or "development" as we learned to call it—became a bigger and bigger part of the museum as the institution matured. Part of that maturation was a change in governance. In 1994, after years of reporting to the Dean of the College of Liberal Arts, the museum asked and was approved to be repositioned under the Office of the Provost, the university's academic head. Our simple rationale: the art museum existed to serve all students, faculty, community members, and visitors. Universities are nothing if not political: the new structure allowed the museum director to hobnob with WSU leaders, increasing the museum's visibility on and off campus. The museum was now, quite literally, invited to the party. Increased visibility plus new access to people and places encouraged new donors. The pinnacle of this trajectory wasn't to reveal itself fully until 2013, when, under the guidance of museum director Chris Bruce, major donors stepped forward to fund a long-standing dream—a new, larger, purpose-built museum at the heart of campus. The pivotal donor was (and is) collector and philanthropist Jordan D. Schnitzer, after whom the museum is now named. It is telling that among the three hundred names celebrated on the donor panel at the new museum's entry are those of many original "Friends."

Before there was development, through the 1970s and '80s, in addition to the Friends, hard-earned grants were a needed means of support. Usually penned during the midnight hours, successful grant applications were a lifeline. The National Endowment for the Arts, the National Endowment

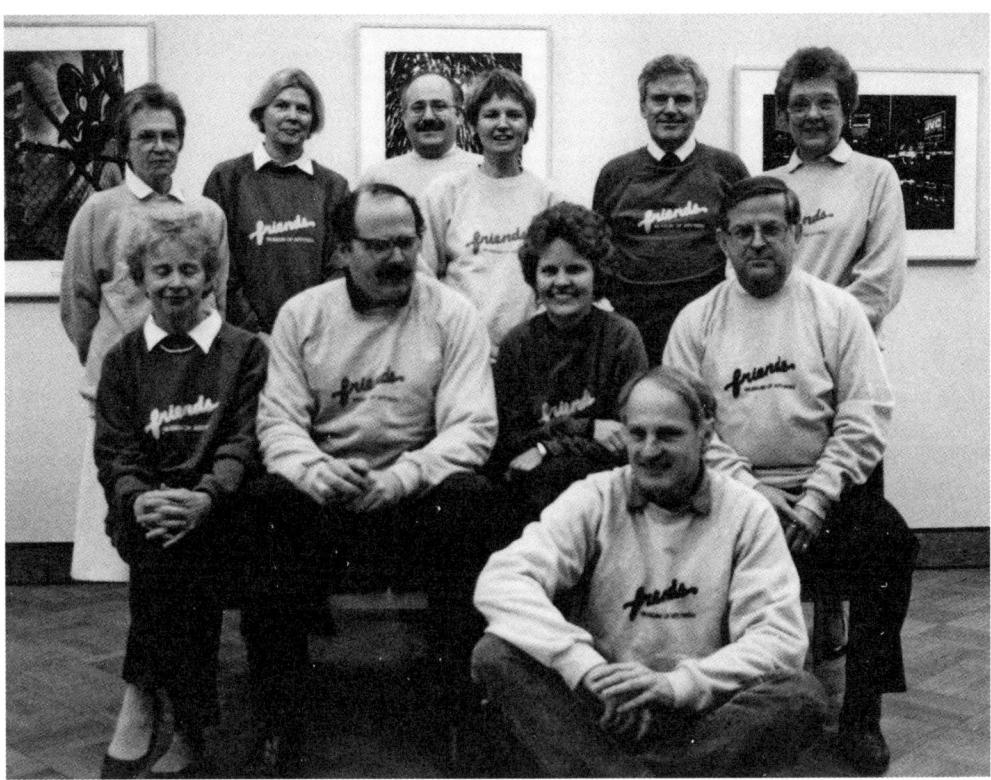

The Friends of the Museum was a group of volunteers who dedicated themselves
to the art museum (shown here in the 1980s)
From left to right: Front: Ken Spitzer.
Second Row: Clarice McCartan, Bob Helm, Barbara Petura, Sam Smith.
Third Row, Jody Sahlin, Pat Smith, Kevin Jacque, Patricia Watkinson, Bob Nilan, and Kelma Short

Photo: Jordan Schnitzer Museum of Art WSU Archives

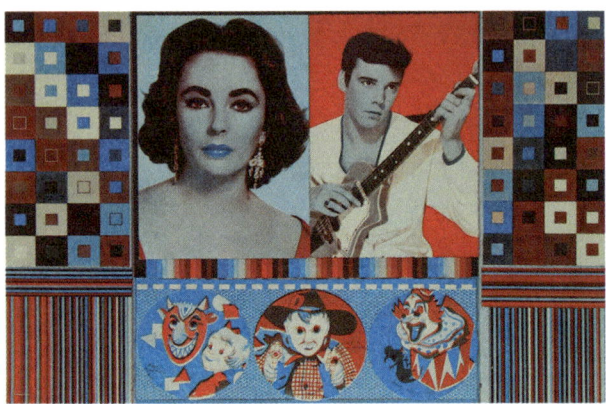

Eduardo Paolozzi, *An Empire of Silly Statistics ...*
A Fake War ... from *General Dynamics F.U.N.*, 1970
Offset lithograph, JSMA WSU Permanent Collection,
Gift of Nicolo Pignatelli

for the Humanities, the Washington State Arts Commission, and the Washington Commission for the Humanities, among others, made museum programs possible. Competition for these funds was fierce and none more so than for those of the coveted Institute of Museum and Library Services. IMLS provided unrestricted "general operating support," which—banal though it may sound—was actually pure gold. It allowed us to meet vital needs, including hiring a registrar. To the envy of museum colleagues across the nation and to the relief of the WSU staff, the museum received IMLS funding twelve times throughout the 1980s and '90s.

We also kept an ear to the ground for intermural competitive sources of funding—from the Dean's office, from WSU's Memorandum of Understanding with the USAID,[6] from the ASWSU Lecture Artists Committee and, above all, from yet another acronym, VPLAC—the Visual, Performing, and Literary Arts Committee. Although now defunct, for over a quarter century this university fund—the inspired brainchild of Dean of Students Art McCartan—brought performers, poets, dance groups, musicians, and artists from across the nation and even the world to WSU's isolated campus.

The art collection grows and outgrows

By far the most significant grant to date came in 2018—from the Henry Luce Foundation. It was the work of Laura Child, development director, and Anna-Maria Shannon, interim director, and it funded a turning point in the museum's life. At 44 years of age, the museum as we knew it was to be superseded by a much-desired, glamorous building, right next door—the Jordan Schnitzer Museum of Art WSU. With Luce assistance, the "old" museum found itself happily recycled into state-of-the-art housing for a growing art collection (4000 + works of art) with spaces for students to study the art and for staff to care for it—the new Collection Study Center.

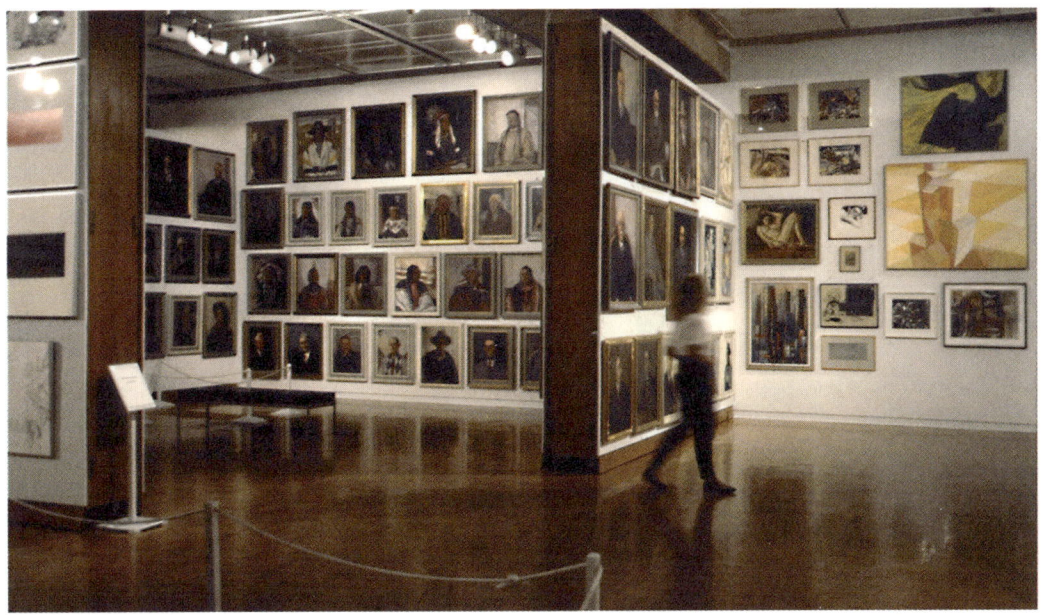

Wandering the galleries, a student observes the museum's permanent collection in the exhibition *Salon for Now*, June 2–July 31, 1992

Photo: Jordan Schnitzer Museum of Art WSU Archives

That number—4000+—comes as a surprise. It seems just yesterday that the fledgling museum housed a small but valued collection. There were American painters from the Holland and Orton collections—Frank Duveneck, Robert Henri, William Glackens, Walter Ufer, *et al*—etchings by Francisco Goya; engravings by William Hogarth; and a smattering of paintings by former WSU artists. Like many universities, WSU has too few funds to buy or care for art. It is totally through the generosity of individuals—artists, gallery owners, dealers, collectors—that desired works of this magnitude have been added to the WSU collection. Sometimes, however, the museum had to resist pressure to accept art that did not meet our collection standards or needs. It would be explained to us that potential donors to select areas of the university could be more successfully cultivated if their art was first accepted by the museum. It wasn't always easy to be the tough guys!

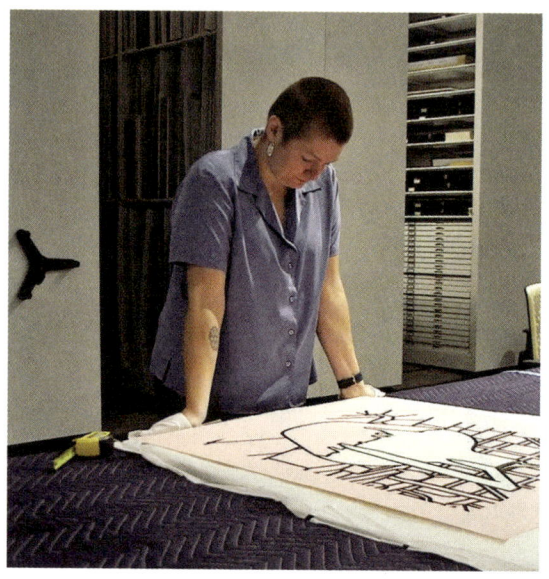

Gracie Brown in the Collection Study Center reviewing a print by Patrick Caulfield, 2019

Photo: WSU Photo Services

Nevertheless, over the years the museum has quietly acquired desired works—by WSU artists, artists from the Pacific Northwest, across the nation, and internationally. Through opportunity and intent, much of the collection has focused on works on paper, original prints, drawings, and photographs. As early as 1975, the museum became part owner of the collection "Works on Paper: American Art 1945–1975" that included work by such notable artists as Robert Rauschenberg, Helen Frankenthaler, and Willem de Kooning. It was a daring partnership described by the National Endowment for the Arts as "unique in the nation." Together with three other regional museums[7] and with inspiration and support from Seattle philanthropist and collector Virginia Wright, the Washington State Art Consortium was formed to "familiarize Washington citizens with the highest standards of contemporary works of art on paper."[8]

This seemed a time when Seattle, with its concentration—albeit a small one—of art institutions, galleries, and collectors, looked toward the rest of the state with a nurturing attitude, willing always to lend a helping hand to rural and less populated areas. By the later decades of the twentieth century, this thinking and the art world were changing. Seattle became more of a player in the national scene, the international art market was a dominant force, and art values skyrocketed as investors often replaced collectors.

In 1983, an influx of original prints came to WSU through the Martin S. Ackerman Foundation. It delivered notable works by Americans Ed Ruscha and R.B. Kitaj, and Britons Eduardo Paolozzi and Tom Phillips. But the infusion par excellence of original prints has been at the hands of WSU fine art alumnus Sean Elwood. His gifts number over 300 and represent an exciting, often intentionally challenging selection of work by contemporary artists from 1968 to today.

The show must go on

Through its changing exhibitions program, the museum has brought a wide world of art, artists, and scholars to Pullman. Whether it was *Greek and Roman Antiquities from the Getty Museum* (1974) or *Amistad II: 200 Years of Black American Art* (1977), whether it was the photography of Eikoh Hosoe from Japan (1994) or the drawings of Austria's Arnulf Rainer (1991), the "world of art" has been interpreted broadly, through a range of art mediums, through artists both established and emerging, through in-depth solo or theme-based group exhibitions. It's judicious to explain this choice as the best way to serve an isolated campus, bringing experiences otherwise unavailable. But a parallel truth is that each new exhibition is a thrill for museum staff. We have the privilege of holding—in our gloved hands—and learning about a wide variety of art: our curiosity is piqued again and again. For days or weeks, we live and breathe a specific exhibition, only to have to cast it aside, like an abandoned lover, for the next love interest.

Note the word "change" in changing exhibitions. When the museum was young and its staff had the energy and enthusiasm of youth, exhibitions changed monthly, resulting in an ambitious eleven shows each year! In time, wisdom and increased professionalism prevailed. Or was it just that we had to allow ourselves extra time to drive to Seattle or Portland to pick up art loaned for the next exhibition? Somehow it was a simpler world where art collectors such as Virginia Wright were willing to let us take her life-size George Segal sculpture *Woman on a Bed*, pack it carefully, load it into a rented U-Haul, and drive it 300 miles over the mountain passes to Pullman.

The Segal was joined by additional borrowed sculptures by Richard Serra, Claes Oldenburg, Louise Nevelson, and twenty-two other artists featured in *Two Decades 1957–1977: American Sculpture from Northwest Collections* (1977). The exhibition was one in an annual series, curated by Bruce Guenther, that addressed, in turn, abstract painting, photography, fiber arts, and drawing—each exhibition accompanied by an ambitious two-day symposium that dealt "with contemporary questions in the fine arts," with speakers from around the nation and attendees from throughout the region.

The generosity of lenders was sometimes augmented by happy coincidence. *Fabric Traditions of Indonesia* (1984) was built around the spectacular textile collection of Tim and Tuti Manring. Tim was

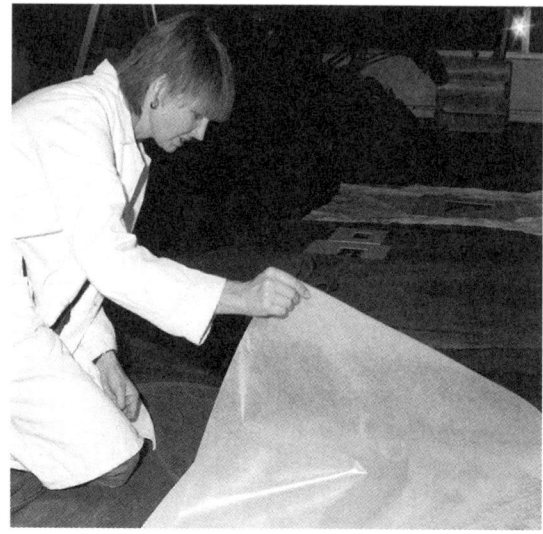

Curator Patricia Watkinson leans over to view an artwork

Photo: Jordan Schnitzer Museum of Art WSU Archives

born in Pullman, a farmer's son and an international lawyer. His mum Betty, a volunteer in the museum gift shop, told us of his collecting. When the university started a federally funded project to develop higher education in Indonesia, the opportunity seemed ripe. We engaged leading textile scholars as curators, and, aided by visiting Indonesians and their families, we presented a film and lecture series, Gamelan music, and celebratory foods to present the diverse traditions and lifeways of this complex nation.

A decade later came another, even more ambitious project, presenting a culture that drew its strength from the very land on which the museum had been built. *A Song to the Creator: Traditional Arts of Native American Women of the Plateau* (1997) started as an idea by former curator Barbara Coddington and grew beyond the museum into a ten-year, university-wide endeavor with thirty scholars, Plateau artists, and museum professionals. Some 250 spectacular garments, moccasins, cornhusk bags, and pieces of jewelry were complemented by woven baskets, horse regalia, painted parfleches, and beadwork, along with rare interviews with the women involved.

There were other opportunities to see and hear about work by artists in the region, whether they were the many outstanding WSU faculty artists or from elsewhere in the Pacific Northwest. Retrospective exhibitions reflecting an older generation included Margaret Tomkins, Wendell Brazeau, and Kenneth Callahan. A sampling of a younger generation included John Buck, Marsha Burns, Deborah Butterfield, Kathy Glowen, Fay Jones, Mel Katz, Lucinda Parker, Norie Sato, and Michael Spafford, to name but a few.

Ultimately, all exhibitions are ephemeral. But an exhibition *catalog* is a different animal. Few regrets are as keen as having no catalog to remember an exhibition by! But lack of funds and of time all too often cause the sorry situation. The museum has a long history of producing publications and

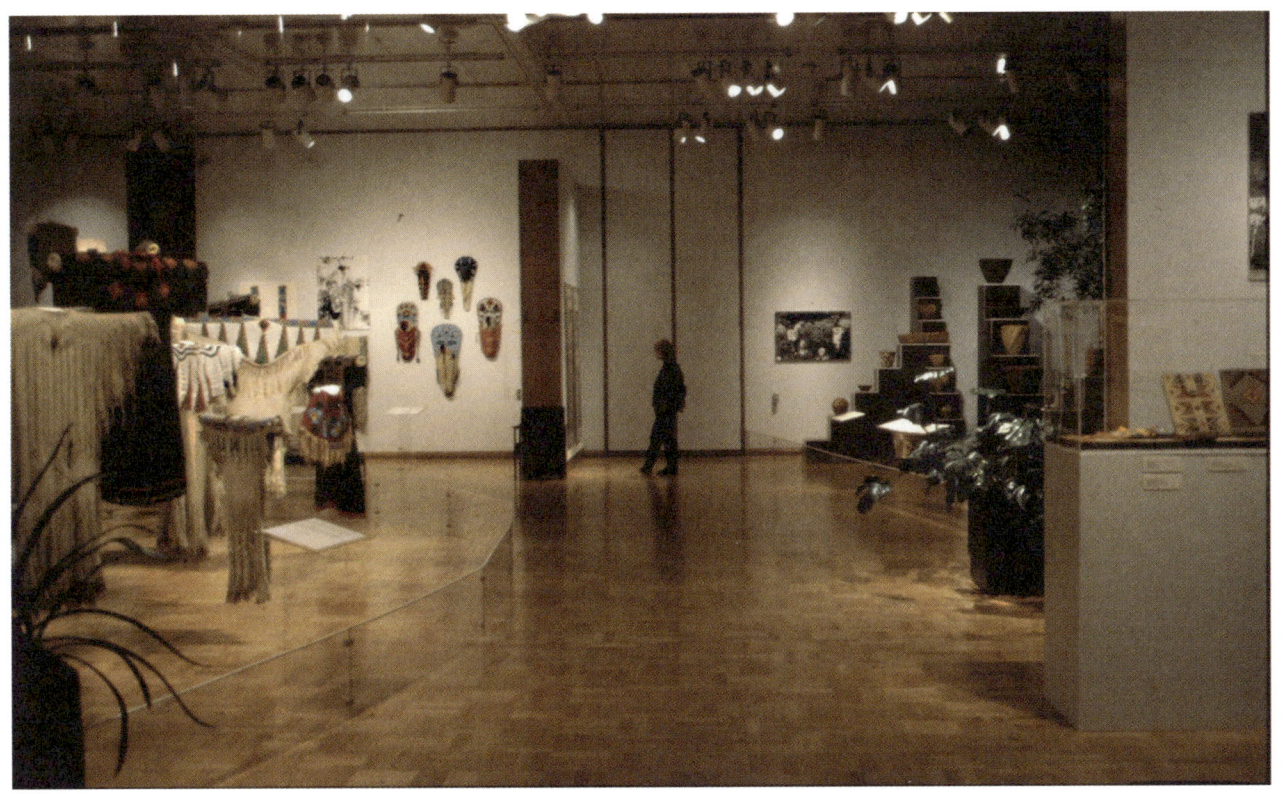

A Song to the Creator: Traditional Arts of Native American Women of the Plateau,
October 14–December 15, 1996

Photo: WSU Libraries' Manuscripts, Archives, and Special Collections

catalogs. Some are slim, well-worn, black-and-white records that still hold keys to the past. Others are more substantial—and colorful—undertakings, with a longer life. For over twenty-five years, until the advent of websites, email, and social media, the museum printed attractive posters to announce its offerings. For all those years, posters and catalogs were creatively designed by Jo Savage, our enthusiastic collaborator at the WSU Press.

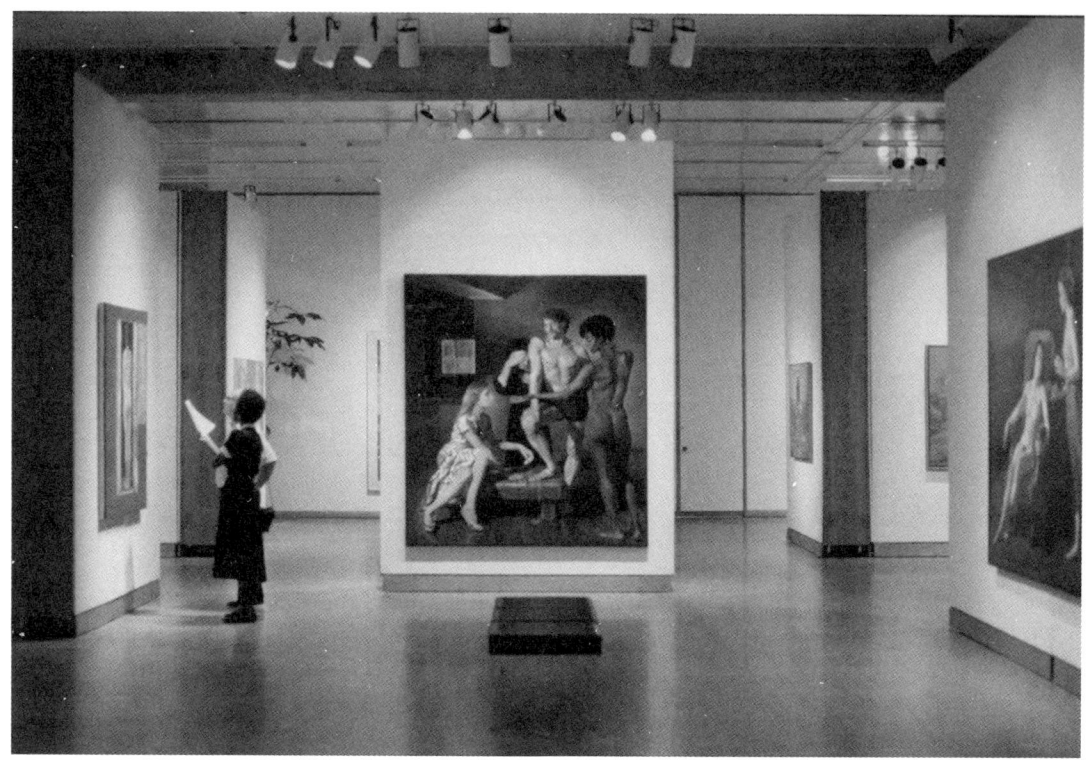

Two museum visitors ponder the exhibition *Modern Myths: Classical Renewal*,
September 5–September 27, 1987

Photo: WSU Libraries' Manuscripts, Archives, and Special Collections

Exhibitions curated at WSU also traveled to other institutions, thus extending the life of the exhibition, the audiences reached, the likelihood of grant support, and the curator's sense that their labors were worthwhile. To tour our exhibitions, we worked with colleagues at institutions such as the Cheney Cowles Memorial Museum,[9] Boise Art Museum, Bellevue Art Museum,[10] Seattle Art Museum, Henry Art Gallery, and Whitman College's Sheehan Gallery. Sometimes a tour took the WSU museum's name farther afield, to Portland, San Jose, Los Angeles, or even Pennsylvania State University. Greater prestige yet came when a WSU exhibition was selected by a national touring

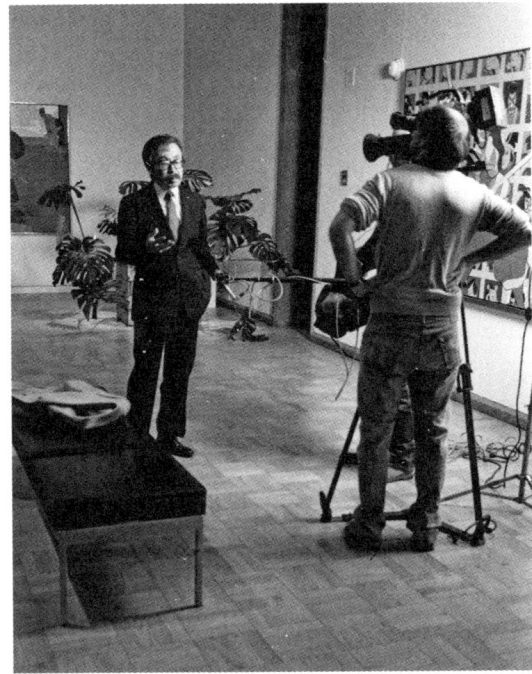

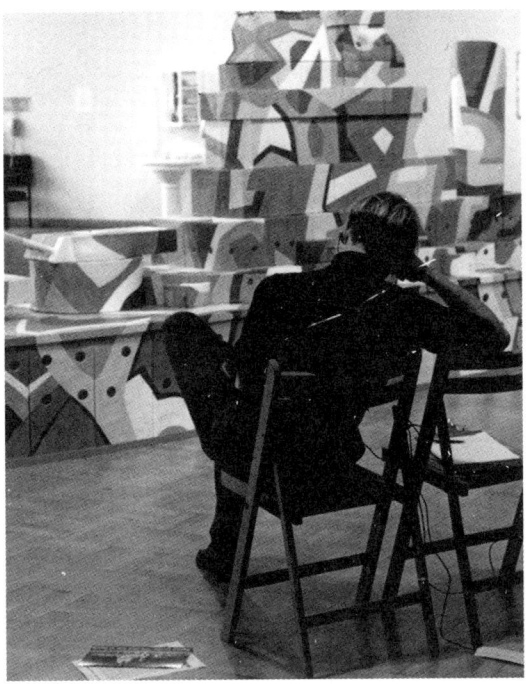

WSU assistant professor Dr. Take Tsurutani is interviewed by CBS in the Museum of Art/WSU during the 1989 exhibition *Where Two Worlds Meet: Masami Teraoka and Roger Shimomura*

Marilyn Lysohir: The Dark Side of Dazzle
September 29–October 28, 1990

Photo: Jordan Schnitzer Museum of Art WSU Archives, Photo credit: Mark Olsen

organization: *Contemporary Metals: Focus on Idea* (1981) was chosen by the Western Association of Art Museums, and *Noritake Art Deco Porcelains* (1982) was chosen by the Smithsonian Institution Traveling Exhibition Service, to be shown throughout the nation.

It has always brought a smile to think of sophisticated scholars and renowned visiting artists bouncing over the Palouse in the tiny Cascade Airlines planes to be met at the as-yet-unimproved Pullman-Moscow airport. You'd glance up from your museum desk, hear then see the plane overhead, and have plenty of time to be on the tarmac to greet the visitor. And what an amazing panoply of the art world has come: scholars such as Linda Nochlin, Albert Elsen, William Gerdts, and Mattiebelle

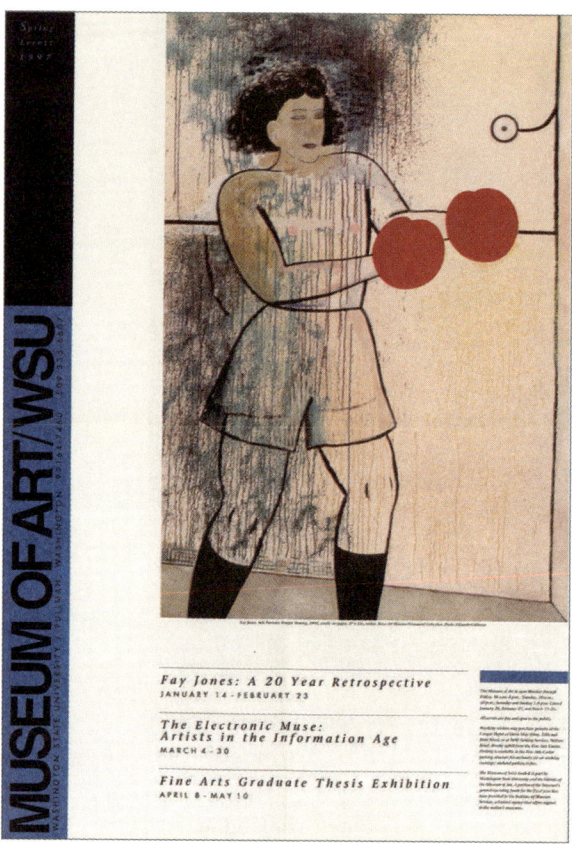

Museum of Art/WSU Spring 1997 poster
Photo: WSU Libraries' Manuscripts, Archives, and
Special Collections

Gittinger; critics such as John Canaday, Matthew Kangas, Hilton Kramer, and Donald Kuspit; writers such as Robert Hughes, Lucy Lippard, Dore Ashton, and Bevis Hillier; and artists such as Robert Motherwell, Lynda Benglis, Fred Wilson, Howard Kottler, Larry Poons, Ed Ruscha, Judy Chicago, and Roger Shimomura.

This is not to suggest that scholarship and renown came from outside only. A popular campus program was "Art à la Carte"—lunchtime talks in collaboration with the Compton Union Building. The series lasted for a quarter century, until 2006, without losing steam or appealing topics. Audiences were entertained and enlightened by WSU faculty, staff, and visitors with talks as diverse as "The Private and Public World of Islam" and "The Roots of Star Wars, or Why Princess Leia Fights like a Girl."[11]

Shock of the New[12]

In the five decades of the museum's existence, the art world has undergone unimaginable changes. The museum seems to have ridden the wave, aware of the changing environment, yet not subsumed by it. Thus, while in the 1970s museum staff might still be explaining abstraction, in the 1990s we were installing *The Electronic Muse: Artists in the Information Age* (1997). And, while President Holland might have been exhorted by university regent Charles Orton to buy only "American paintings on canvas,"[13] before the turn

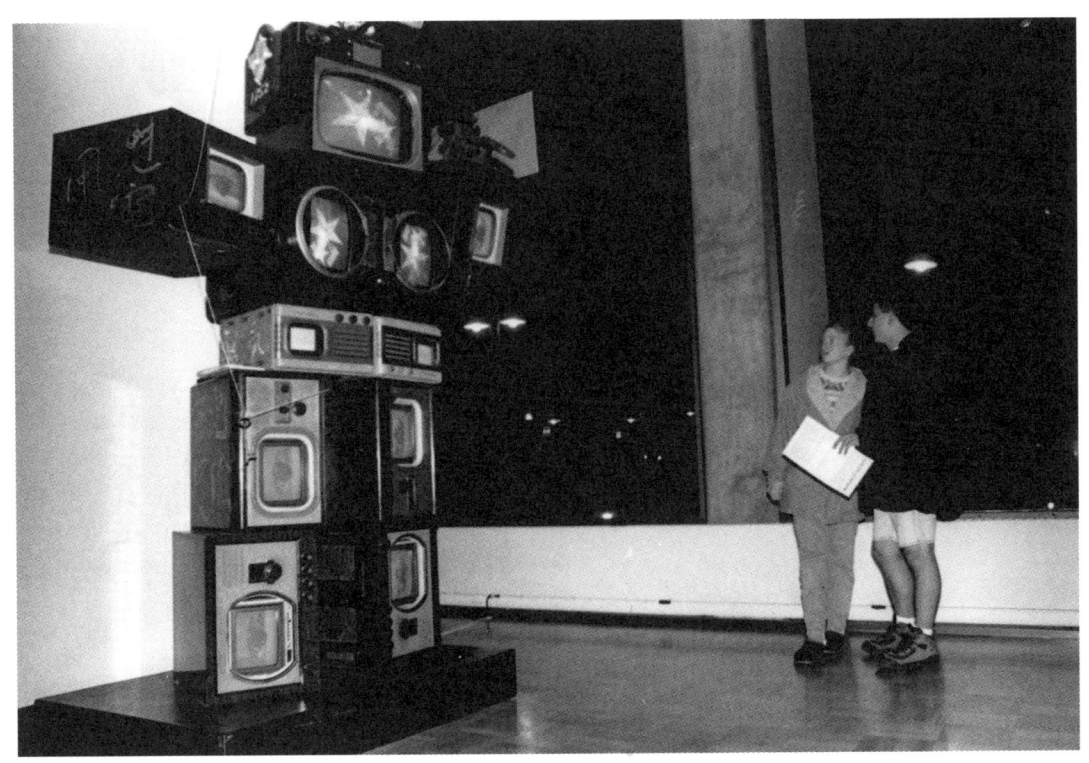

Museum patrons consider a sculpture by Nam June Paik in
The Electronic Muse: Artists in the Information Age,
exhibited March 4–March 30, 1997

Photo: Jordan Schnitzer Museum of Art WSU Archives

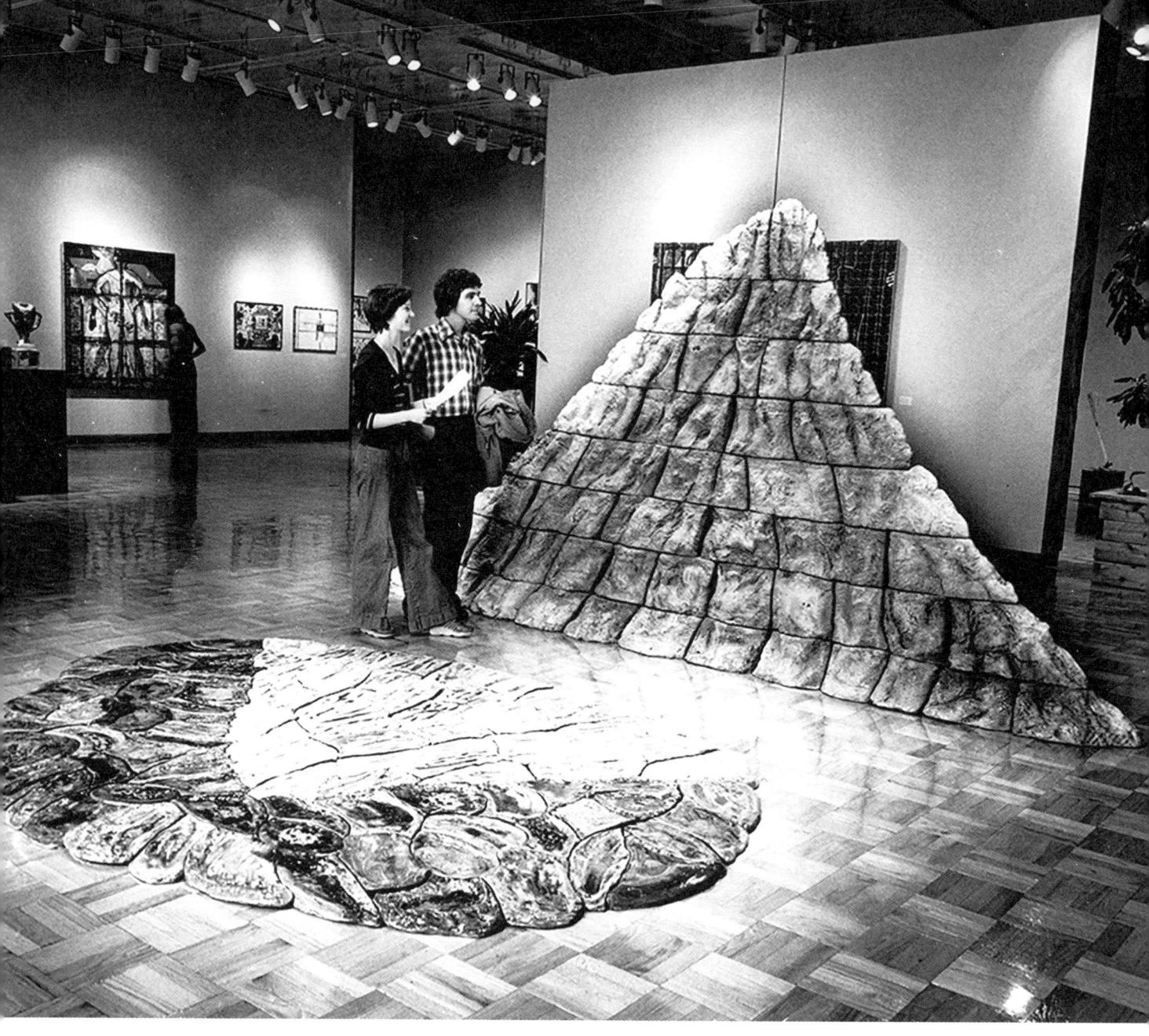

Visitors take in the exhibition *6 from California*, showing Robert Arneson's *Mountain and Lake*, 1975
The exhibition ran from October 29 to November 20, 1976

Photo: Jordan Schnitzer Museum of Art WSU Archives

of the twentieth century, mediums such as textiles, photography, ceramics, glass, the written word, and concepts had entered the artistic mainstream and been exhibited by the museum.

Some exhibitions did rock the boat. Although Andres Serrano's infamous and beautiful photograph *Piss Christ* sailed through the gallery without comment in 1988, the 1976 exhibition of feminist artist Judy Chicago's work, including her hand-painted ceramics with their vaginal imagery, ended in a ruckus. Two "offending" works were removed by director Harvey West; an orchestrated student outcry over censorship ensued, reaching Chicago's ears; she in turn phoned to confront West, who found himself obliged to reinstall the works. A few months later, sculptor Robert Arneson's sexualized ceramic toilet *Herinal* was included in *6 from California* (1976) and curators found themselves at lunch justifying "Bay Area Funk" art to one of the museum's most loyal and formidable supporters, a shocked Catherine Friel. Sometimes it was museum staff who were taken by surprise. Graduate students in the fine arts department had two museum exhibition slots per year and their work often pushed boundaries. While the art installation with live rats was permitted after the student had agreed in writing to tend the creatures, the sculpture that needed an electrical outlet to run its live electric fence had the plug pulled.

Another challenging instance was when *Philip Pearlstein: Paintings to Watercolors* (1985) filled the gallery with large paintings of non-idealized male and female nudes. The museum had just launched its new docent program serving, among others, the local schools, and teachers were fearful of parents' reaction. Director Sanford Shaman made a persuasive presentation at a contentious PTA meeting and ultimately received the schools' blessing. Docents[14] continued the practice of inviting Palouse teachers to preview each new exhibition before school tours were scheduled. But shock, like beauty, is in the eye of the beholder: sometimes it seemed wise—a safeguard—also to invite university administrators to preview exhibitions. One of the more powerful and indeed difficult exhibitions was *A Different War: Vietnam in Art* (1992), curated by Lucy Lippard, with works about the physical and spiritual experience of that devastating war. The museum's ultimate "boss," John Pierce, Dean of the College of Liberal Arts, was visibly shaken as he walked the gallery at our invitation to preview the exhibition.

All hands on deck

There's reward—along with a hint of desperation—in working for a small, ambitious museum in a small town. It's not for the faint of heart...or body. You have the license to do much. And you see the need to do everything! The museum's staff of three or four, occasionally five, individuals shared duties usually allocated in other museums to a much larger cohort of professionals. For some, being a jack-of-all-trades meant there was never a dull moment, with many moments requiring ingenuity or stamina. For others, who longed for uninterrupted hours devoted to scholarship and deep research, the demands were unthinkable.

You needed to be a museum director who would climb ladders, write grants, meet with donors, know the *Chicago Manual of Style*, and respond to security alarms at 4 a.m. Or a curator who would compose scholarly essays, cut mats and frame art, build a shipping crate, teach a class, present a monthly KWSU radio show, and regularly lift weights over 40 pounds. Or an administrative assistant who could take shorthand, balance a budget, understand the peculiarities of art insurance and exhibition contracts, and pack art for shipment. All the while striving for a level of professionalism that encouraged collectors and other museums to loan their prized art works for an exhibition in Pullman or demonstrate to national funders that their financial support was warranted.

The museum and its staff were recognized as museum professionals. They were invited to jury art shows around the state, to take part in selection panels for the National Endowment for the Arts in Washington, DC, or the Seattle Arts Commission, to serve on committees of the American Association of Museums or the Western Museums Conference. Such service brought recognition and essential connections to the university and to the museum, mitigating its geographical isolation and enhancing its professional standing.

Perhaps this is true of all professions, but the backstory of museum life was often a little different from the smooth operation presented to the public. More than once, we greeted guests at an evening opening seconds after finishing the installation. Or, we prayed that tonight's speaker wouldn't drop their slides out of the carousel and then refuse to talk. In the winter, we drove a van full of borrowed art over the icy Cascades, thankfully without incident, only to blow a tire miles outside of Washtucna. We

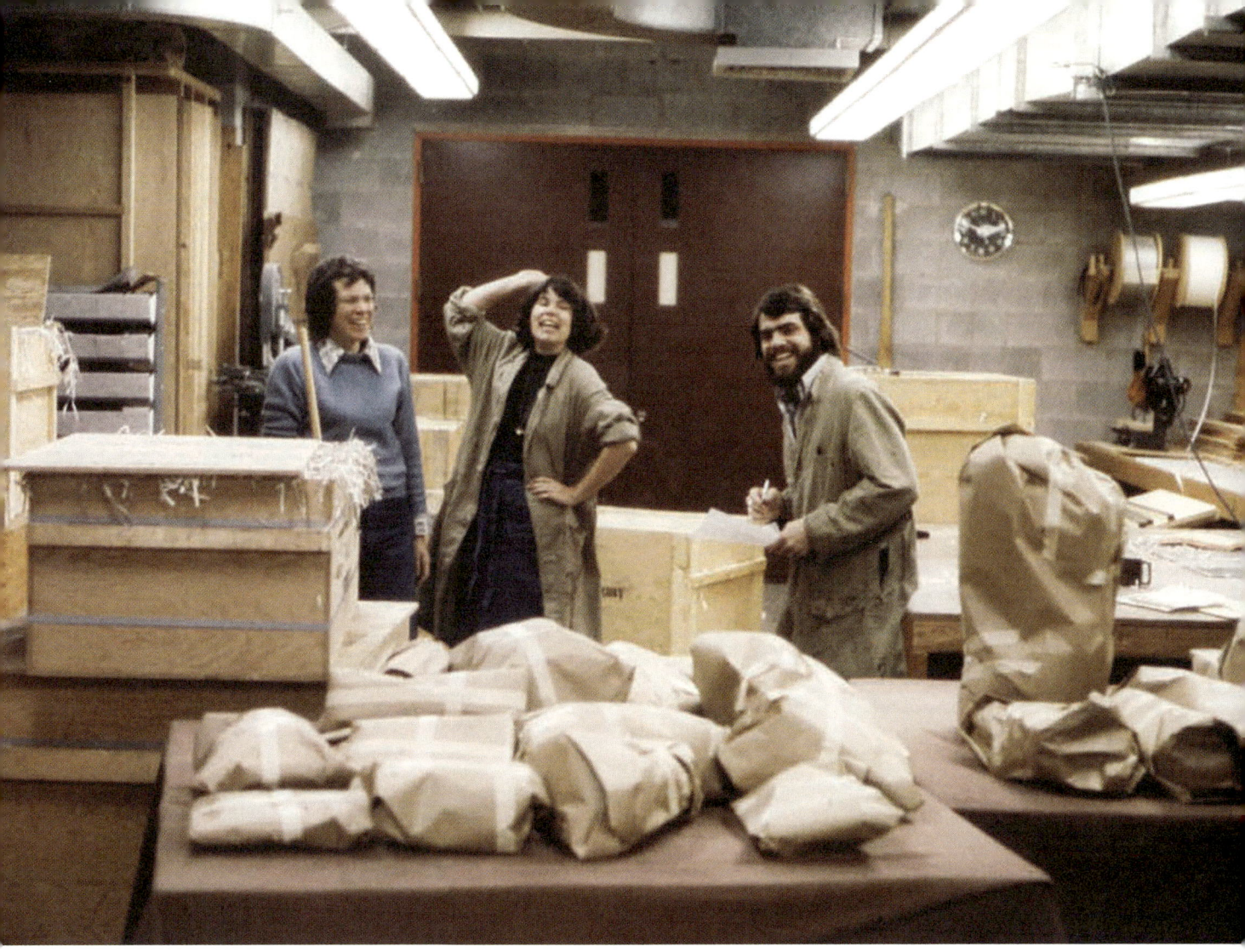

Acting director Bruce Guenther (right) has a laugh with Katie Gorham (center) and Joanna Wilkinson (left) while preparing objects from *Rodin: The Maryhill Collection*, February 1976

Photo: WSU Libraries' Manuscripts, Archives, and Special Collections

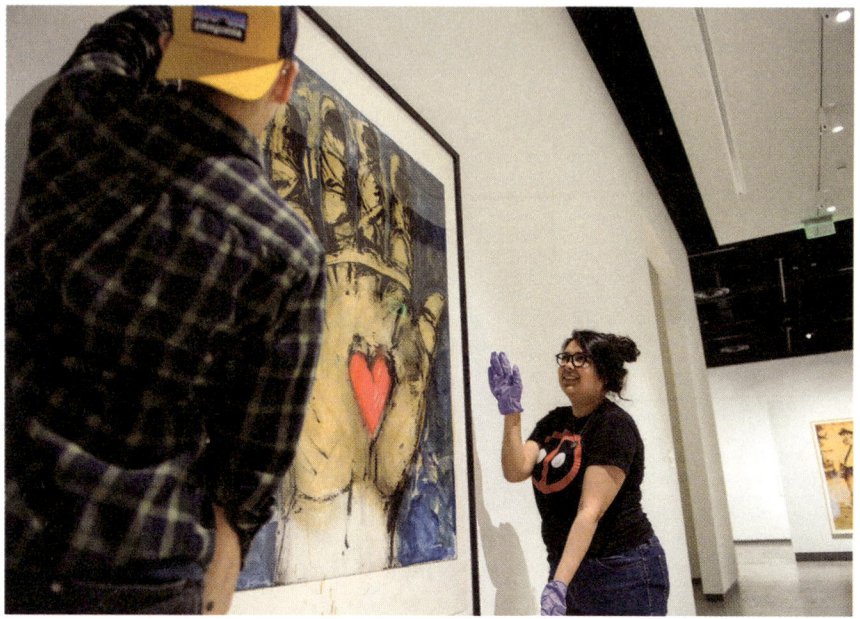

Museum interns installing artwork in the Smith Gallery for the grand opening exhibition *Hearts: Selections from the Jim Dine Print Collection*, 2018

Photo: WSU Photo Services

carefully unloaded the art as the mechanic installed the spare. Another time, we had to quell the doubting voices of Friends seamstresses who'd been volunteering 24/7, sewing hanging sleeves onto Indonesian textiles, hurrying to meet a seemingly impossible installation deadline. Perhaps most memorable was when, unknown to the museum, construction workers penetrated the roof of the Fine Arts Building. Rain came into the museum gallery, luckily without damage to the exhibition. The threat of more rain compelled the museum to mount a round-the-clock watch: the only people available at night were the core staff of three, one with a newborn baby. We each took a portion of the night to stand guard—in a spookily dark gallery in an empty building on a deserted campus—for several days in a row until the roof was finally secured.

As I write this, memories surface of all the individuals, staff, students, and volunteers, the WSU custodians, electricians, and carpenters, who gave beyond expectation or job description or sometimes sleep. It was all worthwhile. Together many people made sure the art museum flourished for its first fifty years and is poised, with the help of a similarly devoted next generation, to thrive throughout its next fifty. The museum is now well on its way to becoming "a permanent institution in the service of society."

1. Excerpt from the definition of a museum by the International Council on Museums, 2019.

2. Keith Monaghan, chair of Fine Arts (1951–72), was instrumental in the new Fine Arts Center. Narramore, Bain, Brady & Johnanson were the architects.

3. Excerpt from President Ernest O. Holland's inaugural address, March 24, 1916. Holland was president 1916–44.

4. From "Forty Years On," a song by Bowen and Farmer.

5. Patricia Watkinson was a charter member of the Advisory Council at the Jordan Schnitzer Museum of Art WSU from 2018 to 2024 and chaired the council 2019 to 2020.

6. United States Agency for International Development.

7. Cheney Cowles Memorial State Museum (now Northwest Museum of Arts and Culture), Spokane; Tacoma Art Museum; and the Western Gallery, Western Washington State College (now University), Bellingham. Later members included the Whatcom Museum of History & Art, Bellingham; the Henry Gallery of Art, University of Washington; and the Seattle Art Museum.

8. From *Works on Paper: American Art 1945–1975*, the Washington Art Consortium publication, 1977.

9. Now the Northwest Museum of Arts and Culture.

10. Now the Bellevue Arts Museum.

11. By Bob Staab and Paul Brians respectively.

12. The title of Robert Hughes' BBC TV series and book, 1980. Hughes was a Friel speaker in 1981.

13. Letter to President Holland from former regent Charles W. Orton.

14. In 1988–89 docents (artists, retired educators, homemakers) toured 3,000 visitors—from preschoolers to university students to senior citizens (per *Museum of Art/WSU Newsletter* no. 4, Fall 1989).

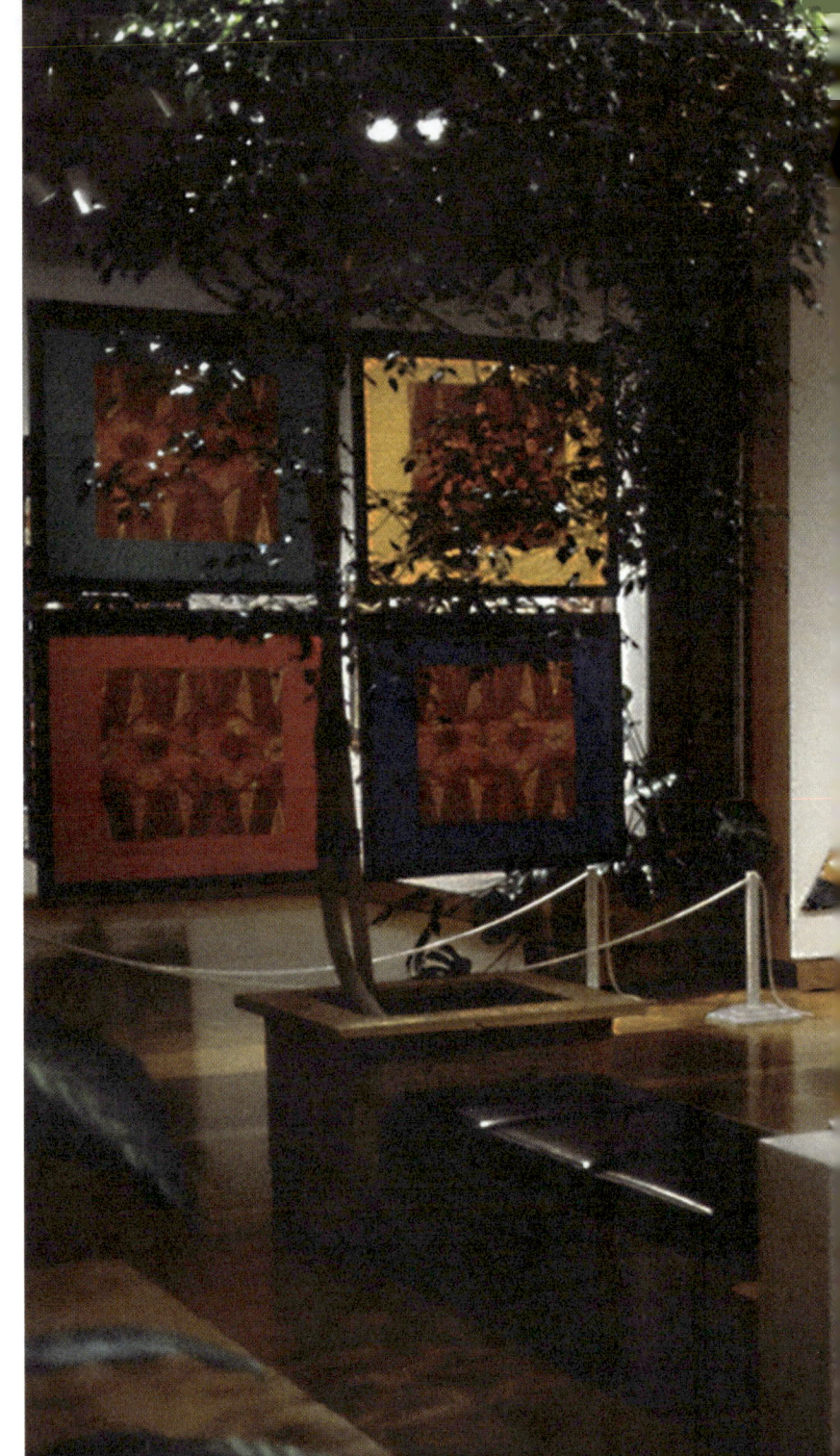

The Definitive Contemporary American Quilt
November 7–December 16, 1992

Photo: WSU Libraries' Manuscripts, Archives,
and Special Collections

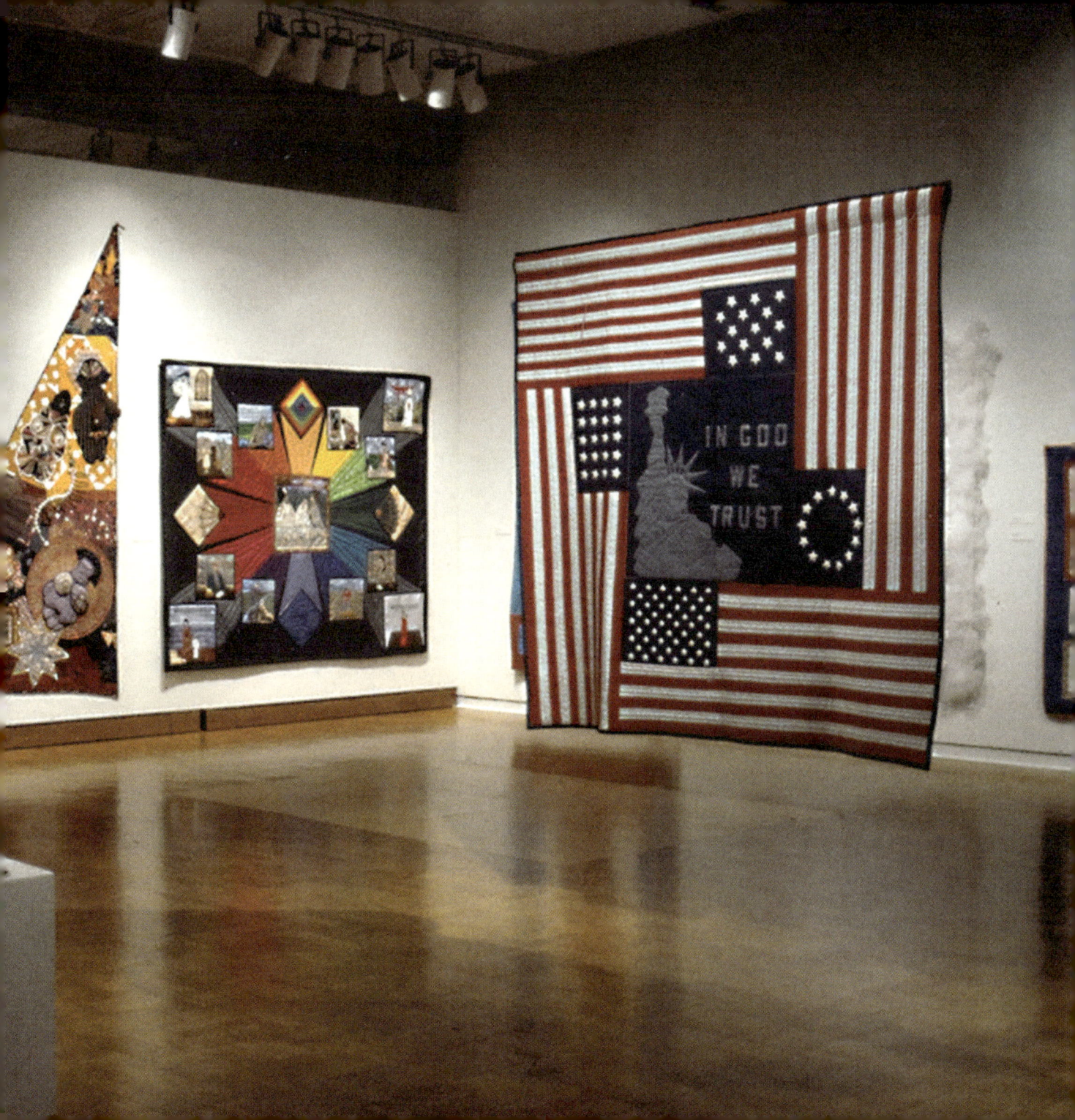

MANY VOICES

Monica Monaghan-Milstein

In 1948, Keith Monaghan accepted an invitation to fill a sabbatical teaching position in WSU's Department of Fine Arts. He was intrigued by the possibilities for art advancement in Pullman and simultaneously astounded to learn that Fine Arts had no designated facilities on campus. The following year he was asked to continue at WSU, in lieu of returning to his position at the University of California, Berkeley. He made the courageous decision to move to Pullman, leaving behind an artistic and teaching environment that strongly supported and legitimized the fine arts disciplines, as well as the influential era of Bay Area art. Keith soon became inspired by the Palouse landscape—a focus that was to continue throughout his lengthy career as an artist and art educator.

In 1952, Keith was appointed chair of Fine Arts and, while assuming new leadership responsibilities and a full teaching schedule, he began fostering momentum for a new facility on campus devoted to the fine arts. As Keith met with university administration over many years, he consistently promoted the concept of this much-needed facility.

The opening of the spectacular, Fine Arts Center in 1972 was a long-awaited fulfillment of Keith's vision and tenacity. A landmark on the WSU campus, the new building featured studios, state-of-the art teaching facilities in many media, an auditorium and exhibition spaces. A large gallery was designed to bring exceptional arts to the university and beyond.

Harvey West, the first director of the WSU Museum of Art, a WSU alumnus, Fine Arts major and longstanding supporter of Keith's vision, was to work vigilantly with university administration, expanding the large gallery concept into a full-fledged museum. The WSU Museum of Art opened in October 1974, launching a seminal era for the newly formed museum, presenting numerous renowned exhibitions, lectures, and annual art symposiums.

After serving his 20-year tenure as chair of the Fine Arts Department, Keith continued to play a major role in teaching at WSU until his retirement in 1986. Keith's tireless dedication to the university and the state of Washington was recognized by Governor Booth Gardner, who proclaimed May 10, 1986, as Keith Monaghan Appreciation Day—a proud day for the university and for our family.

—Monica Monaghan-Milstein (WSU FA)
   Artist and designer & daughter of
   Keith Monaghan

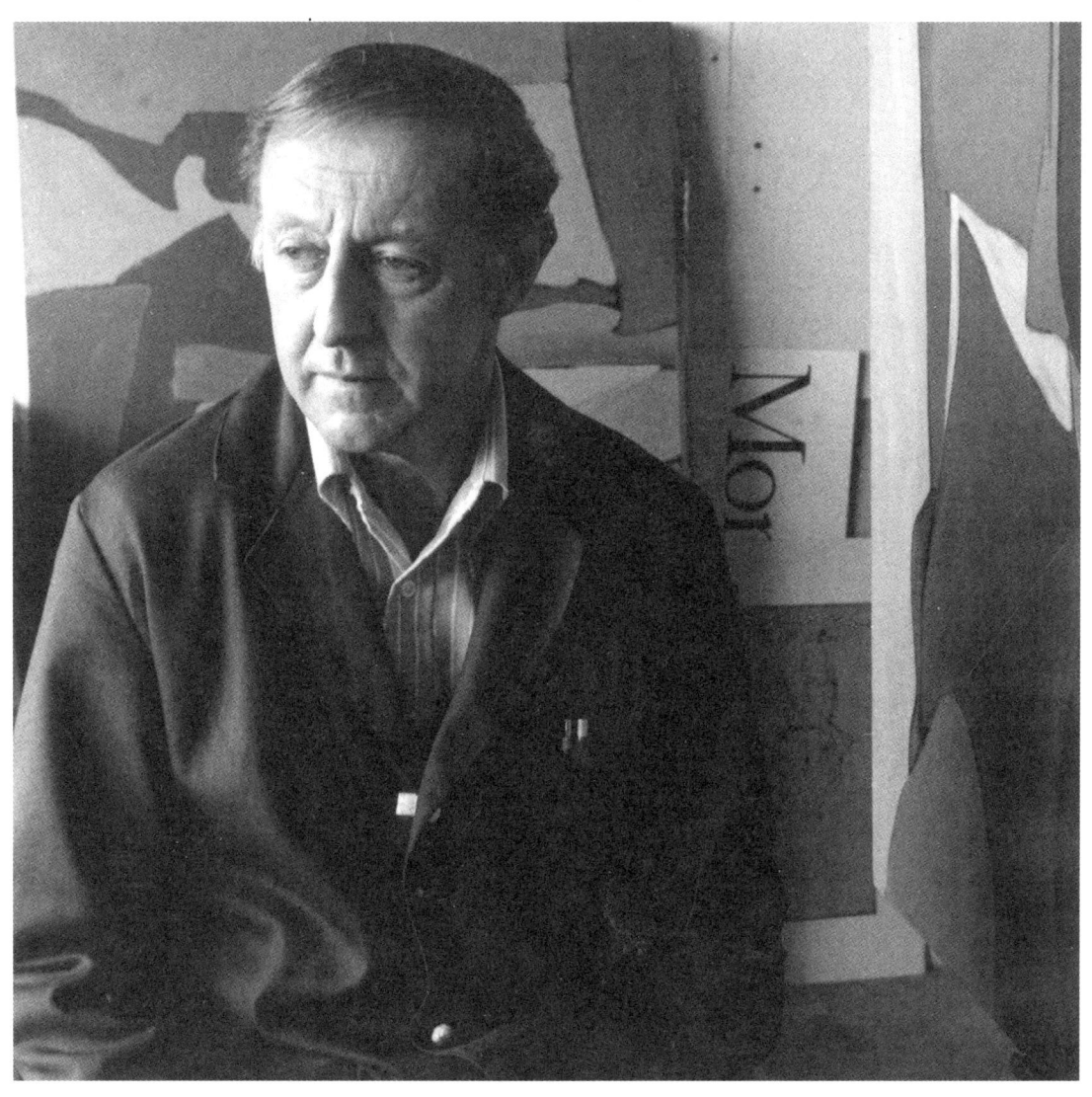

Keith Monaghan, photographed for the exhibition
Northwest Images: Kenneth Callahan and Keith Monaghan, February 10–March 6, 1987
Photo: WSU Libraries' Manuscripts, Archives, and Special Collections

Bruce Guenther

The five years I spent at the art museum in Pullman were an exciting, challenging time. Stepping into the new institution as it began to define itself on campus and develop its inaugural programming was, in many ways, a dream for a young curator eager to build skills and define an aesthetic identity. With a director absorbed in administrative politics and very little art historical background, I was free, within the ever-present budgetary limitations, to outline an ambitious program.

The exhibition program was built around historic media-based survey exhibitions in twentieth century art to nurture students' art education—American drawing, contemporary fiber arts, the American print renaissance, Northwest sculpture, Color Field painting, and photography. We began organizing career retrospectives for major Northwest artists, including two retiring art faculty, as well as exhibitions for the current faculty and a broad selection of contemporary artists, including Robert Smithson, Judy Chicago, Richard Smith, and Alden Mason. The museum's annual symposiums attracted regional audiences; and established lifelong associations for me with Robert Motherwell, Mark Di Suvero, Roland Petersen, Judy Chicago, Mel Katz—as well as art historians Albert Elsen, Richard Field, Riva Castleman, and Mildred Constantine, who all ventured into the Palouse to discuss ideas and art. The distances from Pullman to the major national art centers disappeared in those heady days.

The Pullman museum years taught me how to cold-call artists, dealers, and collectors who had no reason to care about the museum or WSU; develop relationships and solicit donors; work with authors, designers, and printers on art publications; effectively communicate with the general public and the press; along with the carpentry and truck driving that kept us functioning. I became the recognized curator I am today because of the rich "all-hands-on-deck" experiences of the five years and nine days I worked at the Museum of Art/WSU.

—Bruce Guenther
  Curator, 1974–1978
  Acting Director, 1976–1977
  Director, 1978–1979
  Museum of Art/WSU

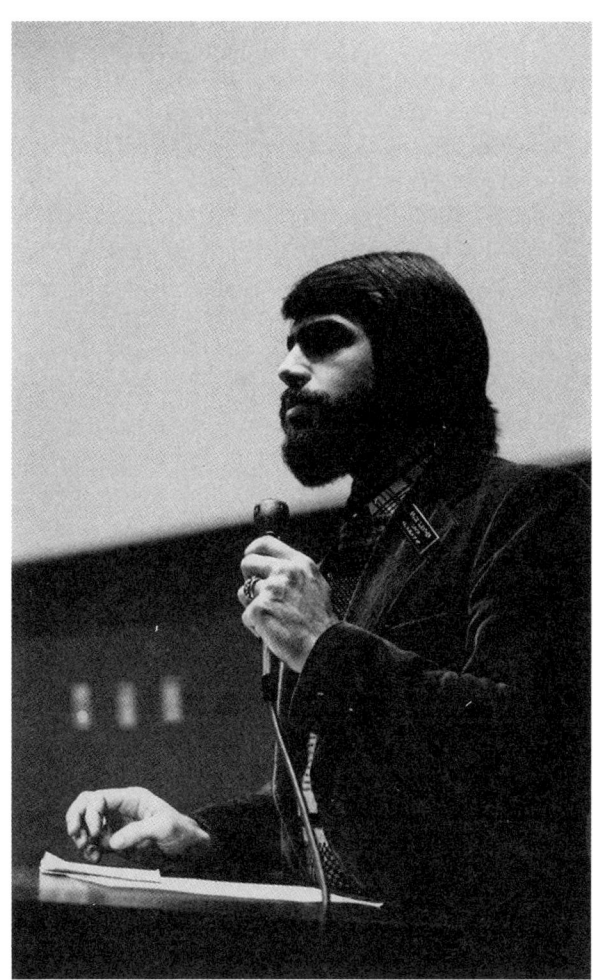

Bruce Guenther speaking at the museum's Rodin Symposium on February 21, 1976, which was a program during the exhibition *Rodin: The Maryhill Collection*, shown February 4–February 29, 1976. Jiri Frel, Curator of Antiquities from the J. Paul Getty Museum, and Walter Hass, professor of Art History at Stanford University, also spoke at the all-day event.

Photo: Jordan Schnitzer Museum of Art WSU Archives

Francis Ho

I became one of the 12-member faculty for WSU's Department of Fine Arts in 1967. Back then, today's Murrow Hall was the home for the department. My colleagues shared offices along a narrow corridor adjacent to the WSU Art Gallery, as it was called, a roughly 35 x 60-foot rectangular exhibition space. Each year, the annual Fine Arts Faculty Exhibition was held in the fall and the Master of Fine Arts Thesis Exhibition was held in the spring. Throughout the rest of the academic year, student class work and invited work by area artists were exhibited in the gallery. The new Fine Arts Center was being planned and would eventually include the Museum of Art/WSU. It was an exciting time to share plans and dreams with my colleagues about what the new facility had in store for us.

—Francis Ho, Professor Emeritus
    Department of Fine Arts, WSU Pullman

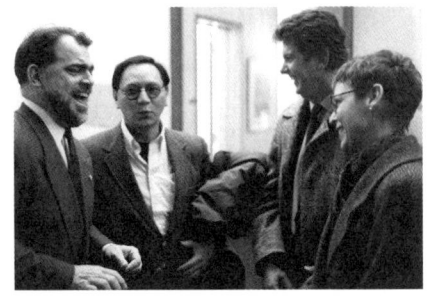

From left to right: Bruce Guenther, Francis Ho, Chris Watts, and Karen Watts at a museum function

Photo: WSU Libraries' Manuscripts, Archives, and Special Collections

Jo Hockenhull

For most of my 25-year Department of Fine Arts appointment in Pullman, I felt the art museum was part of my teaching support system. The exhibitions were educational and exciting—and at our doorstep. The museum nourished the faculty and campus with annual exhibitions of new faculty work, while also hosting graduate student exhibitions.

One extraordinary personal experience, besides my own solo retrospective in 2012, was my involvement in conceptualizing, planning and fund-raising to create the Plateau Project. The project was directed by Barbara Coddington in collaboration with the Museum of Art/WSU, the Anthropology Department, Women's Studies (of which I was director at the time) and the Native American Advisory Board, which was made up of representatives from Plateau Tribes between British Columbia to Northern California.

I can still vividly remember the first day-long planning meeting with around 30 representatives from the Plateau Tribes, in addition to the WSU participants. I sat next to a Nez Perce woman, one hundred years old: Her velvet hand took mine and she introduced herself in her native language.

These initial discussions took place in the late 1980s. The plan was to gather and honor traditional Plateau women's art. In addition to working on two NEH grants for the planning and implementation of the exhibition, I accompanied Ann McCormack, Nez Perce representative, in visiting Northwest private collections, libraries, historical and cultural centers, schools and museums. We sifted through many shoe boxes to choose photos for the exhibition—an amazing experience! I learned about the Indigenous peoples of our region and the complexities of creating this art exhibition, something the Museum of Art/WSU did regularly.

A Song to the Creator: Traditional Arts of Native American Women of the Plateau was exhibited at the Museum of Art/WSU from October 14–December 15, 1996. A superb book associated with the exhibition, with the same title, was edited by Lillian A. Ackerman, WSU Department of Anthropology, and was published by the University of Oklahoma Press in 1996.

—Jo Hockenhull, Professor Emerita, Department of Fine Arts,
    Director of Women's Studies, Associate Dean, WSU Vancouver

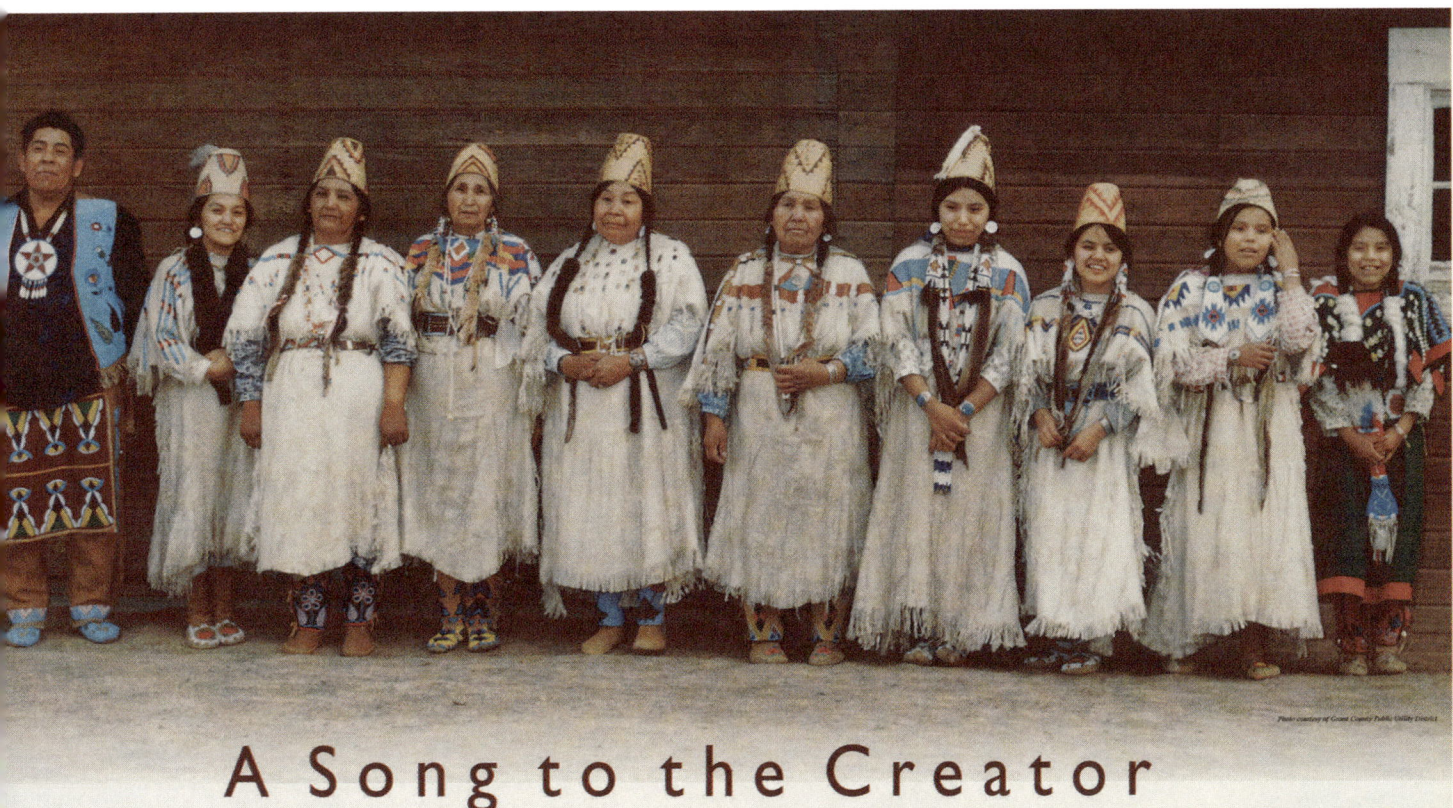

A Song to the Creator

Traditional Arts of Native American Women of the Plateau

This exhibit focuses on women who have kept alive the cultural traditions of their people, creating works of surpassing beauty and spiritual purpose and teaching these art forms to succeeding generations. The objects on display magnificently recreate 100 years of Plateau weaving, hideworking, music, storytelling, and the ornamental arts.

OCTOBER 14 - DECEMBER 15, 1996

MUSEUM OF ART/WSU
WASHINGTON STATE UNIVERSITY / PULLMAN, WASHINGTON   99164-7460   509-335-6607

OPENING
Monday, October 14, 7:30 p.m.,
Compton Union Building Ballroom.
Lecture and poetry reading by
Elizabeth Woody, Plateau poet.
Reception follows in
Fine Arts Center.

The Museum is open Monday through Friday,
10 a.m.-4 p.m.; Tuesday, 10 a.m.-10 p.m.;
Saturday and Sunday, 1-5 p.m.

Closed November 11 and
November 28-December 1.

Poster from the exhibition *A Song to the Creator: Traditional Arts of Native American Women of the Plateau*, 1996

Photo: Jordan Schnitzer Museum of Art WSU Archives

John Pierce

"When it rains, it pours." That phrase applies to WSU's art museum in several ways. First, the museum's growth since its inception at WSU saw a steady outpouring of aesthetic and educational excellence. During my time as dean of Liberal Arts, I was often impressed with director Patricia Watkinson's commitment to supporting the museum's growth in quality and her willingness to collaborate with the academic programs across the university. Additionally, Patricia exhibited a deep concern for the collections themselves. Perhaps the best example was her willingness to stay overnight in the museum in the midst of a rainstorm that produced leaks in the roof, threatening the artwork. Moreover, she took on the task of educating a dean who grew up in a small logging town with little exposure to fine art in his background.

—John Pierce
Dean of College of Liberal Arts
(1986–1997), WSU

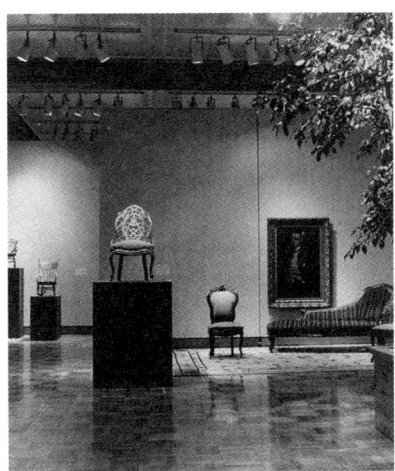

Gallery view from the exhibition
The Chair, 1975

Photo: Jordan Schnitzer Museum of
Art WSU Archives

Curt Sherman

From 1965 to 1980, I served as the lead professor in the Interior Design program at WSU. The program was well-supported by the university, its students, and graduates, enough so that it became the largest and first program in Washington state to receive the coveted accreditation for Interior Design programs. However, we were still distant from the centers of interior design practice, far from the markets where products were introduced and reviewed annually. Students and faculty would travel to Spokane, Seattle, Portland, and even San Francisco for inspiration, but on a day-to-day basis the isolation was deeply felt.

With the Museum of Art/WSU and Bruce Guenther, a miracle occurred. Bruce recognized our virtual design desert and suggested an exhibition of chairs. I hastily agreed! We both scoured Pullman, Moscow, and parts beyond to gather some 100 seating devices. Our earliest examples were an African Chief's Stool and Benin Bronze Chiefs' necklaces in the form of stools. We then highlighted Renaissance Italy, and the sixteenth and seventeenth centuries in France and England. Moving into the twentieth century, all of the seating landmarks were on display: Thonet's bentwood miracles, Rietveld's Red-Blue Chair, Le Corbusier's Chaise, Mies van der Rohe's Barcelona, the Eames's Lounge and their other important pieces, and a whole series of great Danish Modern and Italian works.

The students in Interior Design and Architecture visited and re-revisited the exhibition. I gave numerous tours, and from what I understand, it was one of the most popular exhibitions seen that year. Good design had arrived in the Palouse.

—Curt Sherman
Former Associate Professor, WSU Pullman

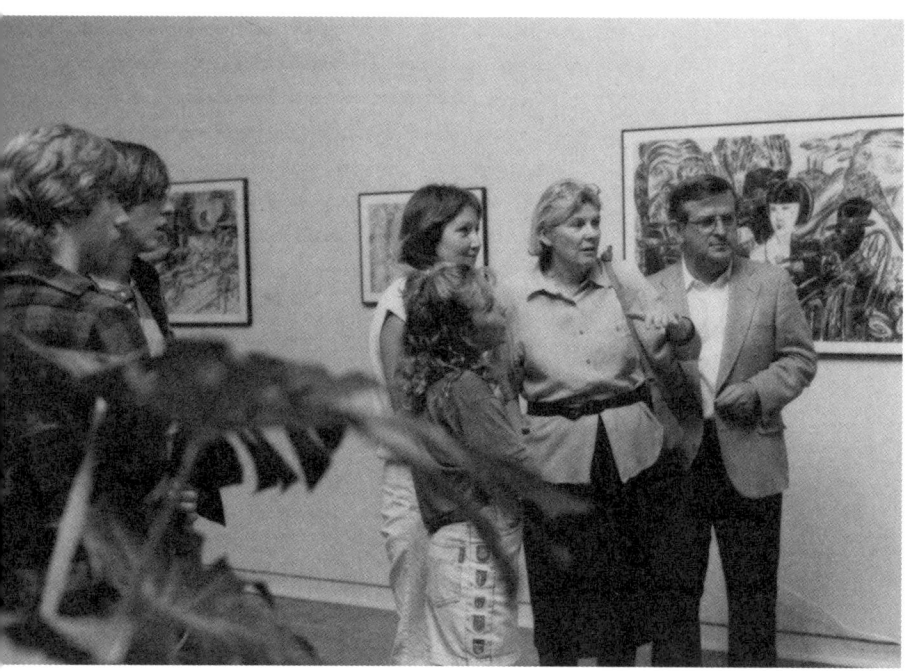

Sam and Pat Smith (right) at a museum reception
Photo: WSU Libraries' Manuscripts, Archives, and
Special Collections

Sam & Pat Smith

Soon after our 1985 arrival in Pullman, we visited the Museum of Art/WSU for a tour. We learned how the exhibits and collection were used in collaboration with disciplines across the campus to enhance and broaden the education of WSU students.

The museum became part of our years at WSU. Viewing the exhibitions and attending the lectures enriched our lives, and we made lasting friendships among the art community. We are pleased to be able to continue support for the museum as it grows and enriches the lives of the campus community today.

—Samuel H. Smith
  WSU President Emeritus,
  1985–2000, and
  Patricia W. Smith

Nancy Spitzer

The impressive *Fay Jones: A 20 Year Retrospective* truly changed how I appreciate and enjoy art. The exhibition was organized in 1996 by Sandy Harthorn, curator at the Boise Art Museum, and then traveled to the Museum of Art/WSU in early 1997.

As a fan of Seattle artist Fay Jones, seeing 43 pieces of her quirky, colorful, mysterious imagery all in one place was exciting and intriguing. After many return visits, I finally bought the accompanying catalog and was captivated by Harthorn's writing style, knowledge, and insights.

Harthorn's interview with Fay Jones about her life and art revealed that the artist grew up in her family's Rhode Island hotel and, as the eldest of six, was put in charge of her siblings. Her hectic family life together with the constant parade of hotel guests provided Jones with a diverse cast of characters and imagery that became personal symbols for expressing emotion. Her recurring symbols of sailors, clocks, palms, and boxing gloves evoke feelings of romance,

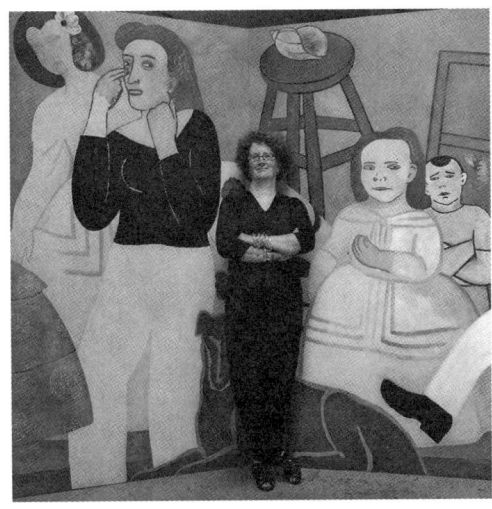

Davis Freeman, *Fay Jones*, 2001
Photogravure, 12 x 11.5 inches
JSMA WSU WSU Permanent Collection,
Gift of Sean Elwood to honor his daughter,
Shannon Strother Elwood

history, exotic locales, and marriage. Sea images convey romance or danger; fish symbolize nourishment. As Harthorn noted "It is a language, once recognized, that gives you a key to the work." What a lightning bolt! Now I could decipher secret emotions in Jones' work. I then realized that this talented curator had not only given me a deeper understanding of Fay Jones' art, but also a new appreciation for the curator's work. I am so grateful for that gift. Congrats to the Jordan Schnitzer Museum of Art WSU for 50 years of revelatory experiences!

—Nancy Spitzer
   Jordan Schnitzer Museum of Art WSU Advisory Council and
   Pullman Community Member

Karen Weathermon

The Jordan Schnitzer Museum of Art WSU looms large in my art experiences. My very first visit to an art museum as a child was to the Museum of Art/WSU in the early 1970s to see an exhibition by faculty member Gaylen Hansen, and I still recall the whimsy of his many iterations of works involving striped socks. Returning to WSU as a graduate student and eventually as a staff and faculty member, the museum has been the starting point for interesting student assignments, the source of personal enjoyment, and a valued partner with the Common Reading Program in creating opportunities for wider student engagement.

Some standout experiences for me have been the eclectic, joyful wonder of *Petland*, the privilege of seeing civil rights history through the photographs and stories of Benedict Fernandez's *Countdown to Eternity*, the sobering impact of Chris Jordan's depiction of consumer waste in *Running the Numbers*, and the array of monumental art displayed across campus from the Walla Walla Foundry. In these, and so many other exhibits, the museum has broadened my own perspectives on artistic forms, on the creative imagination, and on human experience. It is always a joy to introduce students to these important ways of knowing!

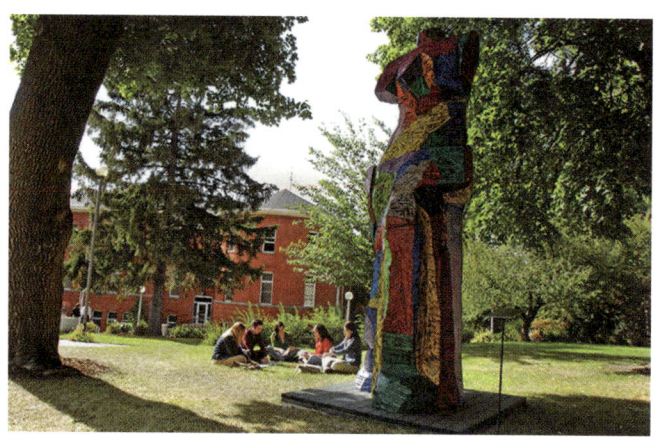

From August through October 2004, the Museum of Art/WSU presented works of Jim Dine and sculpture from the Walla Walla Foundry across the WSU Pullman campus

Photo: WSU Photo Services

—Karen Weathermon
  Director of First-Year
  Programs in the Division of
  Academic Engagement and
  Student Achievement,
  WSU Pullman

Michael Holloman

On a trip to Pullman in 1991, I found myself wandering through the Museum of Art/WSU. I became transfixed by a series of oil paintings by Worth D. Griffin, a former chair of WSU's Department of Fine Arts. These stunning portraits from the museum's permanent collection depicted Native Americans and were painted at the advent of the 1937-41 Nespelem Art Colony on the Colville Indian Reservation. While I recognized some of the individuals, I knew little about the art colony itself, which was co-founded by Griffin and junior faculty member Clyfford Still.

Upon my return to the Colville Indian Reservation, I immediately asked my grandmother if she remembered the art colony. It took time for her to recall those days before WWII and all that had transpired within the tribal community. I told her names of people who were painted, and she became animated, relating wonderful stories of each person. In contrast, many of Griffin's contextual notes were challenged by their dated tropes of a vanishing race.

Recently, I have had the pleasure of working closely with the museum to create expanded label copy for many of these same paintings. On these labels, tribal descendants of individuals who were painted by Griffin offer more detailed, culturally compassionate, and personal narratives of their ancestors.

—Michael Holloman
(Confederated Tribes of the
Colville Indian Reservation)
Associate Professor,
Department of Art,
WSU Pullman

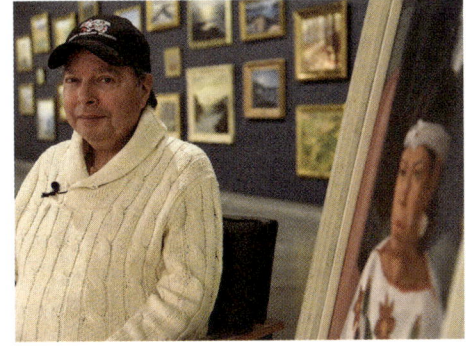

Michael Holloman guest-curated
Follow the River: Portraits of the Columbia Plateau in 2021

Photo: Kristin Becker

Ana Maria Rodriguez-Vivaldi

I grew up surrounded by art. My extended family was comprised of an eclectic group of museum goers, artists, and passionate collectors of artworks. From Puerto Rican artists to many of other cultural and national backgrounds, our homes showcased that diversity of taste and love for the arts and crafts in their many expressions. Thus, for me, to be within a space such as the Jordan Schnitzer Museum of Art WSU is like being home. I strongly believe in the arts in general, and the WSU art museum in particular, as being both a literal and a symbolic bridge among cultures: A magical space where we can lose ourselves and explore things that, while being unique—the artist's own vision—still represent humanity in a plethora of ways. In that space of exploration, we undertake a voyage where the many ways of being human and expressing ourselves may be witnessed and understood. In this magical space, we share in the experience of looking into the mind and soul of people with different backgrounds, ethnicities, and life experiences. In doing so, we come together in a spark of recognition, identifying new means of seeing and a shared language that is inclusive, accepting, and safe. I've always felt and said that the arts sustain me, and we are privileged indeed to have a museum that promotes such a joyful gathering of diverse minds and souls.

—Ana Maria Rodriguez-Vivaldi
    Emerita Associate Professor of Spanish, American Studies and Culture, and Film Studies;
    Former Associate Dean of Student Affairs and Global Education,
    College of Arts & Sciences, WSU Pullman

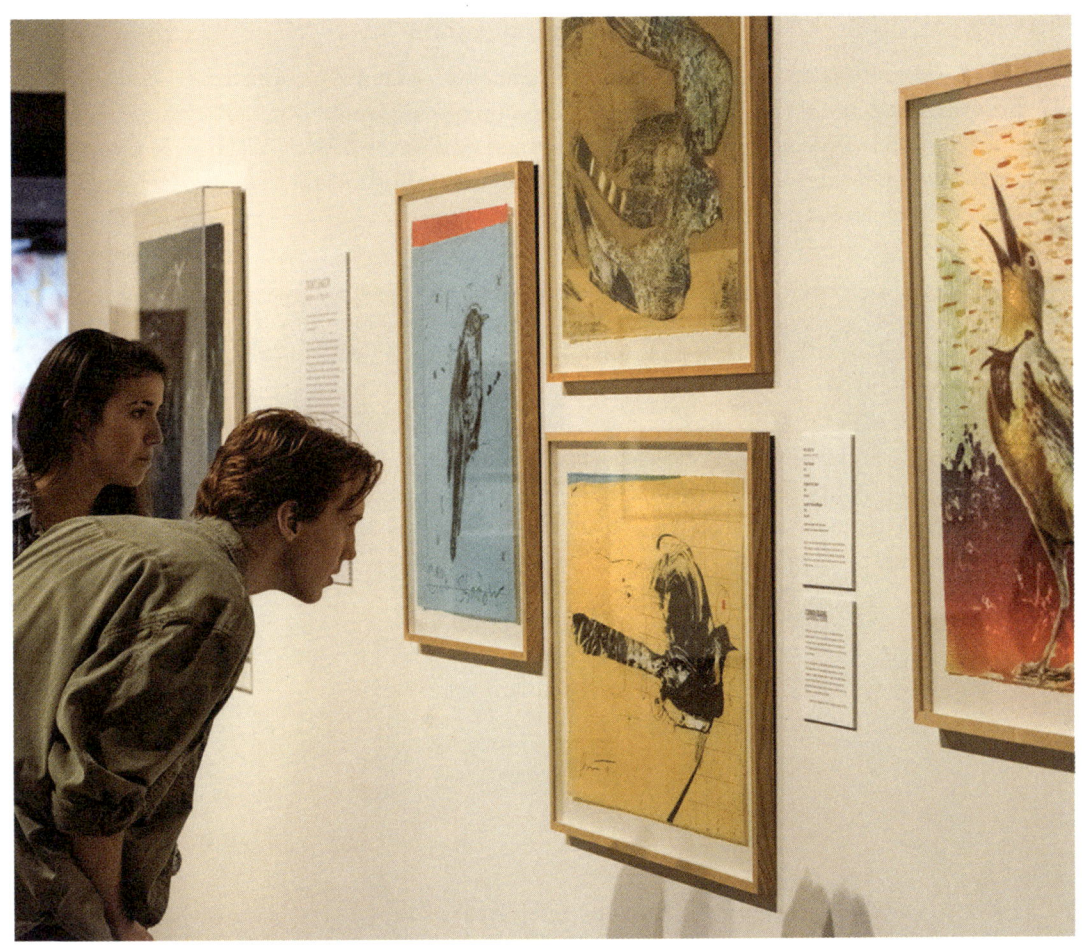

Visitors enjoy several of Rick Bartow's prints from the exhibition
Here in a Homemade Forest: Common Reading Connections
at a program for first-year experience students and faculty on September 12, 2023
Photo: WSU Photo Services

Anna-Maria Shannon

The Museum of Art has been much more than a workplace for me; it's been a cherished home filled with unforgettable memories and extraordinary individuals. My journey began with a simple step into volunteering, warmly welcomed by director Patricia Watkinson. Over 20 years, I transitioned from a library volunteer to Associate Director and later Interim Director, marking profound personal growth.

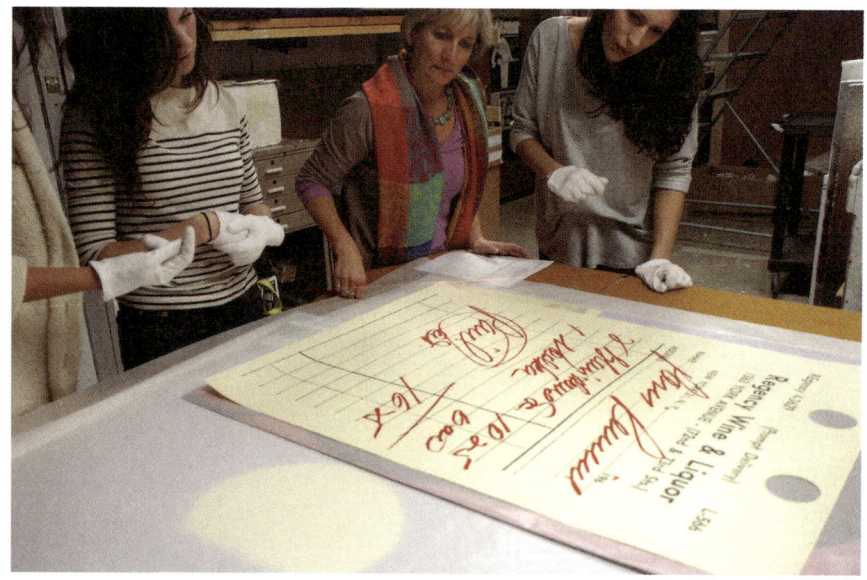

Anna-Maria Shannon (center) and museum studies students accessioning Andy Warhol's *Paris Review* (1967) into the permanent collection from the Andy Warhol Legacy Project in November 2013

Photo: Zach Mazur

Leaving the museum wasn't just bidding farewell to a job; it was parting ways with a beloved family. The heart of this family lay in its people—artists, curators, directors, faculty, volunteers, and students—who shaped my very essence. Directors like Patricia Watkinson, Ross Coates, and Chris Bruce provided invaluable guidance and vision.

The creative brilliance of curators like Roger Rowley and Keith Wells brought exhibitions that garnered accolades and inspired admiration. Keith's passing left a void only few could begin to fill, and Ryan Hardesty seamlessly stepped in, alongside dedicated team members such as Laura Child, Zach Mazur, Ann Saberi, and Debby Stinson, all instrumental in the museum's success.

Reflecting on my time, I recall countless stories etched into the museum's walls—stories of art, encounters with transformative artists, and unwavering support from those who believed in the museum. My journey wasn't just about preserving history but becoming part of it—a custodian of the past and contributor to the future.

As I enter the doors of the new museum, I feel a sense of belonging and gratitude for the leadership of Ryan Hardesty, the stewardship of Ann Saberi, and the enthusiastic museum team. To new staff, I encourage you to embrace the unique experiences awaiting you. My time was a whirlwind of emotions—wild, fun, challenging, and enlightening—but above all, it was about forging bonds with an extraordinary family, the true heartbeat of the art museum.

—Anna-Maria Shannon
    Volunteer and Docent, 1996–2001
    Assistant Director, 2001–2006
    Associate Director, 2006–2016
    Interim Director, 2016–2019
    Jordan Schnitzer Museum of Art WSU

THE PERMANENT COLLECTION

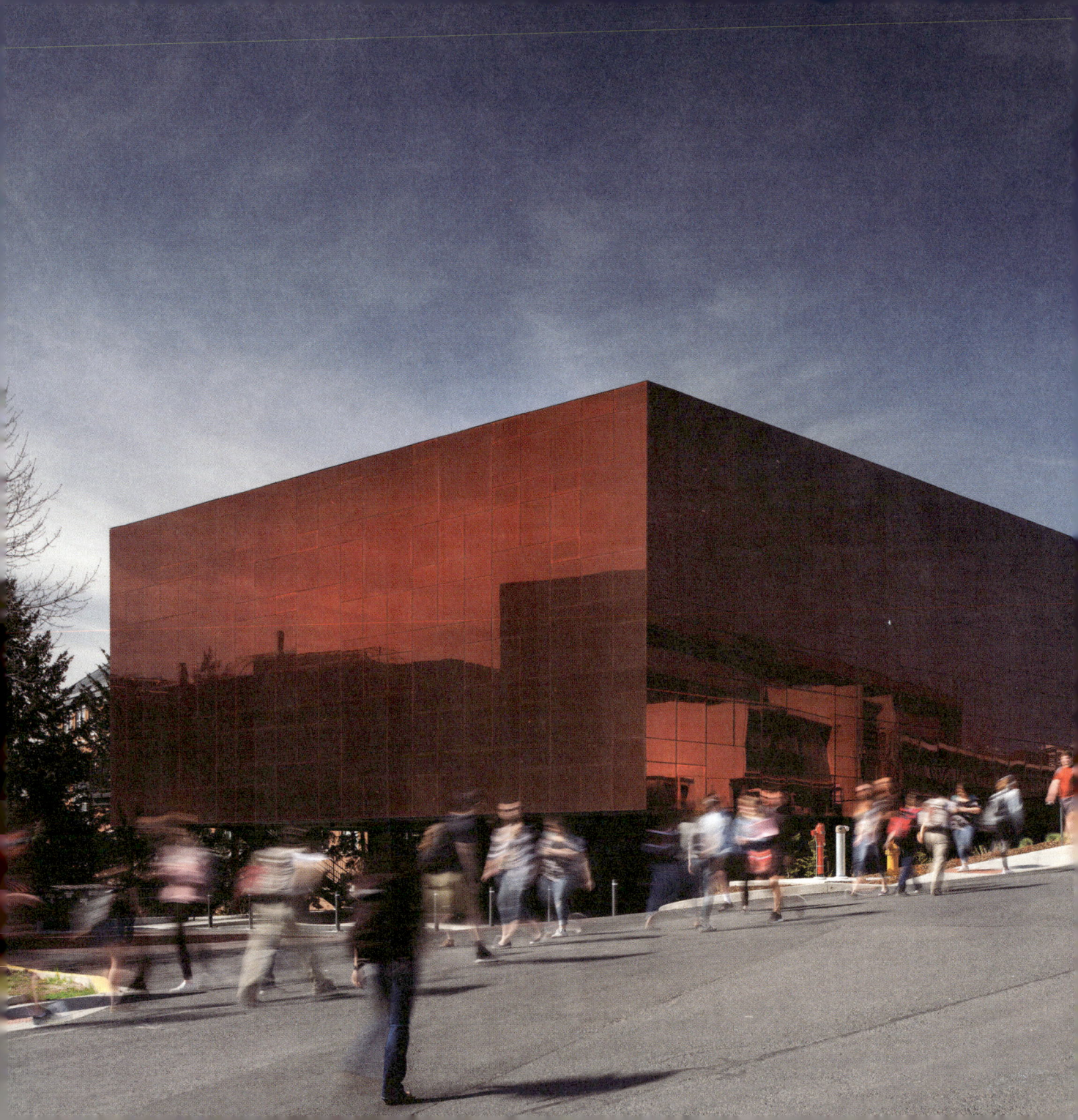

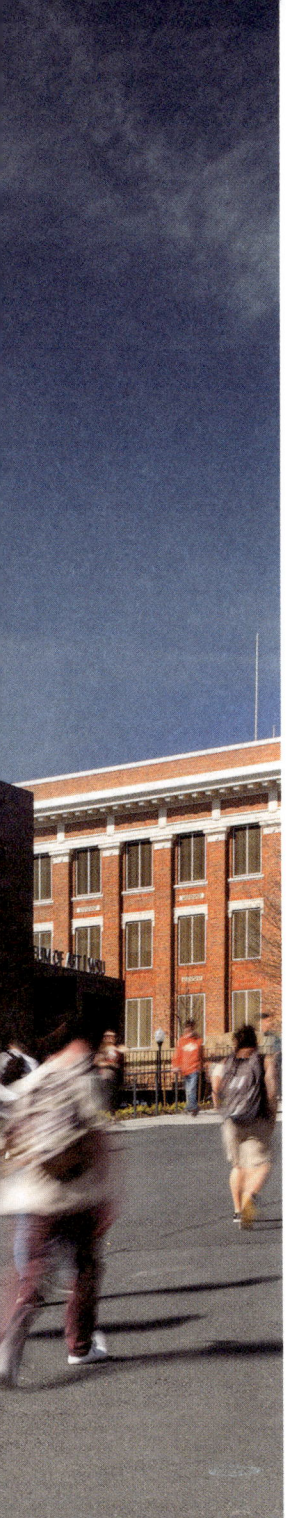

A JEWEL BOX, A MIRROR, AND A TIME MACHINE

Sean Elwood, Museum Supporter

While honored to be asked to write about the collection for the Washington State University art museum's 50th anniversary, I wasn't certain how to approach the assignment. The task is challenging because the collection is substantial and because the museum and its collection are personally significant for me.

I was born and raised in Pullman, my parents and their friends worked for the university, I received my bachelor's degree in fine arts at WSU, and I've maintained a relationship with the place all my life. I've known every one of the museum's directors. And because I pursued (or fell into) the career I did, I was able to buy, trade, publish or otherwise receive many works of art, sometimes by artists of substantial standing. As a result, I was also able to give modest gifts of art to the museum, each one credited to honor my wife, my daughter, or my parents.[1] Over the years the museum and its holdings have become the most enduring connection I have with my home place.

In his invitation, director Ryan Hardesty gave me considerable latitude for how I might approach the topic, suggesting I could reflect and highlight the origins and the directions in which the collection has grown since Harvey West (somewhat controversially) gathered the Orton and Holland collections[2]—then scattered around campus—to form the core of the museum's current holdings. Or I could write about how the collection coalesced through intention and opportunity into the current body of works by hundreds of artists, accumulated through occasional purchases and donations from collectors and institutions, and how it has grown to contain over 4,000 objects. I could expound on the museum's holdings breadth and depth. How it is particularly strong in works on paper (drawings, prints,

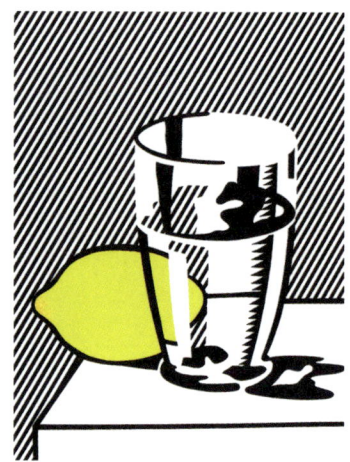

and photographs) and how the museum holds representative collections of Northwest artists from western Washington and inland Washington, as well as from the regions of northern Idaho and western Montana. The museum has gathered significant holdings of works by Indigenous artists as well as art and artists representing diversities of all sorts. It has acquired works by the art stars of the contemporary canon and lesser known—but no less serious—artists from across the United States and the world. There are surprising collections of British prints, Northwest glass, impressive works by historically important artists, and solid and gratifying examples of artworks by past faculty of the university. The story of how all these things came to be gathered in the heart of the Palouse is fascinating, but it is a topic for some other, more qualified author.

I know this is meant to be a retrospective celebration, but if permitted to look forward as well as back as we celebrate, I think it's interesting to contemplate where the collection might be going based on these 50 years of prologue.

A few years ago, with Ryan's permission, I embarked on an entirely self-inflicted task, to familiarize myself with the collection to define a "scope of collections," that is, determine if there was an overarching theme (or themes) represented within the museum's holdings. I thought I would then draft guidelines for what, how, and why the museum might continue to collect going forward, based on those themes. Let's just say it was 2020, I was retired, COVID-19 was everywhere, and I had time on my hands.

I found that, despite my connections to the place, the museum's collection was largely undiscovered territory for me, full of new revelations or reminders of things I had forgotten. I never found that

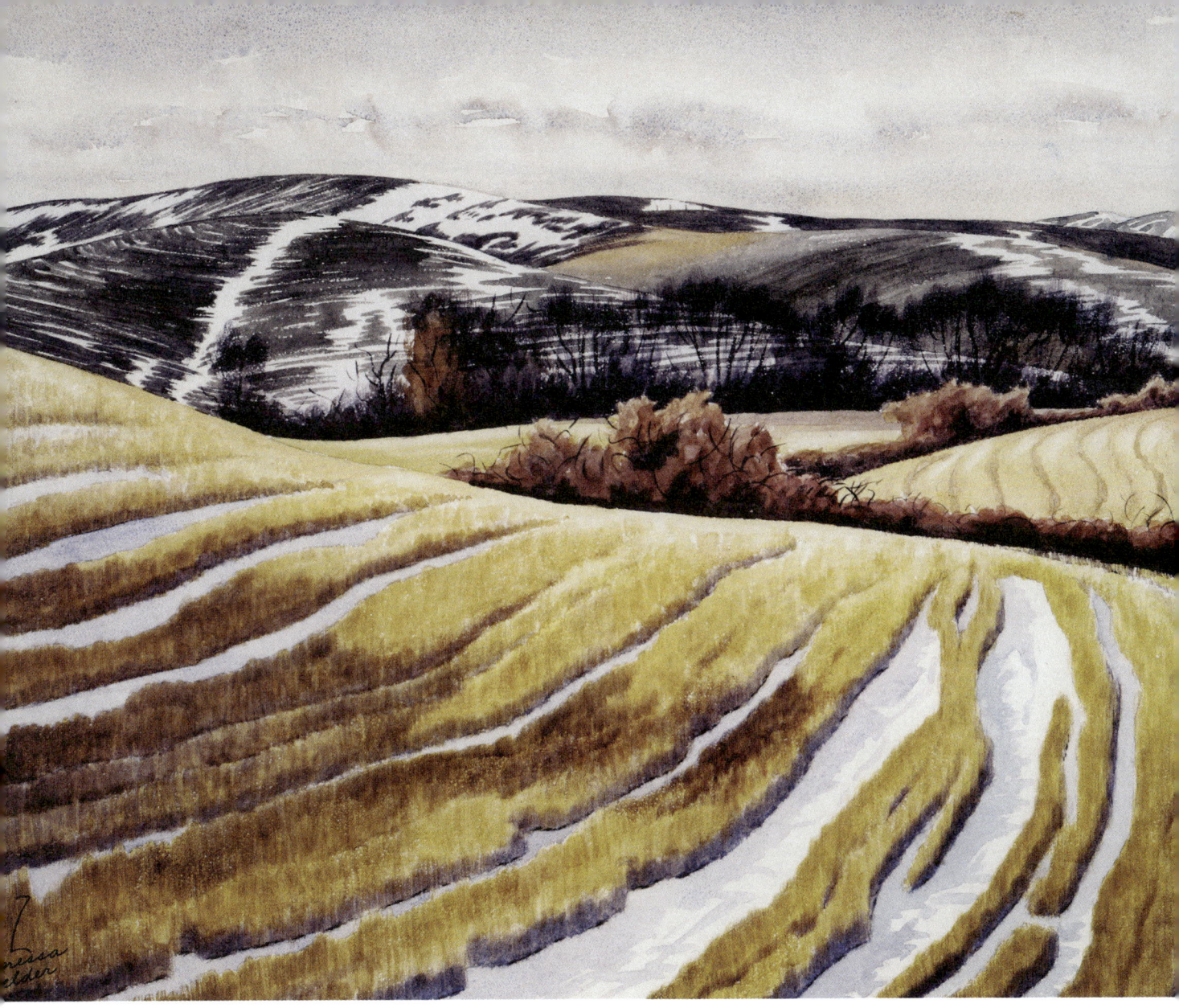

Z. Vanessa Helder, *Snow and Stubble*, 1939
Watercolor, 30.5 x 33.5 inches
JSMA WSU Permanent Collection,
Gift of Charles and Virginia Orton

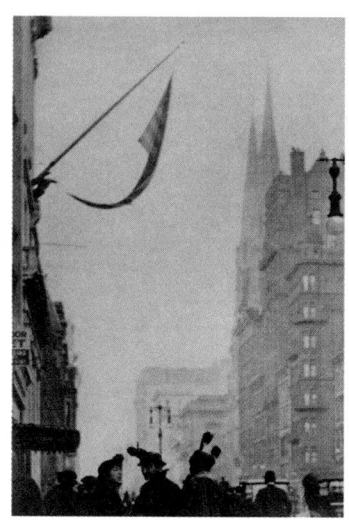

Paul Strand, *Fifth Avenue, New York* from *The Formative Years, 1914–1917*, 1915

Hand-pulled dust-grain photogravure, 12.5 x 8 inches

JSMA WSU Permanent Collection, Gift of Timothy Bradbury

overarching single through-line that connected all the works in the collection. Instead, I was overwhelmed by the variety I discovered. There was no easily defined overall organizing principle, or at least not one evident to me. As I delved into the holdings, I began to consider the collection less as a monolith and more as a collection of collections. There were numerous threads to follow, and it didn't have the focused themes I expected, or maybe I should say, not the themes I had wished to impose upon it. It was its own thing.

I did discover (or re-discover) areas of richness, quirky outliers, and apparent gaps in the museum's holdings. In short, The Schnitzer at WSU had many of the strengths and idiosyncrasies common to museum collections that develop over time—if they have been doing their job. After all, university museums are (or should be) charged with reflecting and interpreting changes in our culture, while trying to acquire and preserve objects relevant to serving the multiple roles it finds itself playing within its community, its region, as well as remaining credible and useful to the educational facility of which it is a part. Add to those the inevitable staff changes, institutional opportunities and challenges that arise as a museum matures—all these inevitably get reflected in its collection.

Those realizations complicated my notion of defining and suggesting a cogent "collection policy." I knew that the Jordan Schnitzer Museum of Art at WSU could not and should not try to be an encyclopedic collecting institution. That is, it couldn't collect artworks from time immemorial to the present, or from every region on the planet. I understood the advisability of collecting works from specific historical eras. I respected those sub-collections that focused on one artist, school

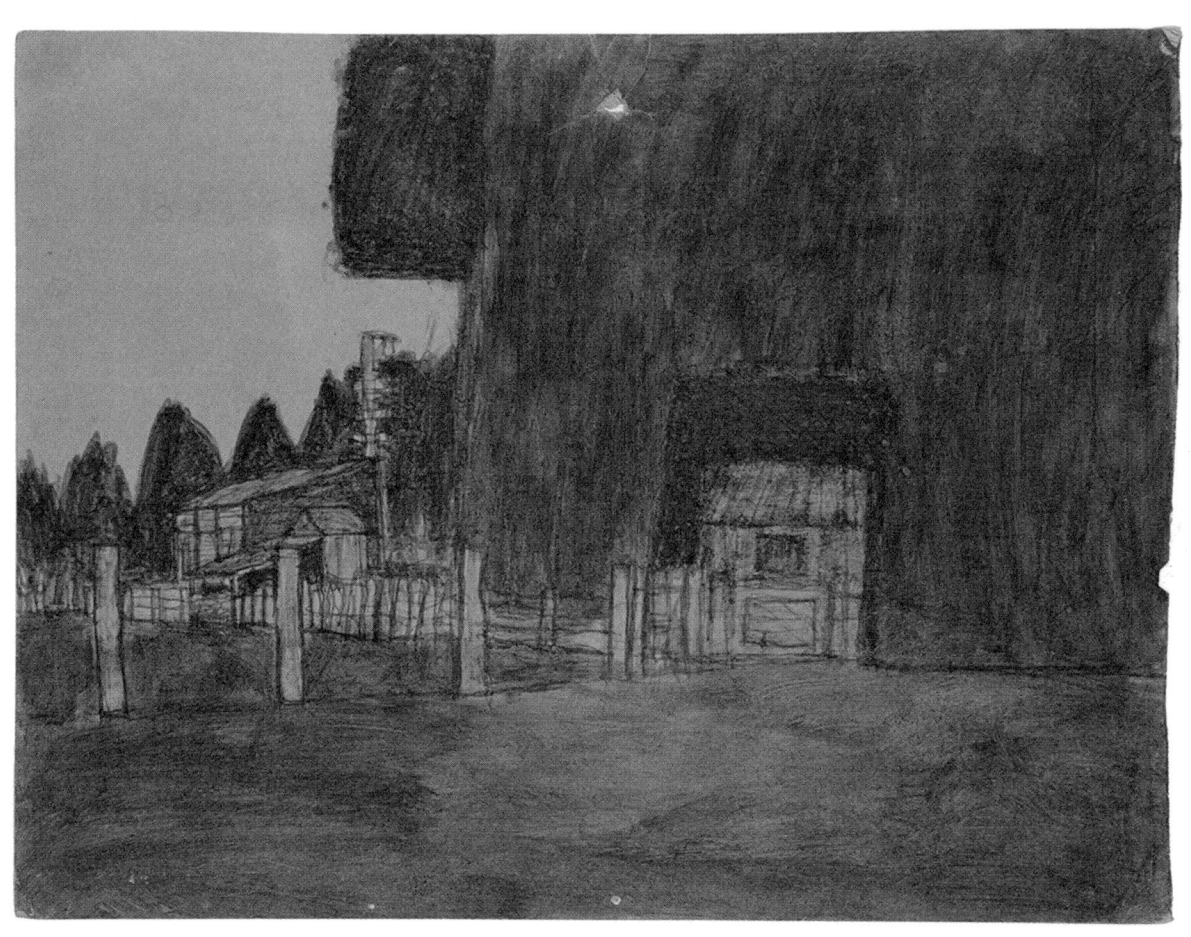

James Castle, *Untitled*, n.d.
Drawing with soot
JSMA WSU Permanent Collection, Transfer from WSU Libraries

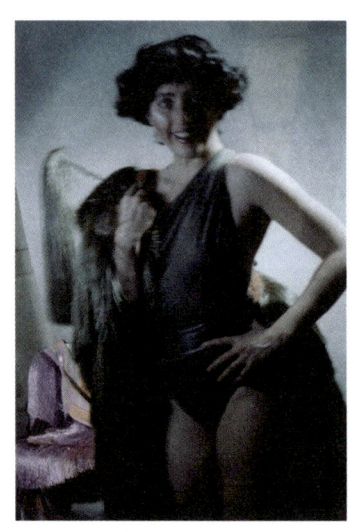

Cindy Sherman,
Untitled (Bathing Suit), 1983/2000

C Print, 35.5 x 24 inches

JSMA WSU Permanent Collection,
Gift of Ronald and Frayda
Feldman to honor Karen E.
Elwood & John R. Elwood

of artists, style of art or medium. And I admired the things that had been donated from a particular artist's estate and/or a single-minded collector.

But in the end, I fell back upon my personal experience of the collection. That is, my fondness for the unexpected, those rough edges of the dominant culture, the un-canonical, and for content expressed with humor, passion, irony and occasionally anger. And almost always, with some innovation and energy of visual expression—those artworks with the volume turned up to 11 or expressed in a visual language of severely disciplined restraint. I like surprises.

Ryan recently closed one of his emails to me saying that: "I've always liked the way artworks collapse time too as they are seen across time and space—with us yesterday, today, and tomorrow." I liked his notion of artworks existing as being reflective of their times, while also able to float through time, morphing and potentially accumulating additional meanings with each new viewer—creations both emblematic of their period and capable of evolving in meaning as they age.

As for that suggested "scope of the collection"?

I'd advise remaining cognizant of trends and collect things with which you and your communities connect. But seek to collect things by artists whose works reflect personal, idiosyncratic, visionary, critical or esoteric approaches to their creations—and while I acknowledge and celebrate the museum's collection for its holdings of works on paper, its understandable concentration on works created since 1890 (the year the institution that would ultimately become Washington State University was founded), and its focus on Pacific Northwest art. I hope going forward the institution will also envision a collection that includes and expands upon its existing

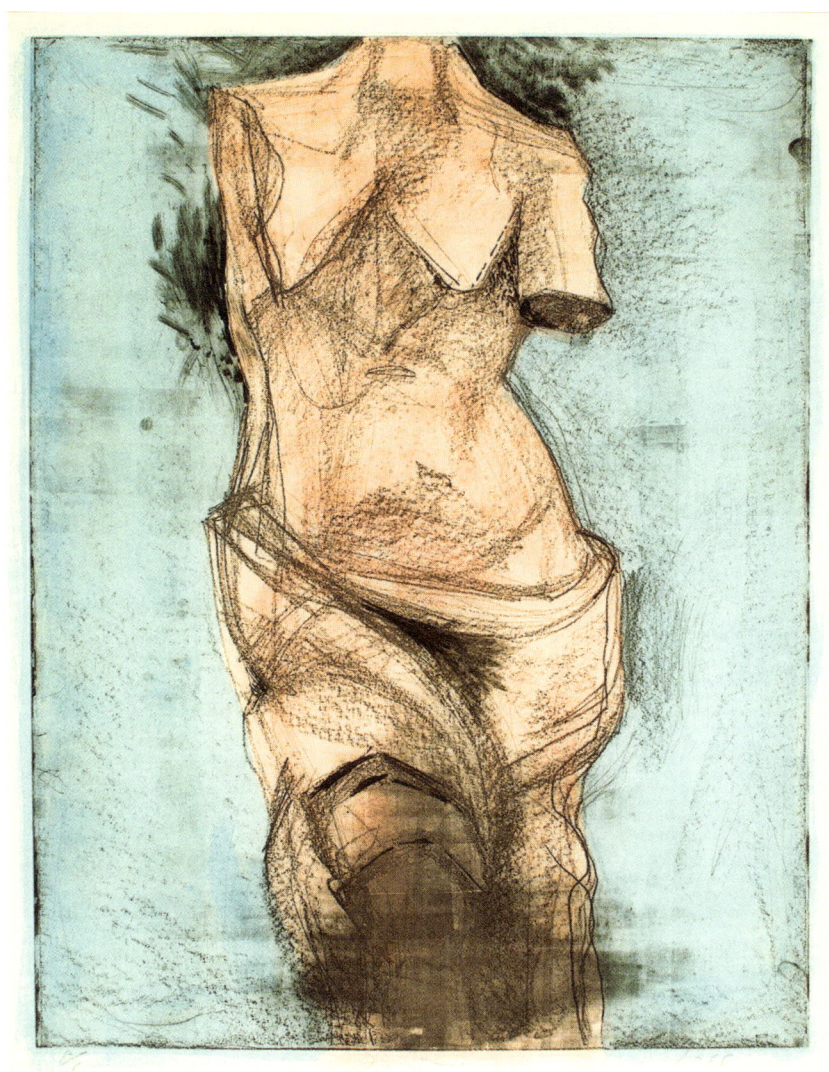

Jim Dine, *Venus at Sea*, 1985
Etching and hand printing, 40 x 32 inches
JSMA WSU Permanent Collection, Gift of Jim Dine

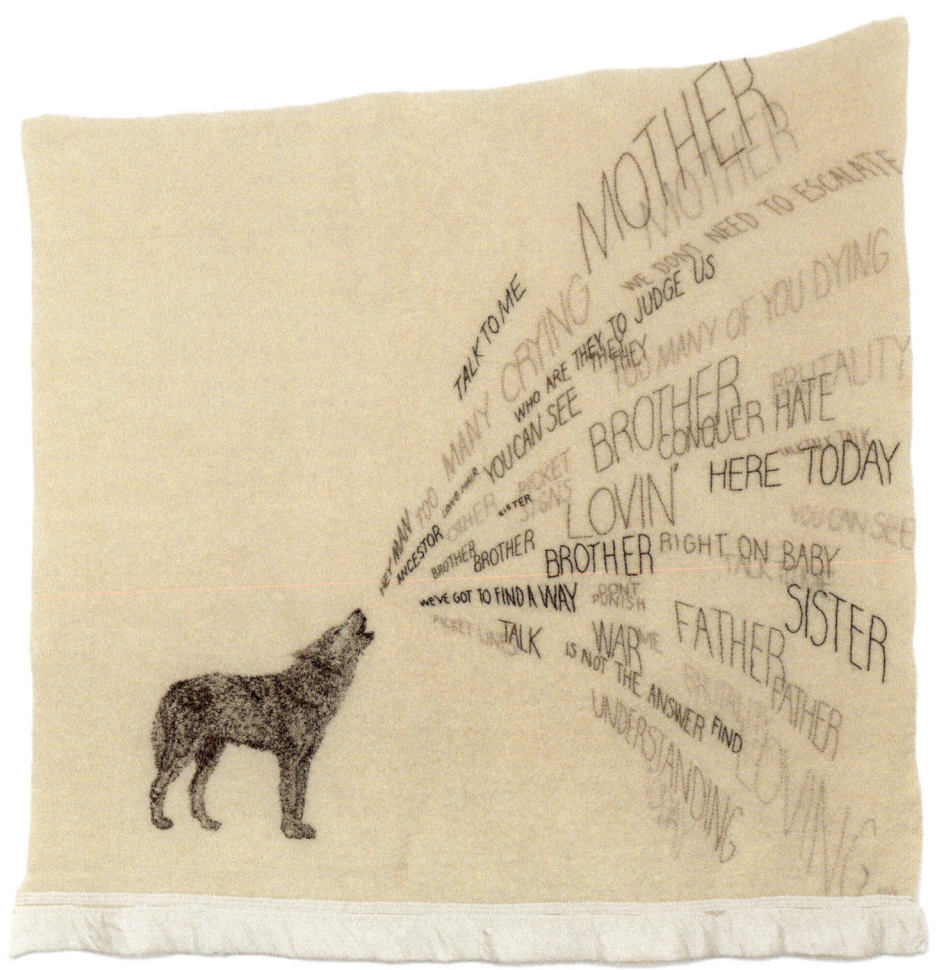

Marie Watt, *Companion Species Calling Companion Species*, 2018
Reclaimed wool blanket, stitching, 36.5 x 37 inches
JSMA WSU Permanent Collection, Museum purchase

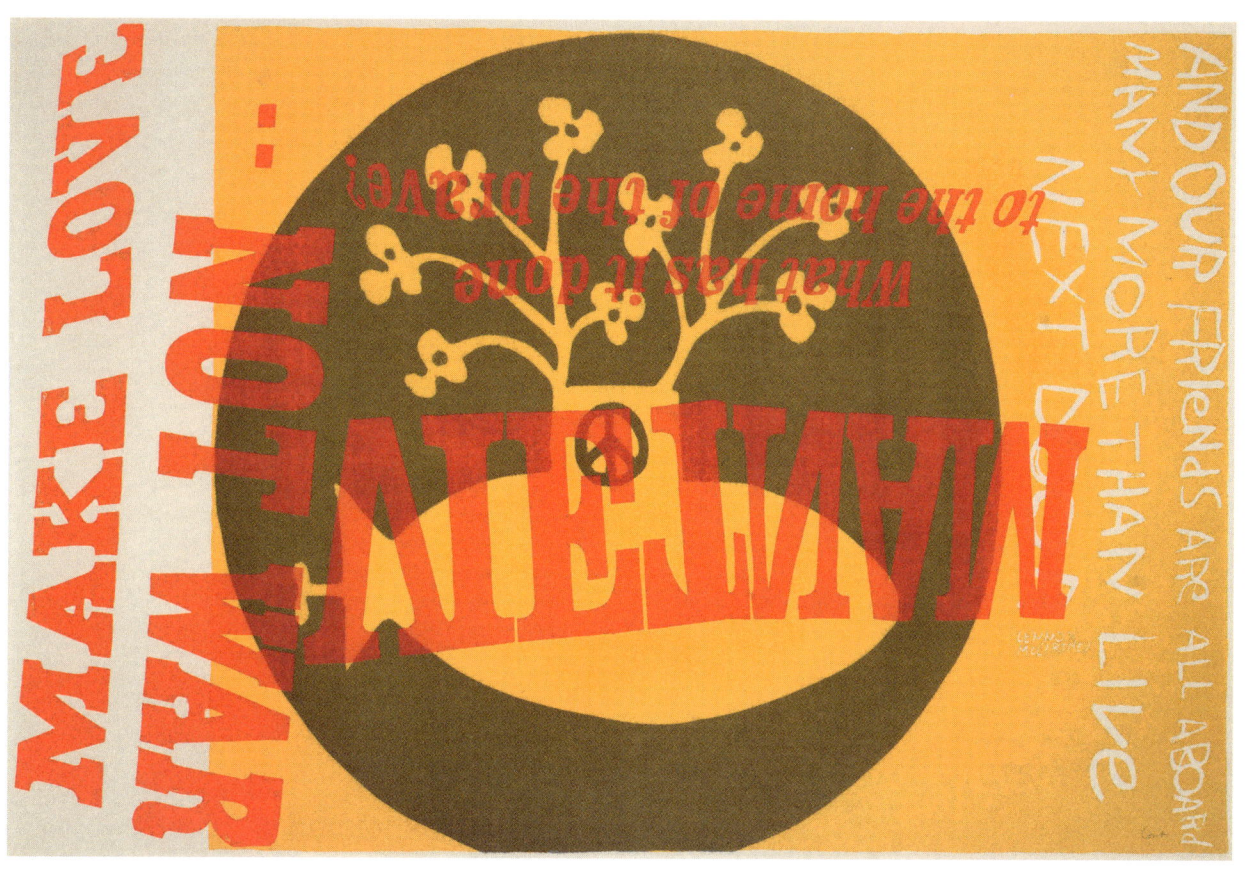

Corita Kent, *yellow submarine*, 1967
Serigraph, 23 x 35 inches
JSMA WSU Permanent Collection,
Gift of the Patterson Family

holdings by introducing, in a measured and reasonable way, a plan for the collection that is ambitious, appropriate, and aspires to be singular in its scope. That it differentiates and distinguishes itself by embracing types of work already represented in the collection which focus on ideas, artist intention and content rather than upon media, region, and historical period as the primary means of guiding its continued growth. It seems reasonable to feature, collect and preserve well executed artworks by artists who seek to chronicle, critique, or celebrate the world in which they live, concerning themselves with the substantial ideas relevant to their era. If done thoughtfully, the museum and its collection can stand out as a conceptual jewel-box, a repository for artworks representing the past and present, reflecting history, culture, and providing insights for those who may consider the works in the future.

Continue to strive for quality, innovation and ideas in the collection, your exhibitions and programming. And don't abandon your foundational obligations as an evolving institution where the intimate and experimental, the attractive and challenging can safely meet.

In other words, congratulations on your anniversary, and keep up the good work.

[1] The Elwood Collections began in 1987 and have grown to more than 300 objects across three sub-collections: The Karen E. Hardin & John R. Elwood Collection is named for Elwood's parents, both esteemed former WSU faculty members, and includes work by artists from outside the state of Washington. The Shannon Elwood Collection is named for Elwood's daughter and features artists living in the state of Washington. The Yvonne Puffer Collection of Visual Culture, named for Elwood's wife, includes objects, ephemera, and resource materials.

[2] Totaling close to 100 paintings, the Ernest O. Holland and Virginia and Charles W. Orton Collections were originally acquired through purchase by President Holland of then Washington State College. The longest serving president in WSU history, Holland's tenure stretched from 1915 to 1945. During those years, and throughout the Great Depression, he worked to assemble a collection of art he hoped would identify the greatest painters of the day and inspire faculty, staff, and students. Financial support came from Regent Charles W. Orton, who contributed funds to support Holland's ambitious collecting efforts at a time when resources were scarce. In his will, Holland gave his prized art collection to the College with a stipulation that a suitable exhibition gallery be formed.

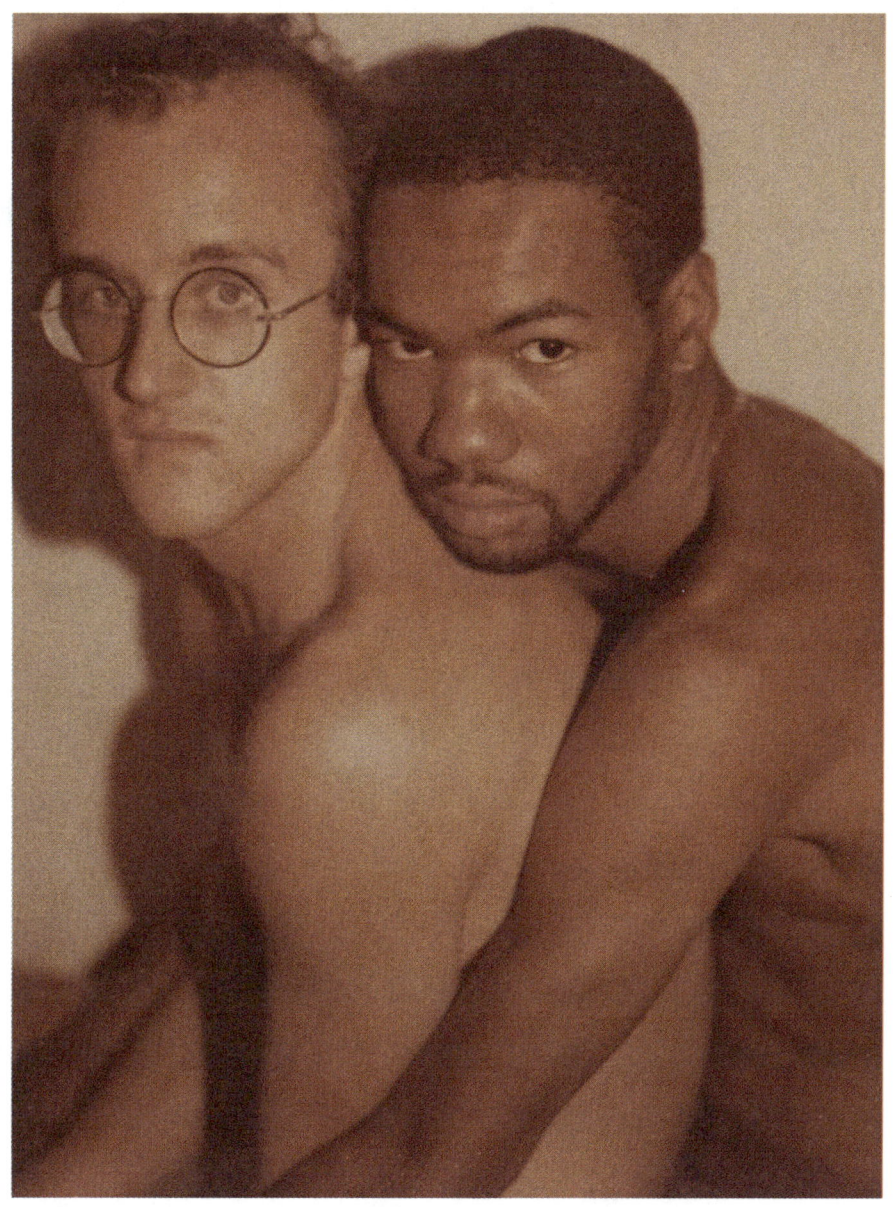

Andy Warhol, *Keith Haring and Juan Dubose*, 1983
Polacolor ER, Polaroid 11.25 x 9.12 inches
JSMA WSU Permanent Collection, Gift of the Andy Warhol Foundation for the Visual Arts

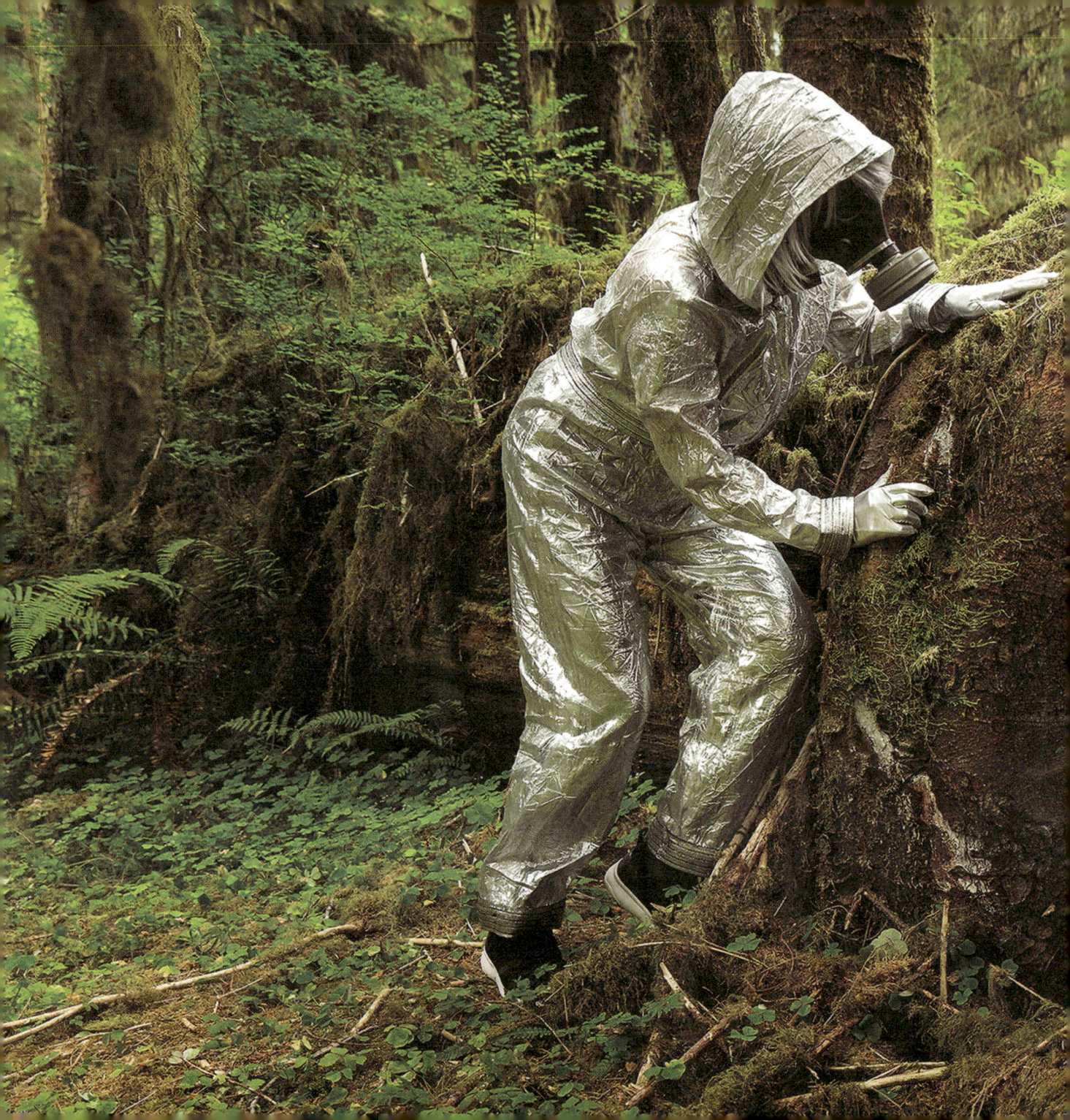

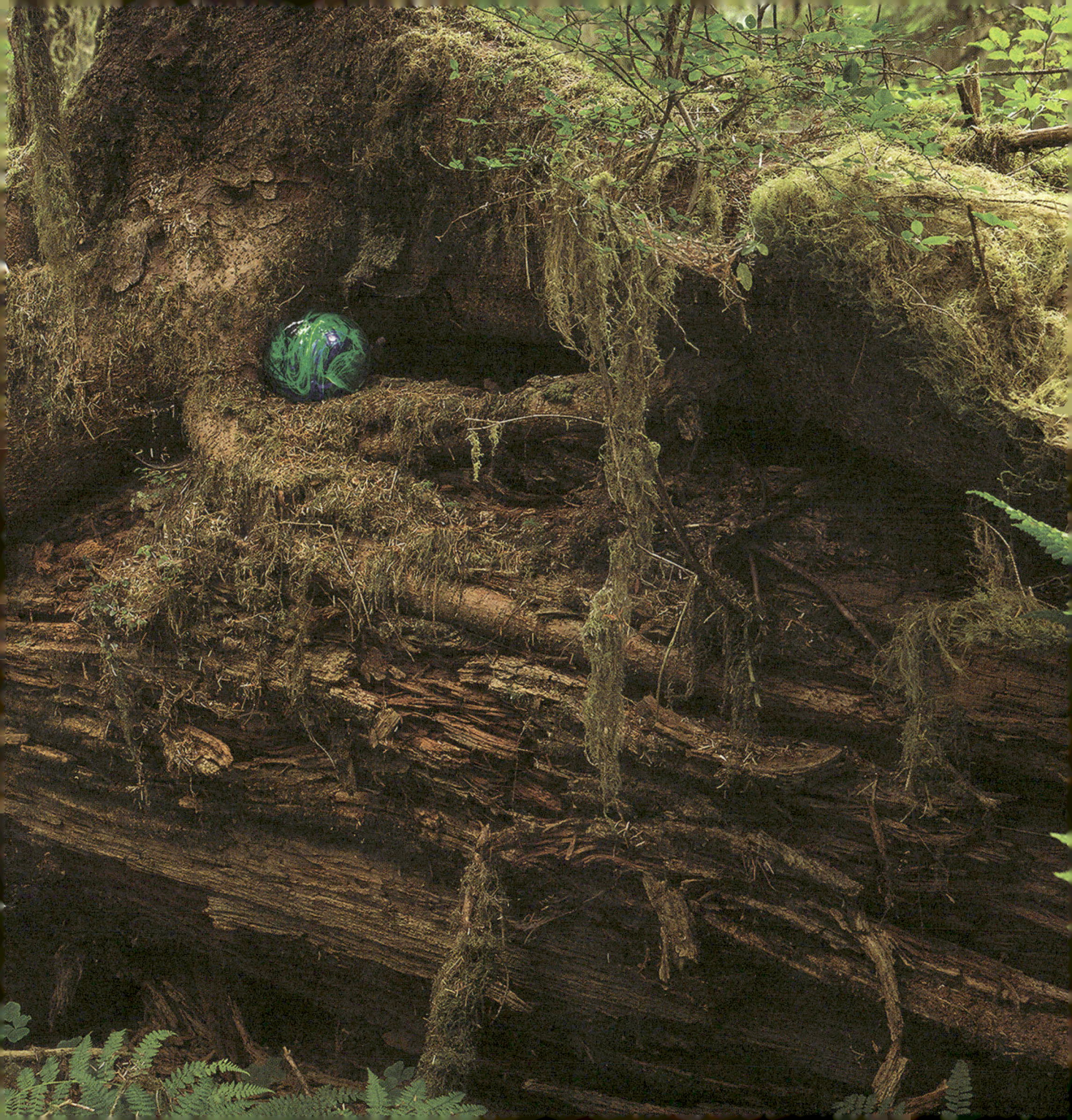

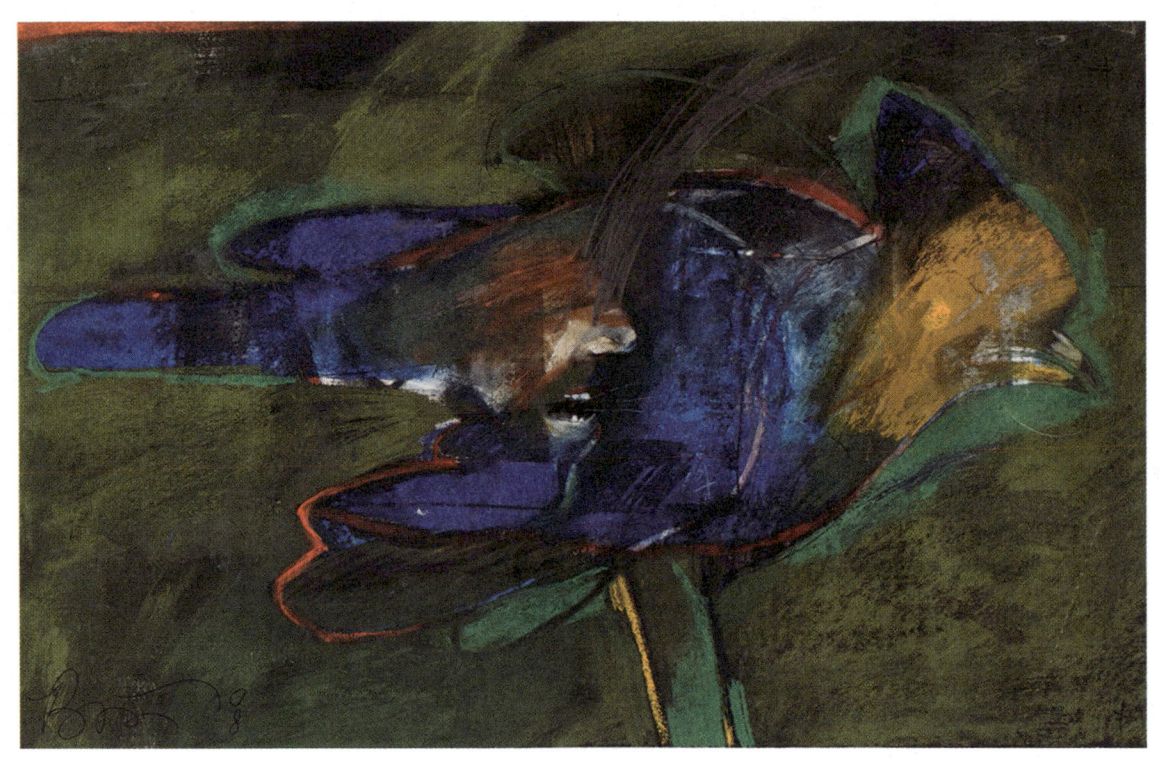

previous spread | Etsuko Ichikawa, *Vitrified*, 2018   Rick Bartow, *The Stellar Jay*, 2008
Film, 7 minutes 30 seconds   Oil pastel, 30.75 x 44.5 inches
JSMA WSU Permanent Collection,   JSMA WSU Permanent Collection,
Gift of the artist   Gift of the artist and the Froelick Gallery

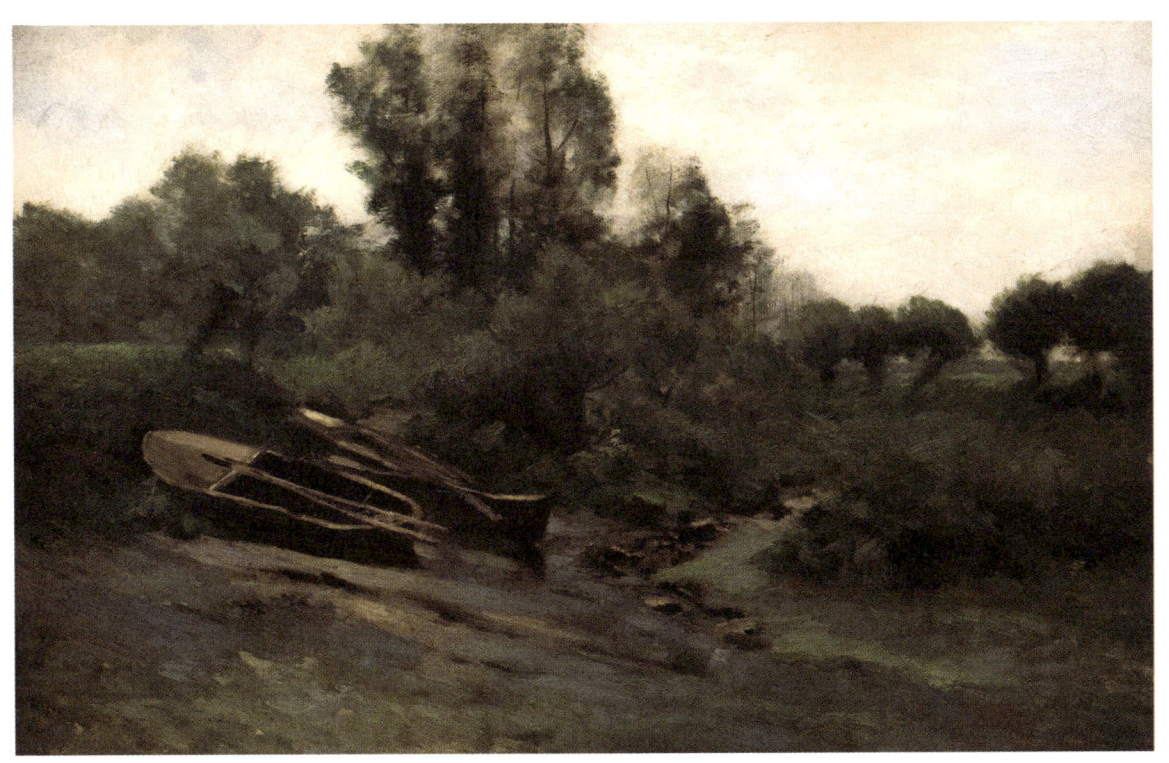

John Henry Twachtman, *Green Landscape*, c. 1890s
Oil on canvas, 30.5 x 33.5 inches
JSMA WSU Permanent Collection, Bequest of Ernest O. Holland

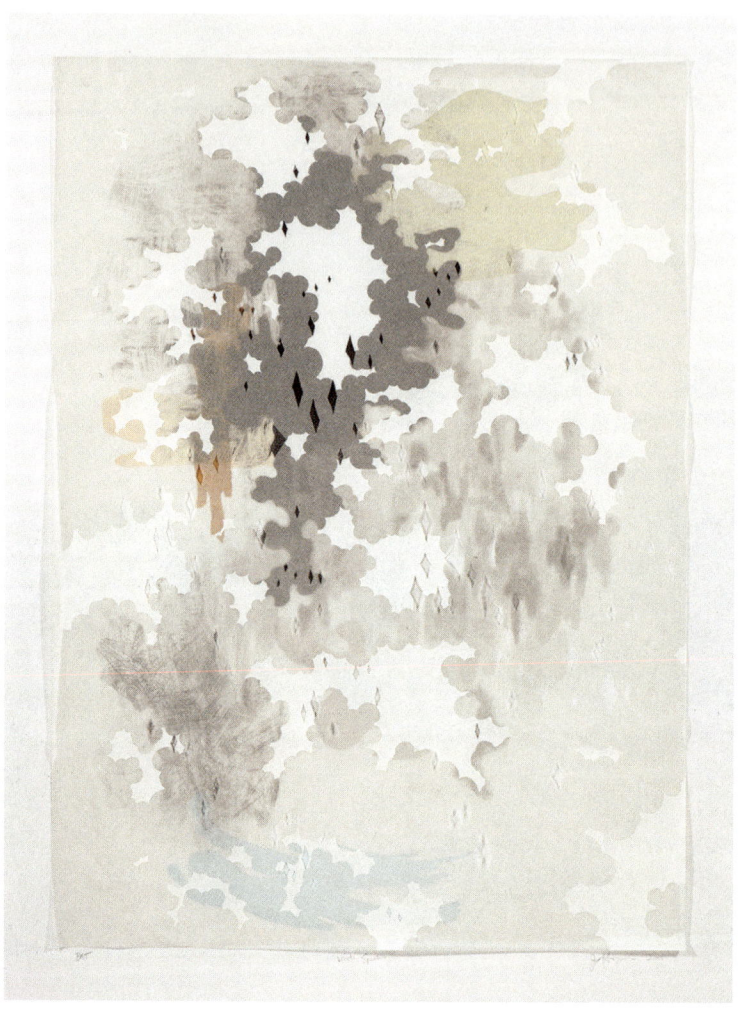

Jim Hodges, *Winter Speaks*, 2015

Intaglio, screen print, chine collé
with hand-cut collage, 44.12 x 34.28 inches

JSMA WSU Permanent Collection,
Gift of J. Scott Patnode in memory of Craig Ducote

facing page | Jim Hodges, *Finally* (detail), 2017

Intaglio, screen and pigment print with chine collé
hand-cut, folded and assembled holographic foil
element, 44.12 x 34.28 inches

JSMA WSU Permanent Collection,
Gift of J. Scott Patnode in memory of Craig Ducote

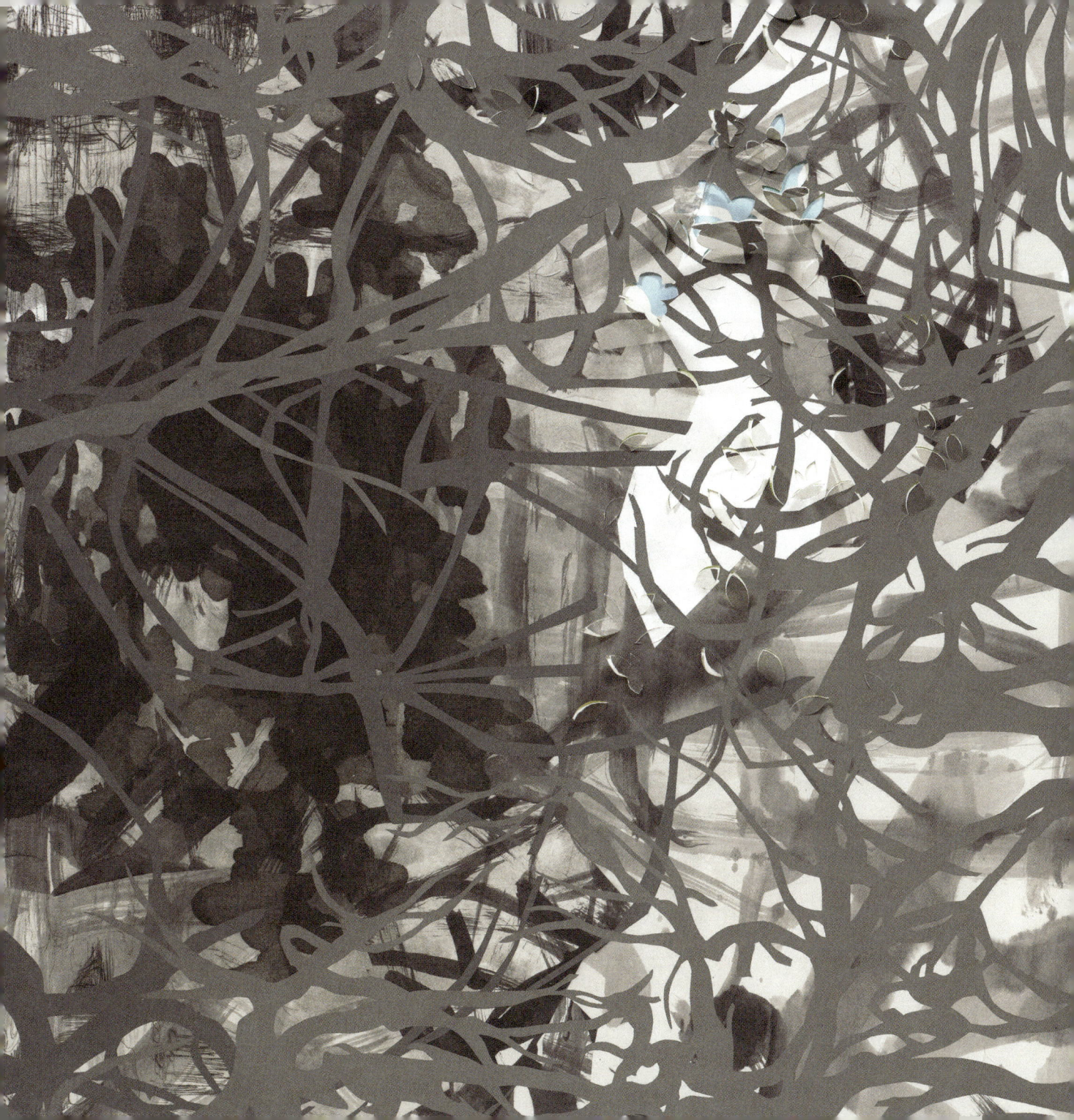

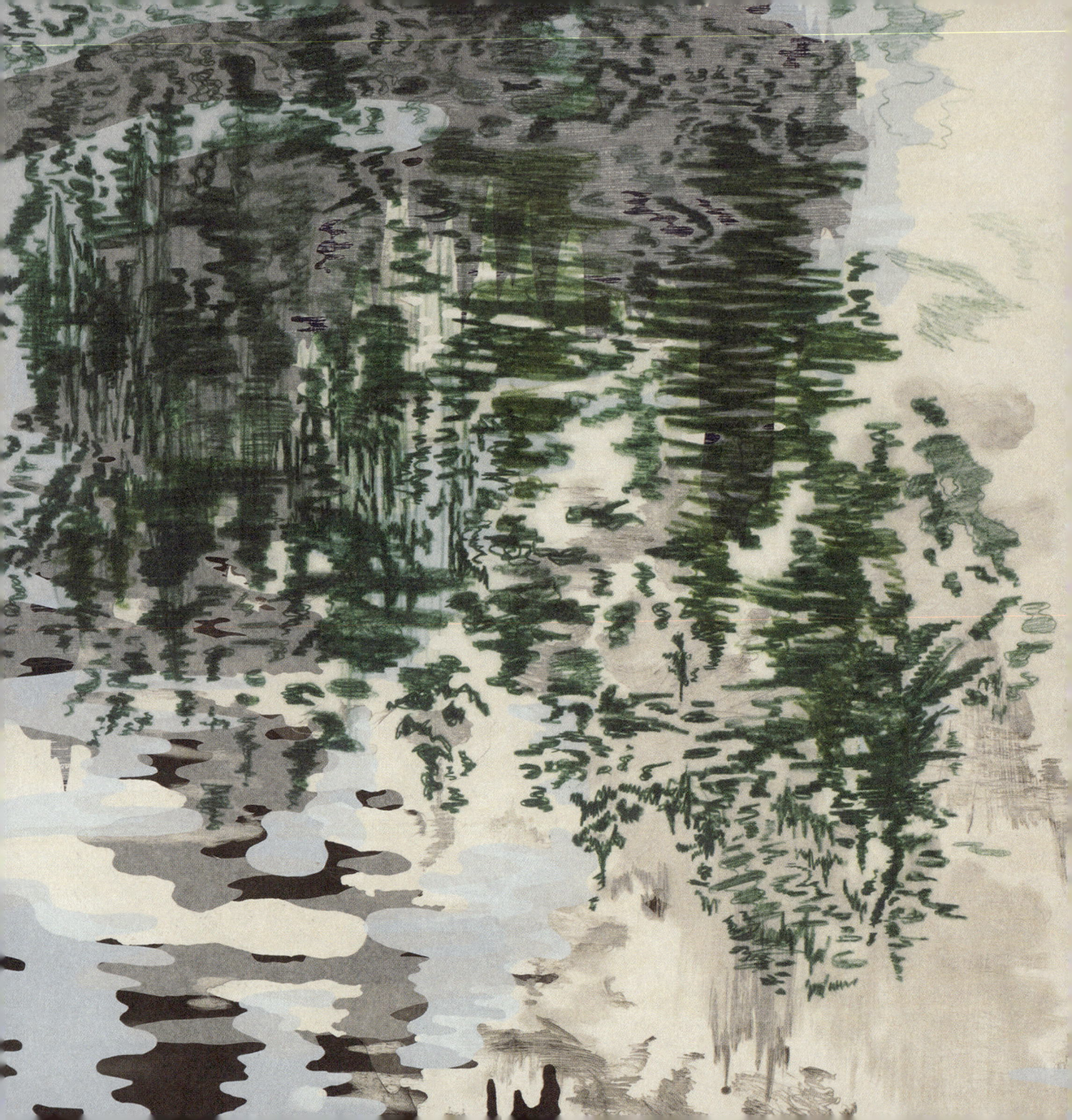

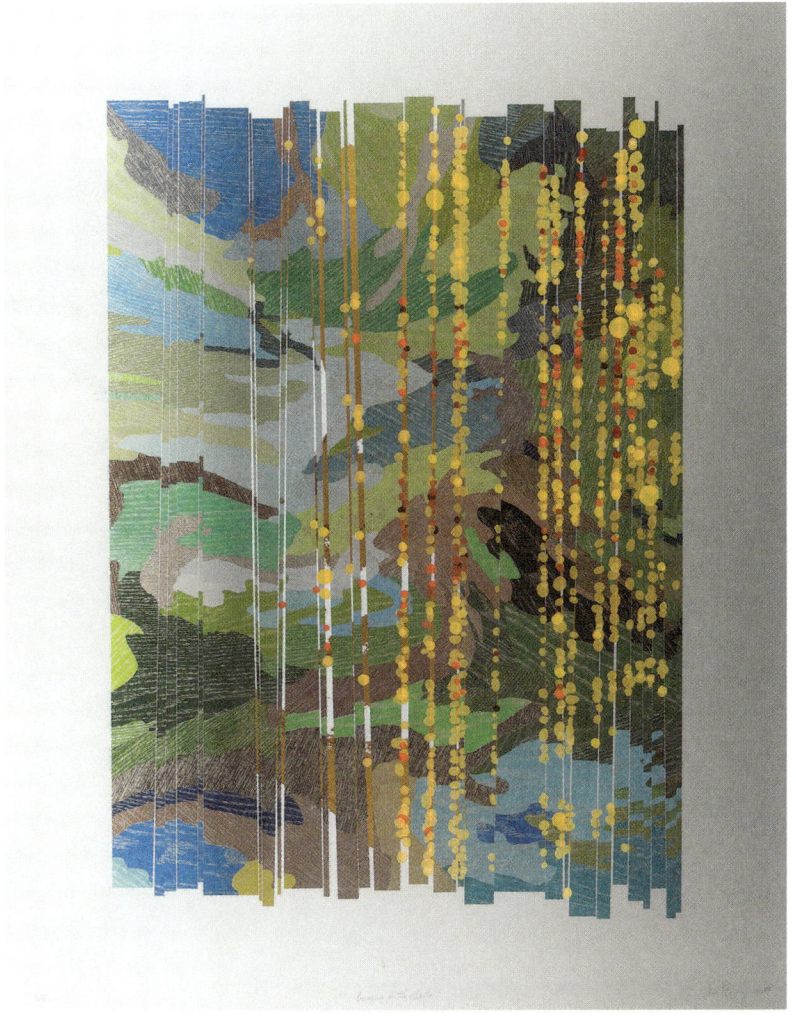

facing page | Jim Hodges, *Of Summer* (detail), 2016

Intaglio, screen relief and
pigment print with chine collé
and collage, 44.12 x 34.28 inches

JSMA WSU Permanent Collection,
Gift of J. Scott Patnode in memory of Craig Ducote

Jim Hodges, *Bringing in the Ghosts*, 2019

Lithograph with seventy-nine colors, screen and
pigment print with hand cutting, collage
and metallic foils, 44.12 x 34.28 inches

JSMA WSU Permanent Collection,
Gift of J. Scott Patnode in memory of Craig Ducote

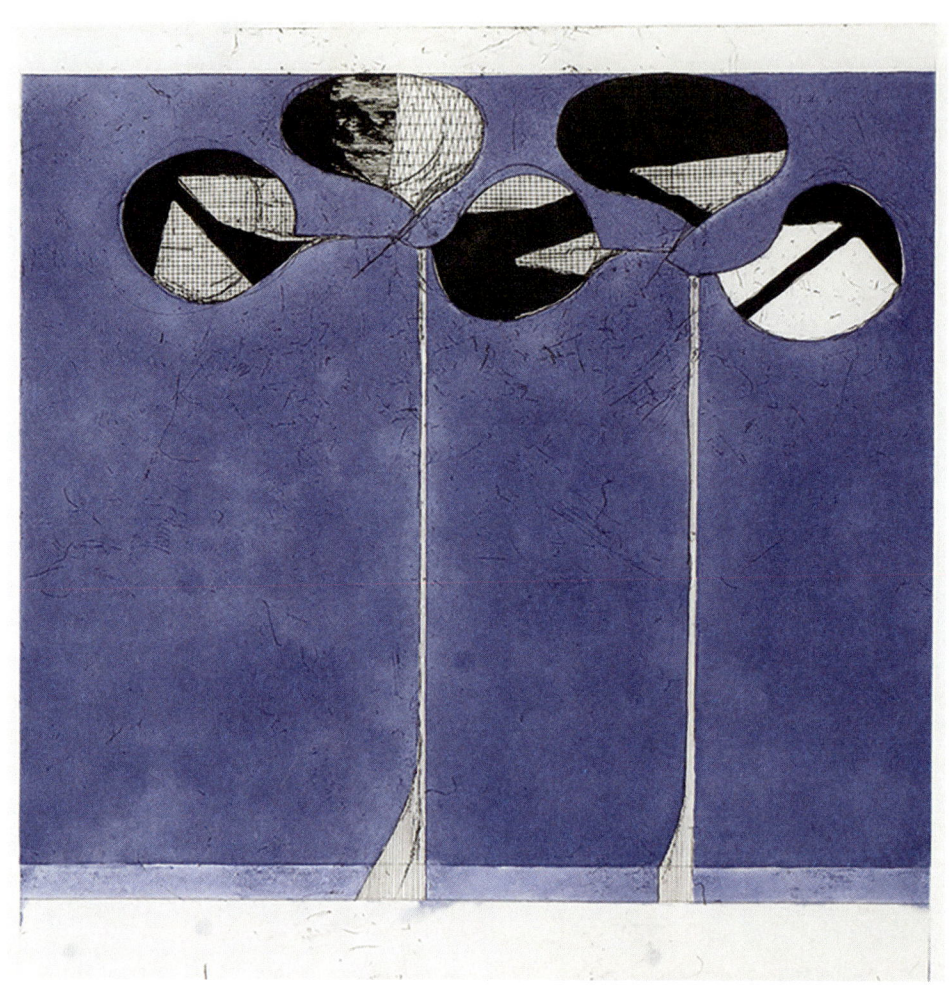

Richard Diebenkorn, *Clubs, Blue Ground*, 1972
Etching, 40 x 32 inches
JSMA WSU Permanent Collection, Gift of the WAC through Richard and Margaret Aiken

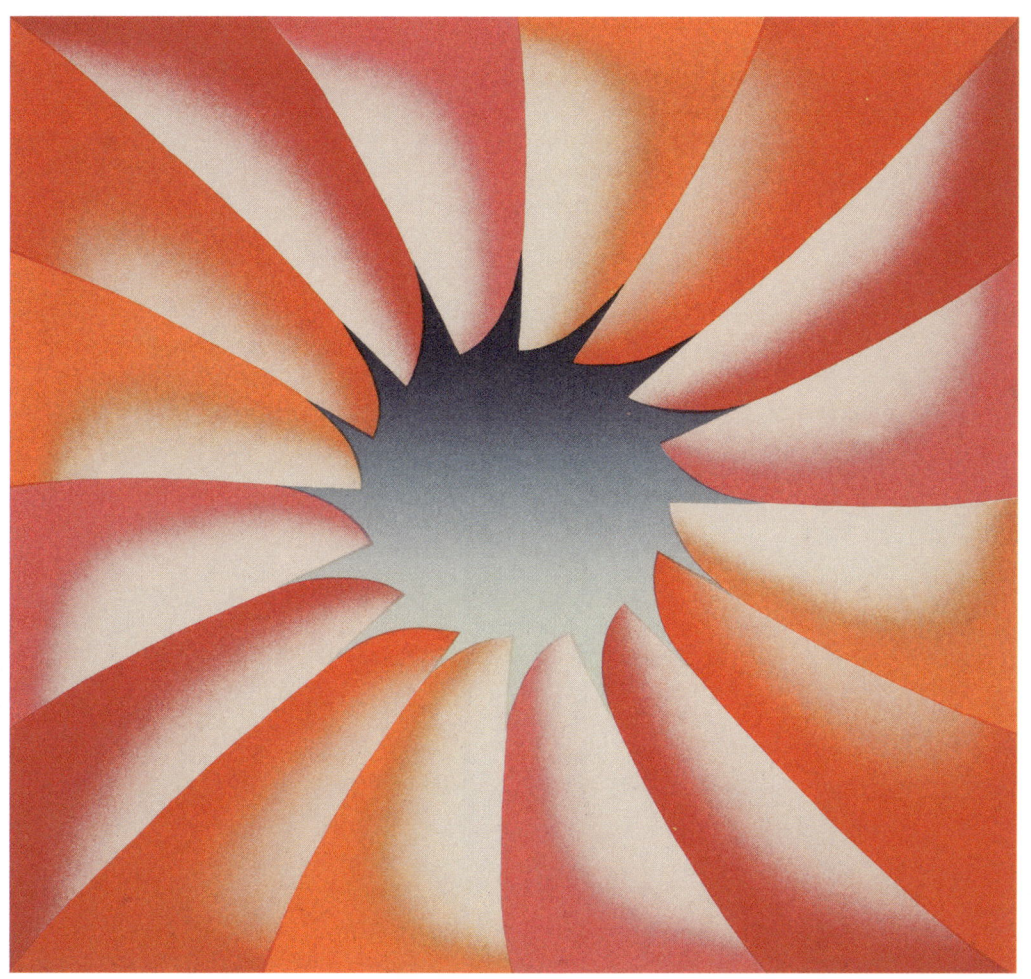

Judy Chicago, *Through the Flower #3*, 1972
Lithograph, 22 x 22 inches
JSMA WSU Permanent Collection, Gift of the Friends of the Museum

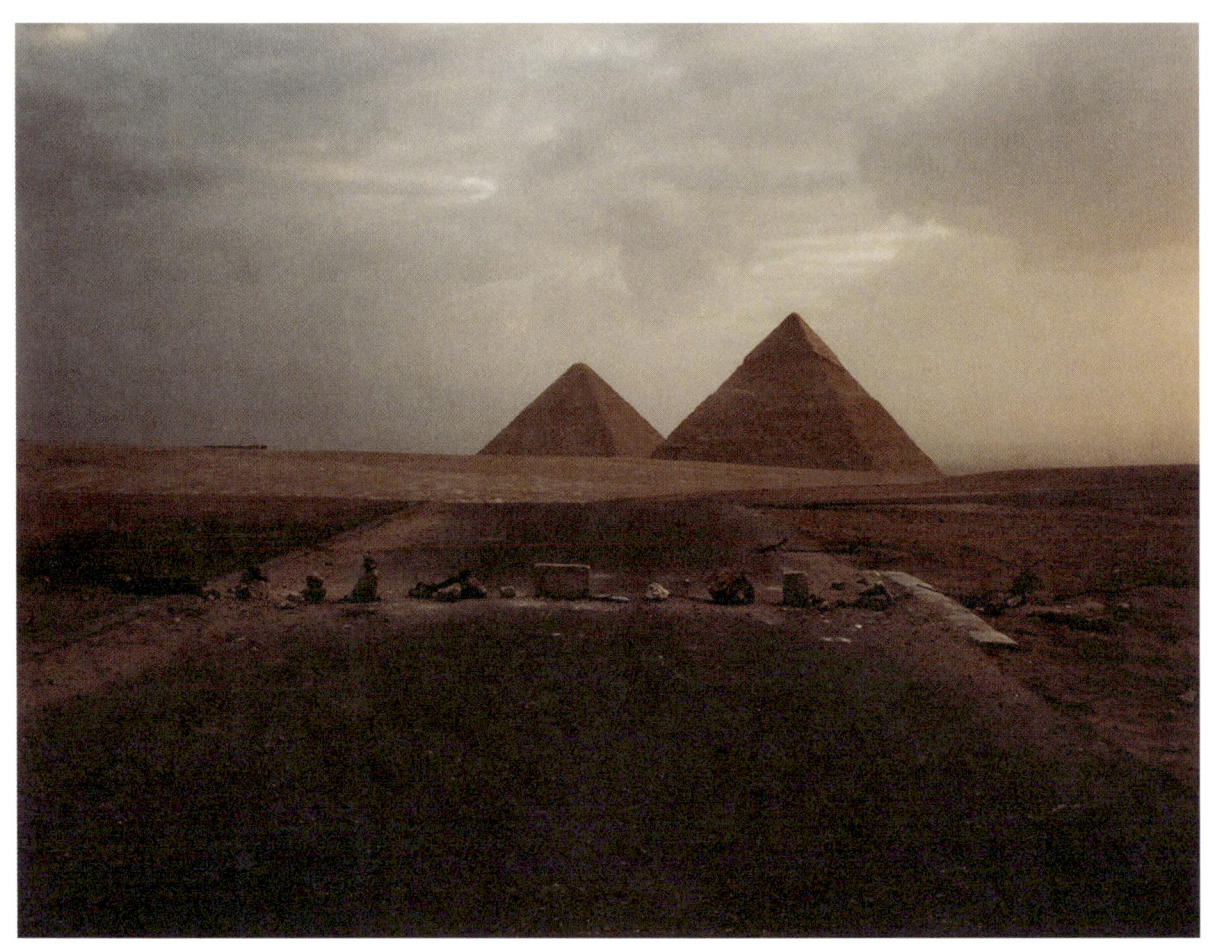

Richard Misrach, *Road Blockade and Pyramids*, 1989
Ektacolor print, 9.5 x 12 inches
JSMA WSU Permanent Collection, Gift of Timothy Bradbury

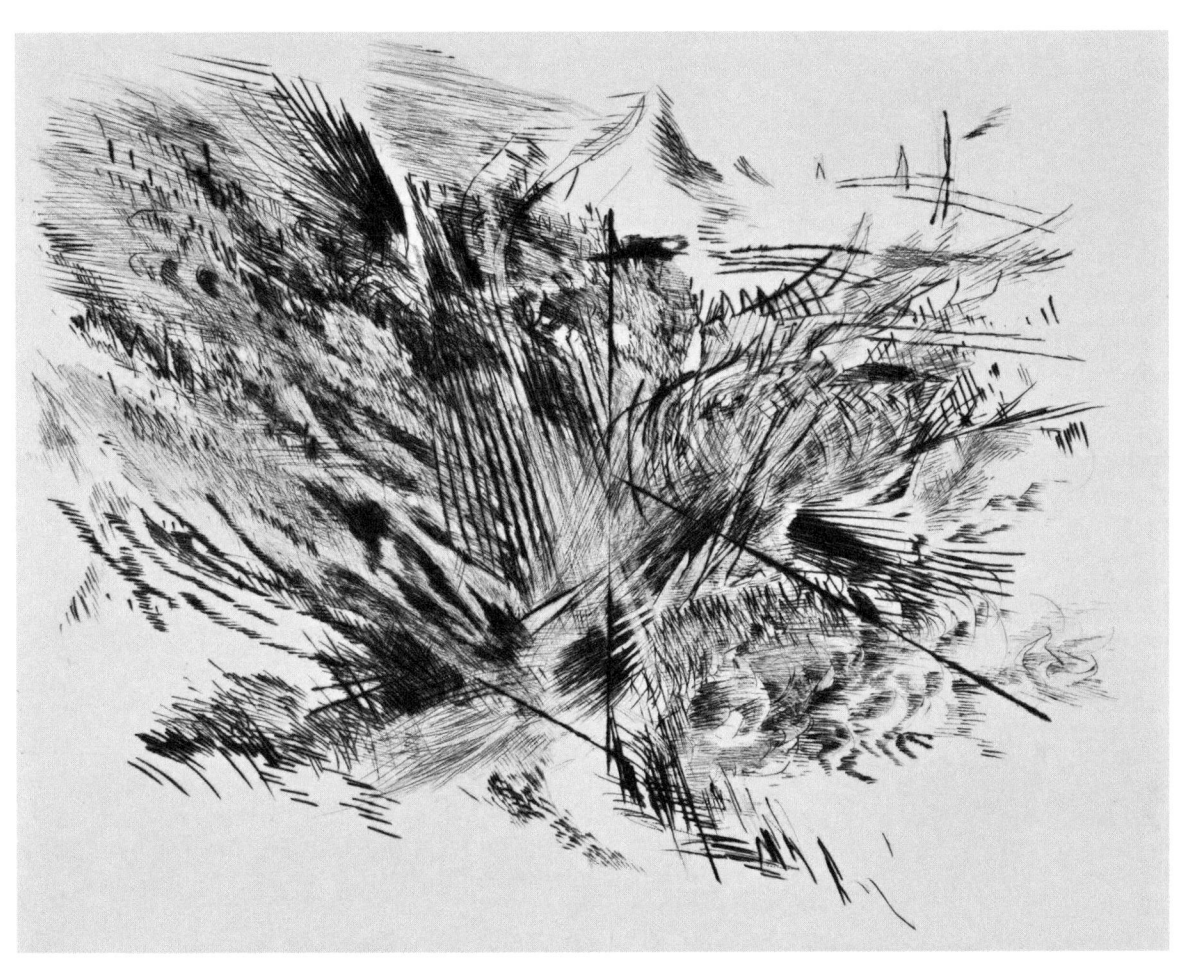

Julie Mehretu, *Untitled 1 (amulets)*, 2008
Drypoint and engraving in black with chine collé, 12 x 14 inches
JSMA WSU Permanent Collection, Gift of J. Scott Patnode in honor of Harold and Rosemary Balazs

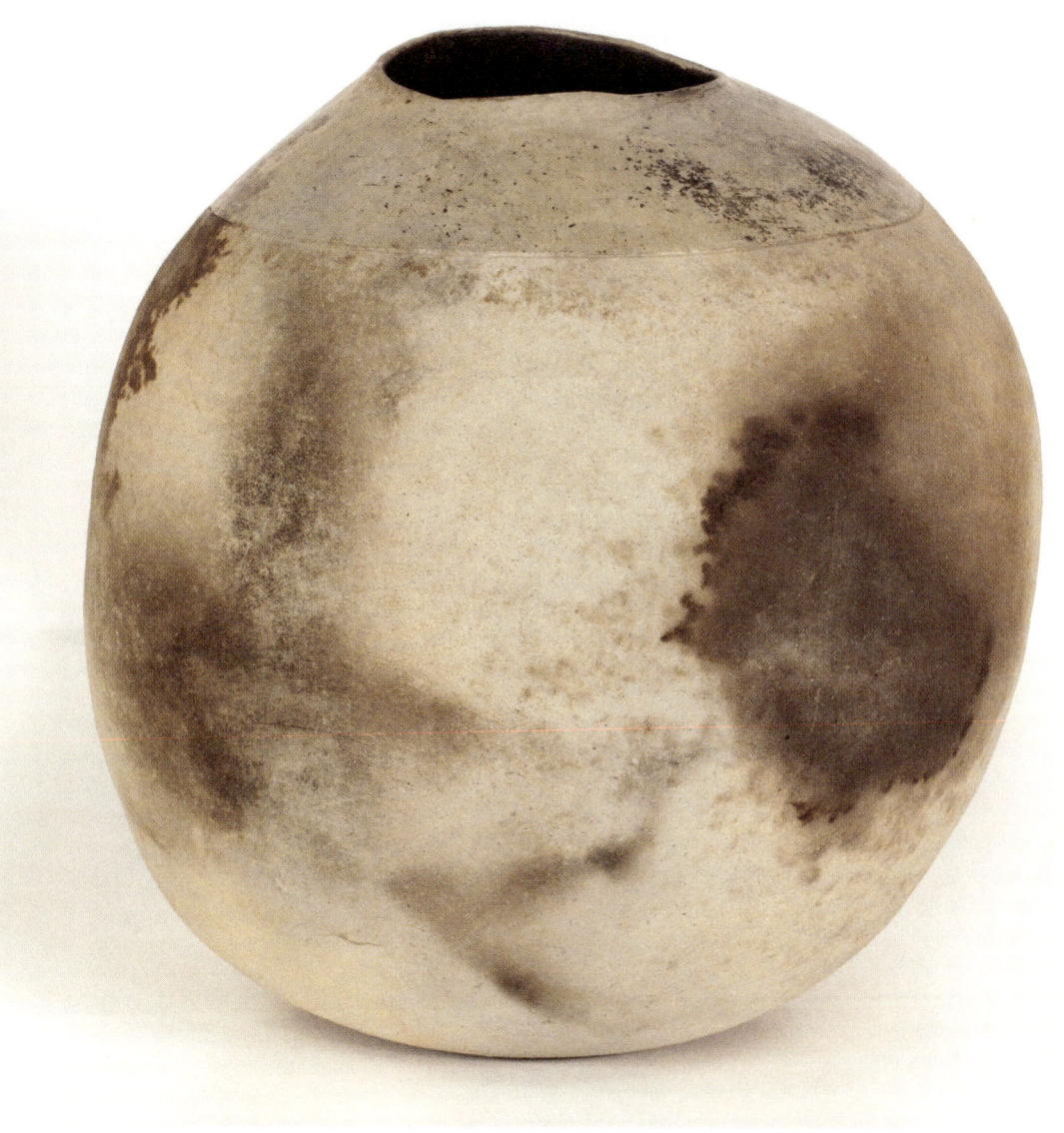

Betty Feves, *Bonfire Pot*, c. 1981
Ceramic, 12.5 x 12 inches
JSMA WSU Permanent Collection, Gift of Alan and Laurie Feves

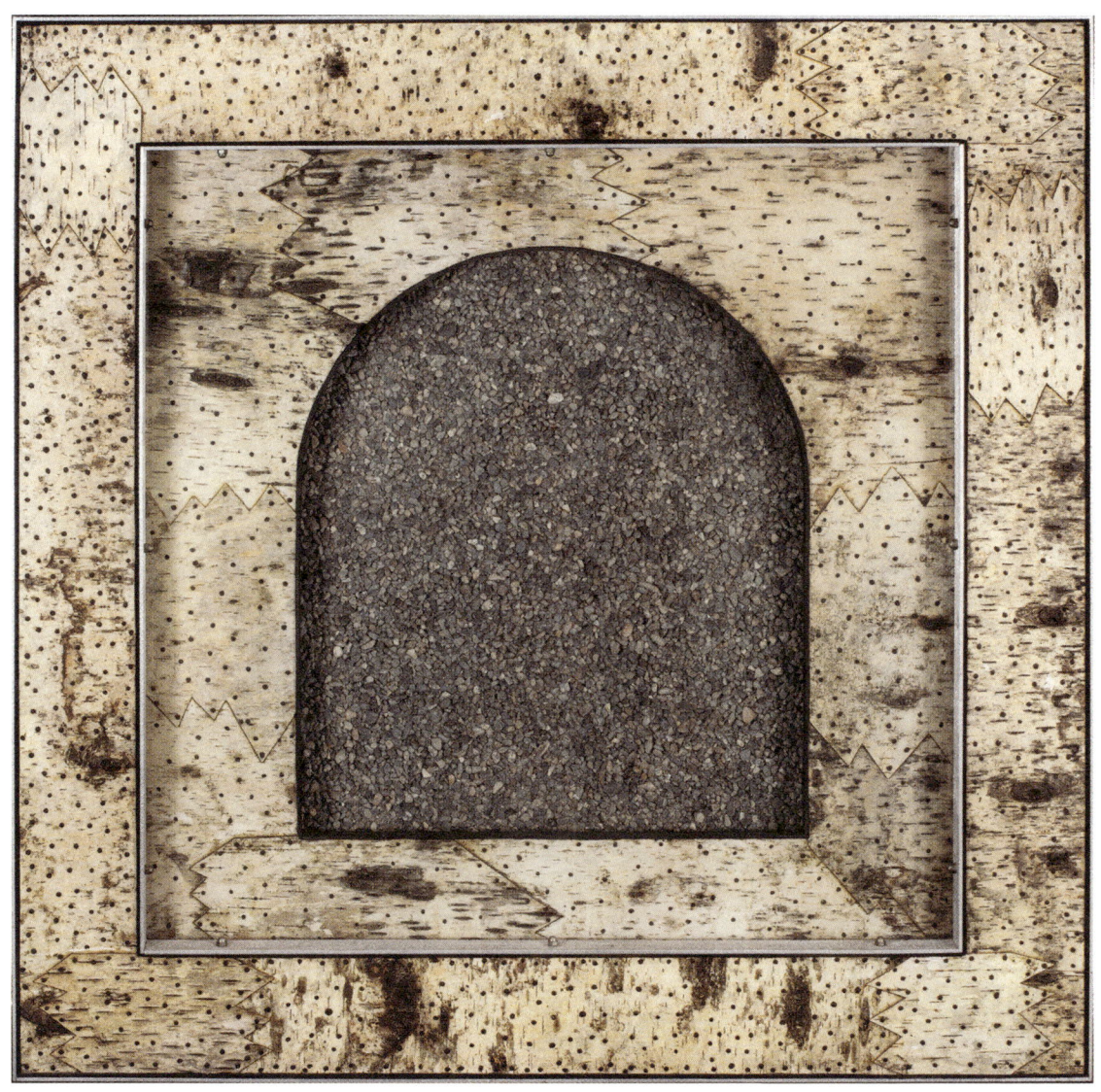

Robert Helm, *Untitled,* from *Timed Pieces*, 1977
Glass, leather, birch bark laminated to wood, gravel, and metal, 35.5 x 35.5 inches
JSMA WSU Permanent Collection, Gift of Robert R. and Jean B. Ecker

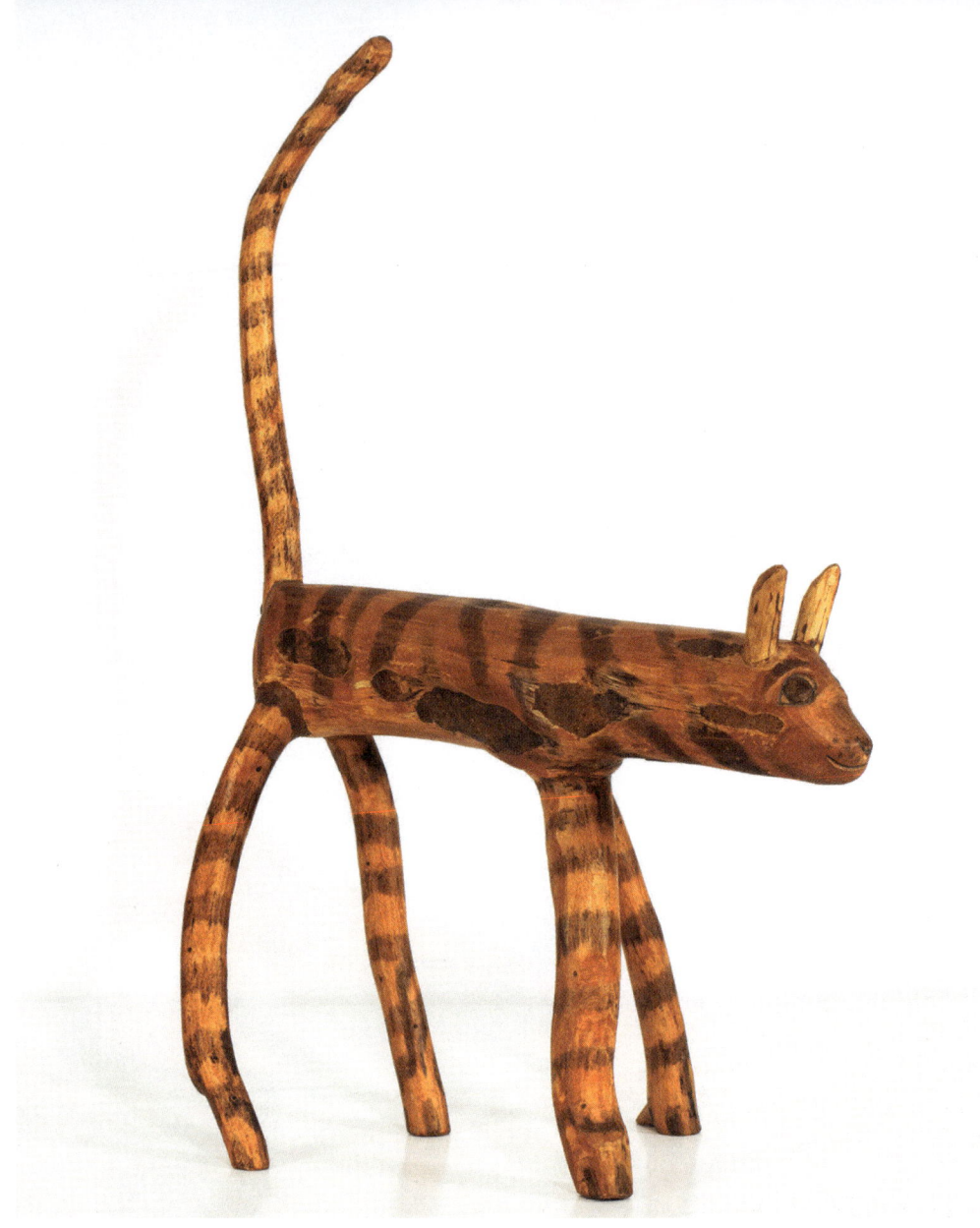

Victor Moore, *Striped Cat*, c. 1993
Wood, paint, 21.5 x 8.5 x 13.5 inches
JSMA WSU Permanent Collection, Gift of Roberta Moore

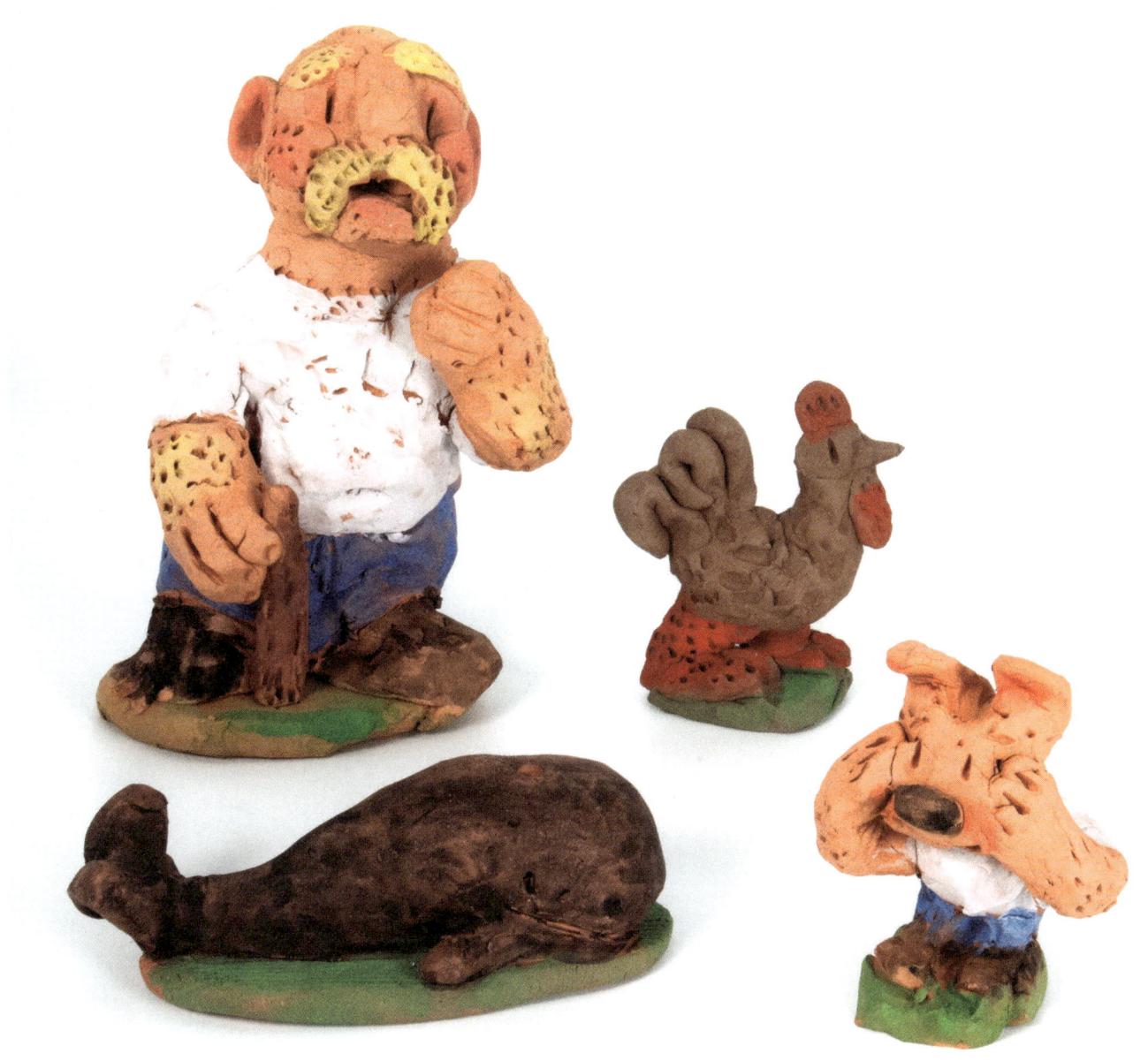

Jeffry Mitchell, *The Death of Buddha* (detail), 2018
Ceramic, various dimensions
JSMA WSU Permanent Collection, Museum purchase

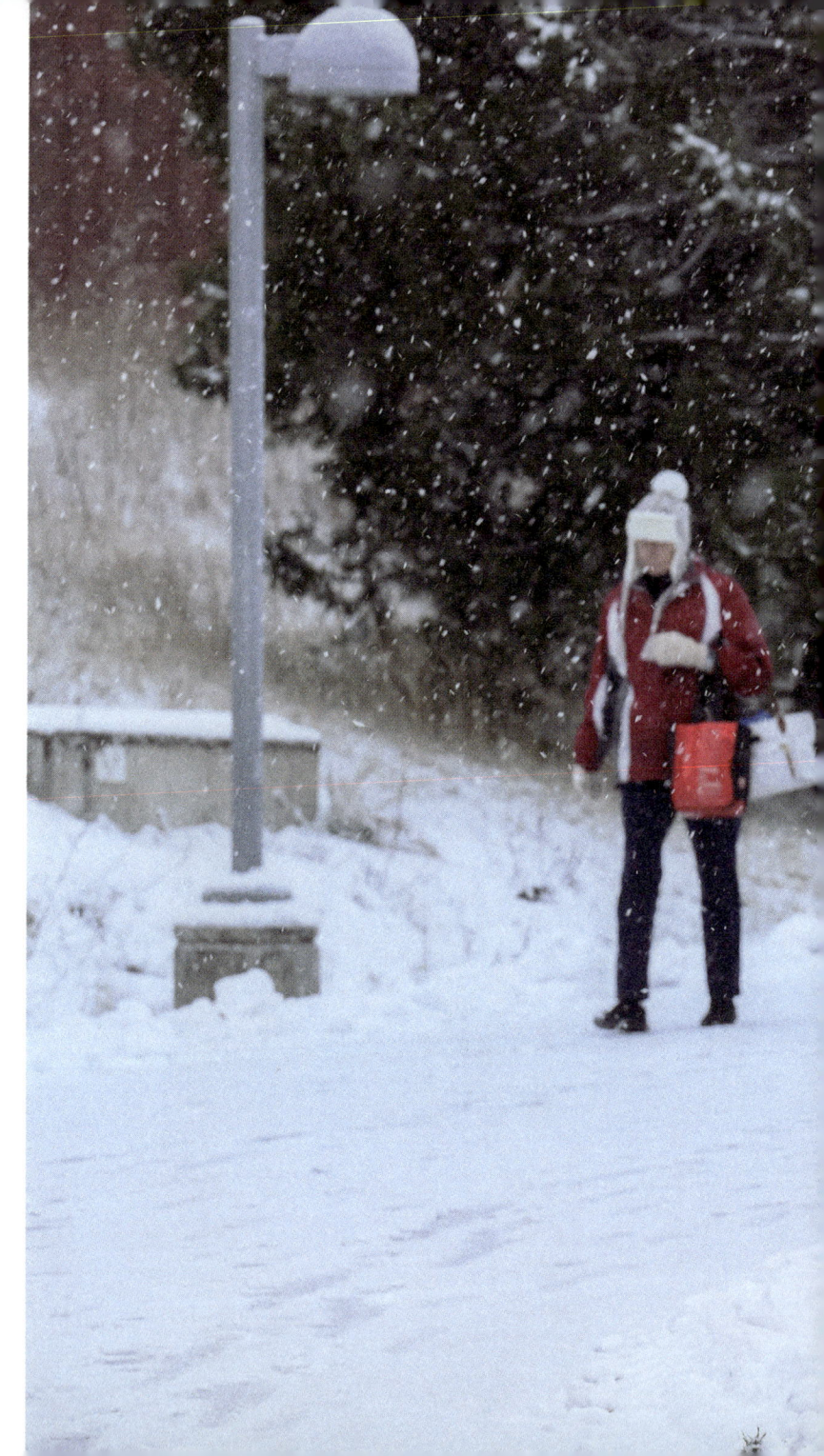

Deborah Butterfield, *Red Forest*, 2013

Cast bronze with patina,
90 x 105 x 70 inches

JSMA WSU Permanent Collection,
Gift of Howard Wright III in memory of
Theiline Scheumann

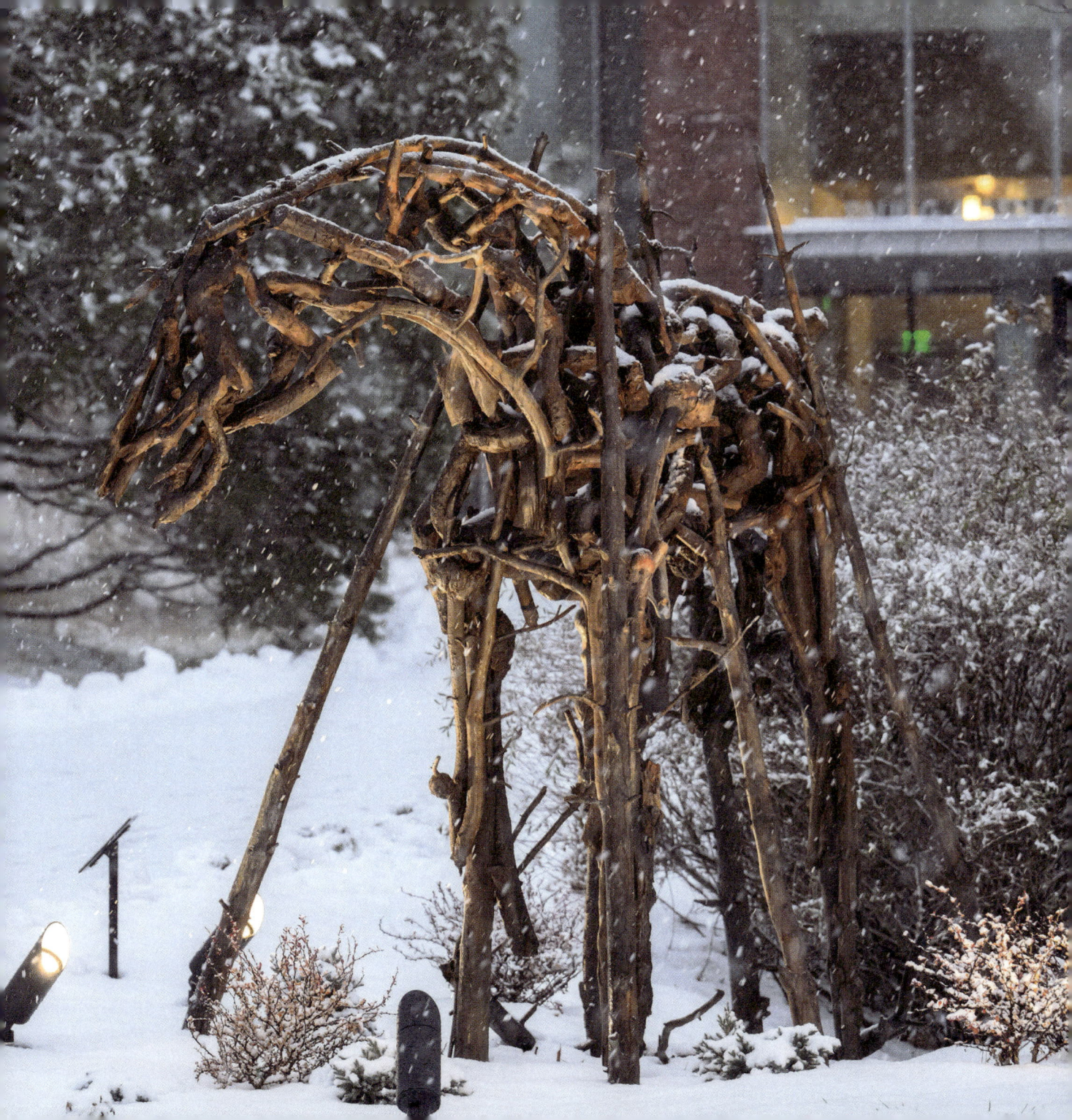

JORDAN SCHNITZER
MUSEUM OF ART WSU

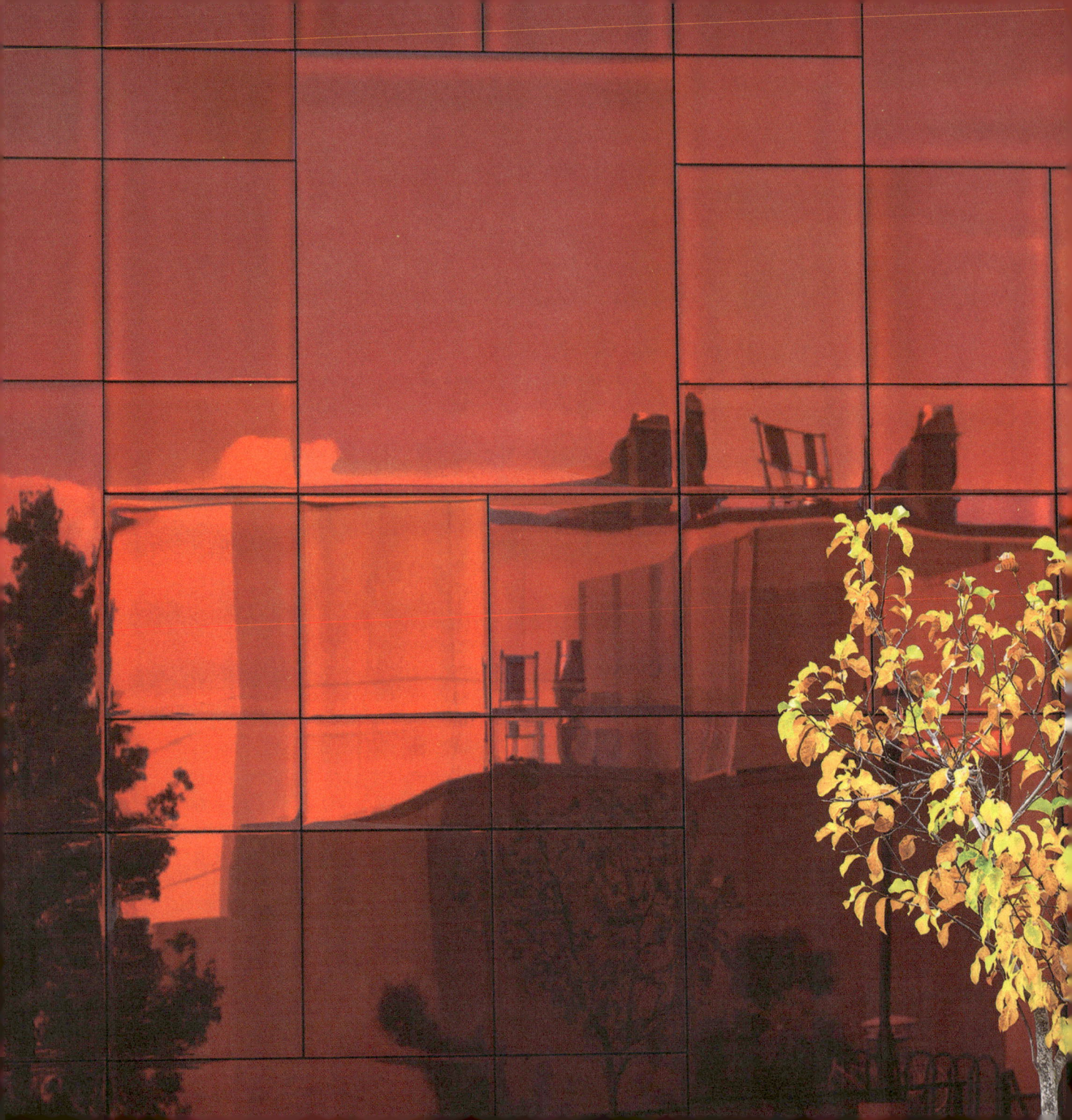

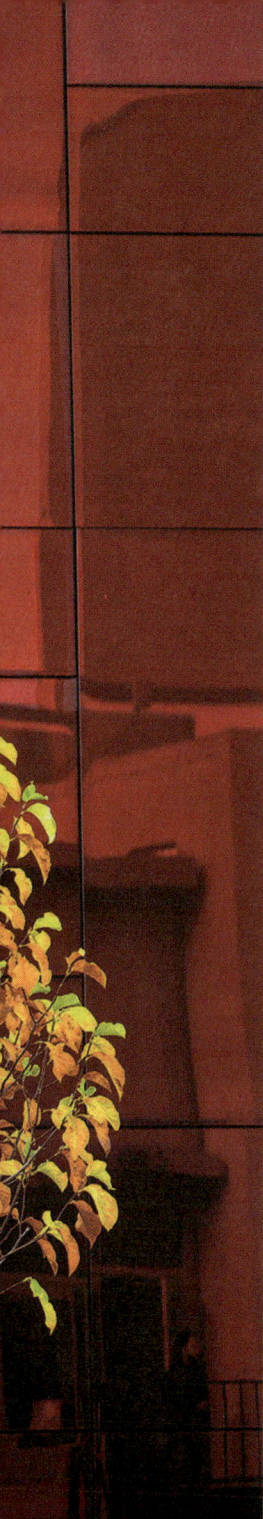

BUILDING A CAMPAIGN TO BUILD A BUILDING FOR ART

Chris Bruce

The challenge

Let's be clear. Over the course of time, "Art" was rarely the first word that popped into most minds with the phrase "Washington State University." Indeed, I've often spoken with Cougar alums who said, "I didn't know there was an art museum on campus! Where was it?"

Without a signature presence, art is vulnerable. If our "crimson cube" weren't there, what else might exist on this former site of the fire station? How would whatever-that-was have changed the look and feel of that area of the campus? Where would we be celebrating the fiftieth anniversary of the Museum of Art, now the Jordan Schnitzer Museum of Art WSU?

If we had failed to deliver this beacon of creativity into the heart of campus, who knows? Cultural activities can all too easily be shrugged off as peripheral to more urgent priorities. They are also the hardest to get back once they're gone. (Who now remembers the Theater and Dance departments?) Without the presence of this building, the museum program could fade into the background, all too susceptible to neglect or even dismissal in tough financial times.

Thus, the goal of the Building Campaign was not simply the construction of a new edifice on an old site. Rather, it was intended to be a make-no-mistake-about-it statement: art is a meaningful part of the human endeavor. With this building on this site, the legacy and promise of those past fifty years is secure, and the Pullman campus community can continue to be inspired, provoked, and stimulated by whatever future generations call "art."

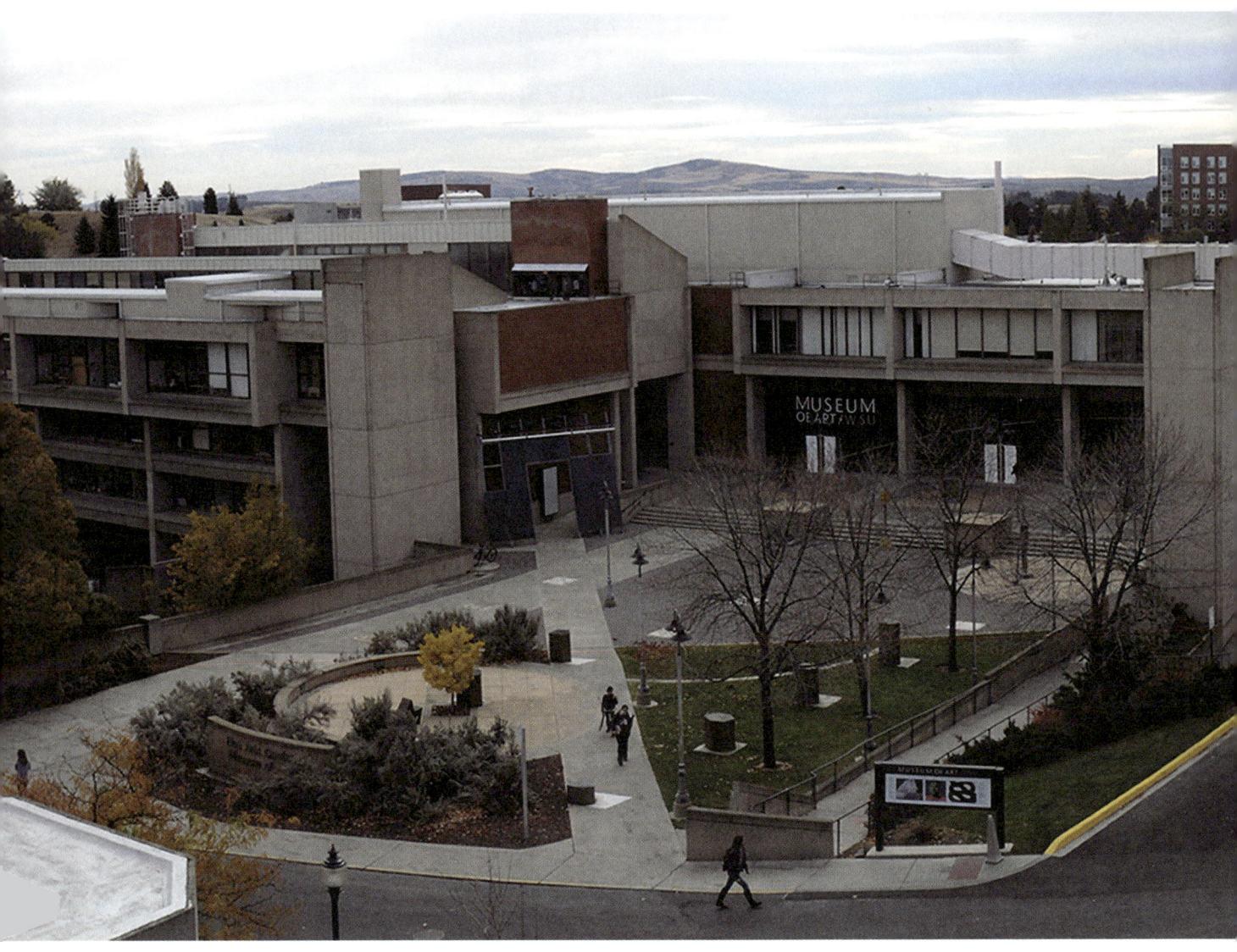

In this 2012 image, the Fine Arts Center housing the Museum of Art/WSU is shown on the left and the Public Safety Building on the right

Photo: Zach Mazur

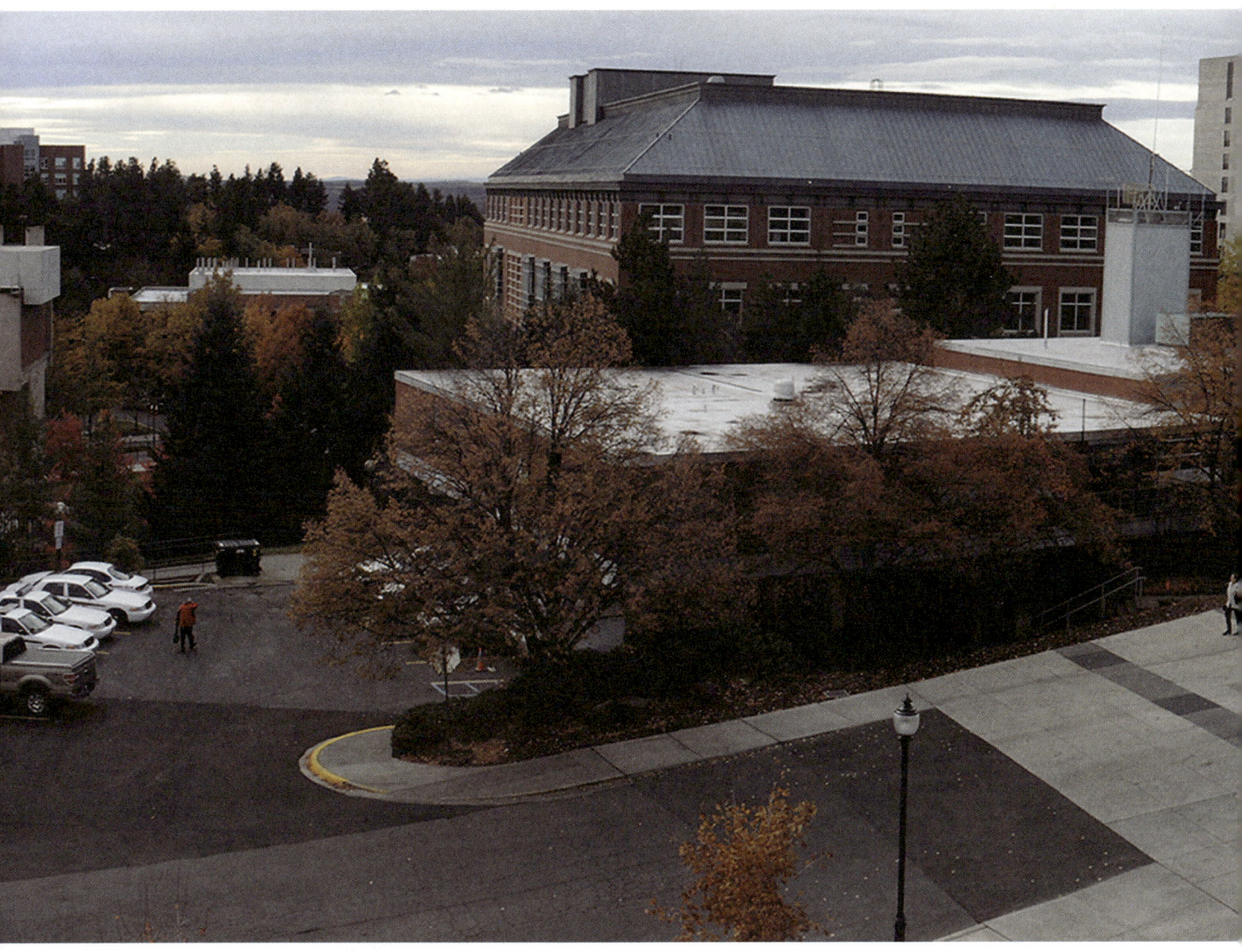

following spread | A 2016 concept rendering by Olson Kundig architects showing the
future Jordan Schnitzer Museum of Art WSU

Image: Olson Kundig

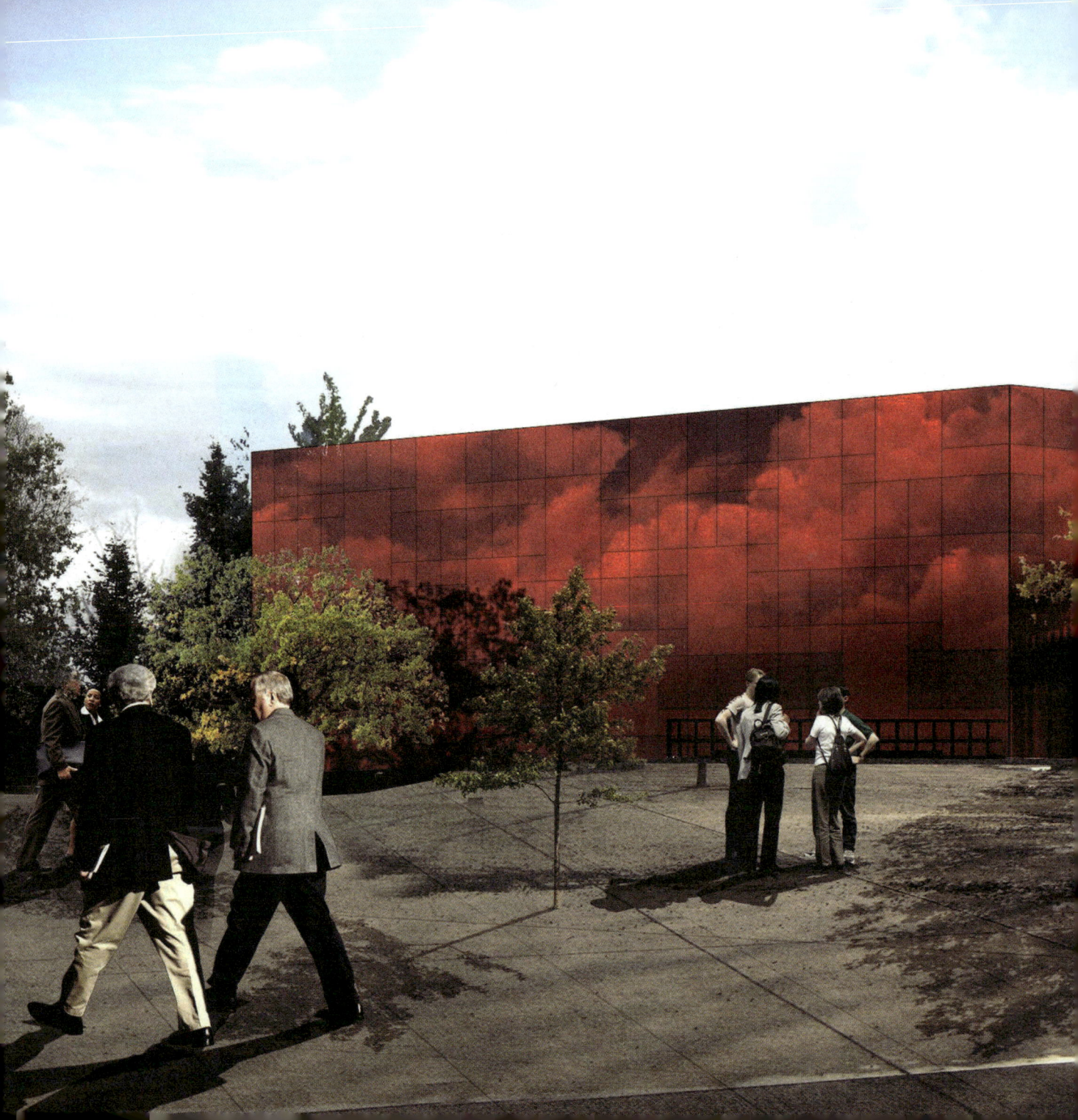

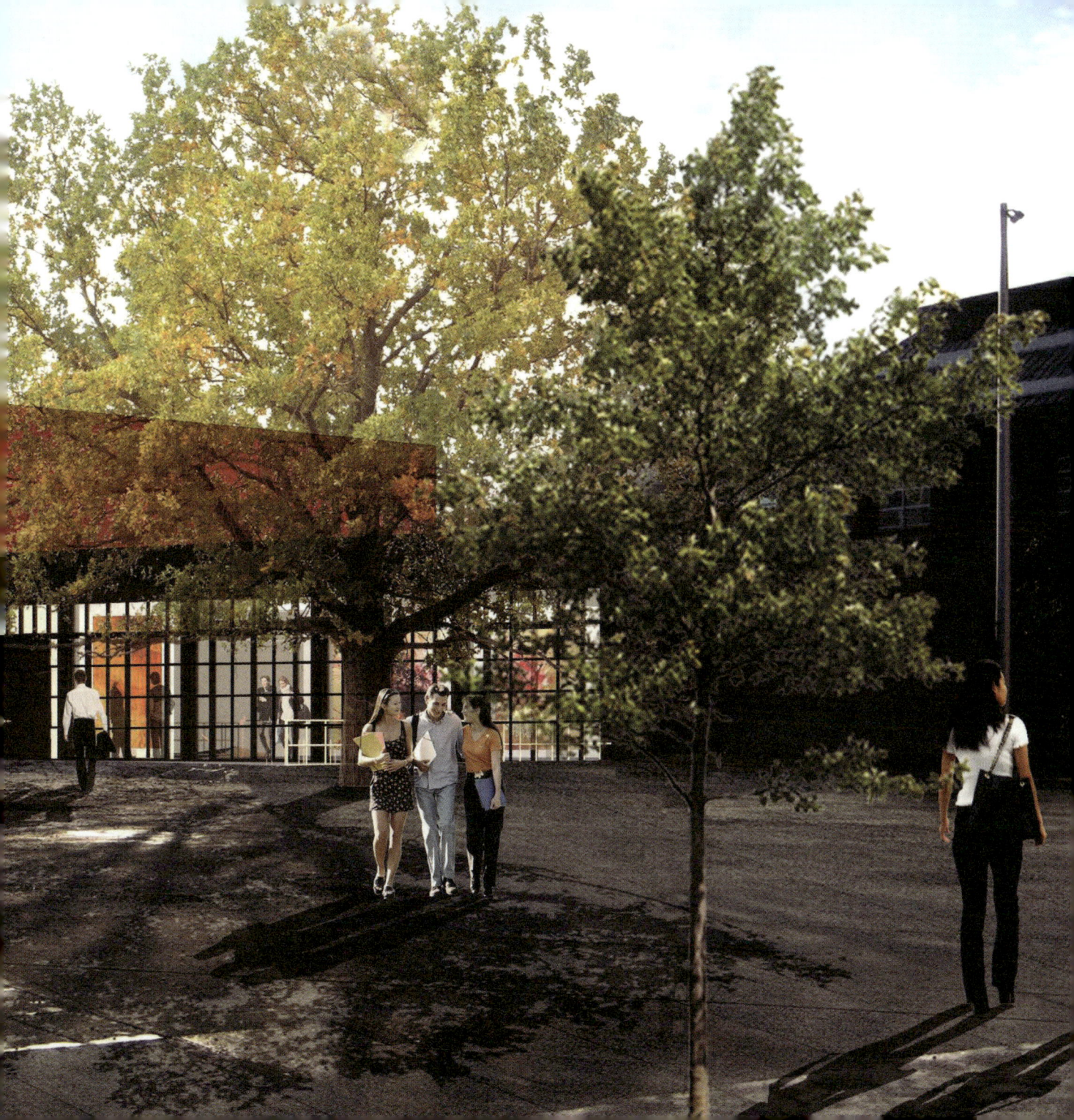

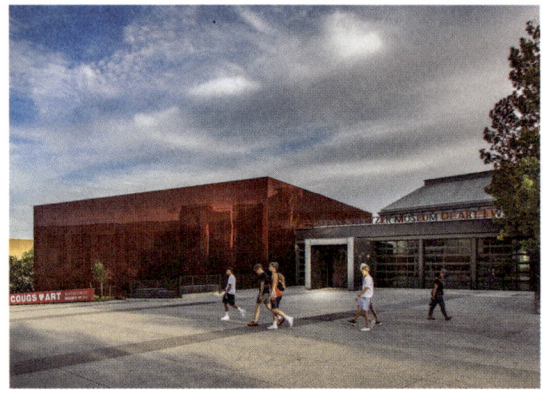

WSU Pullman students enjoy an early summer afternoon on Terrell Mall outside the entrance to the Jordan Schnitzer Museum of Art WSU, 2019

Photo: Kris Faulkner, courtesy of Design West Architects

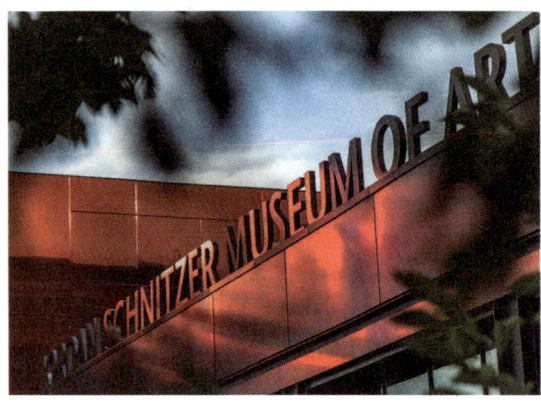

The mirrored glass reflects sunlight onto the charcoal façade of the Jordan Schnitzer Museum of Art WSU, coloring everything it touches crimson, 2022

Photo: WSU Photo Services

How did we get here?

A stand-alone building for an art museum was never a given, but a key decision by former WSU President Samuel Smith (1985–2000) made it a *possibility*. Director Patricia Watkinson positioned the museum program to be a direct report to the Provost (as opposed to being a small tangent in a college dean's org-chart), which gained Sam's eventual blessing. This move certified the museum as an independent entity that could essentially set its own course.

In a sense, I came to WSU in June 2003 to test that potential—to grow the program and build a building. I met with then-President Lane Rawlins, and he said, "Okay, Art Guy, go ahead." (Raise the money.) I figured, "Give us five years." Well, snap your fingers, click your heels, and *fourteen* years later the building was under construction!

Not that anyone was counting, but we're talking over 5,000 days, during which a lot of things had to fall into place, all within the context of a lot of questions: Where will it be? What will it be? Who will pay for it? Why do you need a new building?

My feeling was that, initially, we needed to prove ourselves worthy of investment. In our case, that meant expanding the presence of the program. The museum staff embraced the challenge.[1] We installed public art throughout campus, so even if you never entered the gallery, you'd come in contact with art. We organized exhibitions that travelled nationally. We produced publications that won

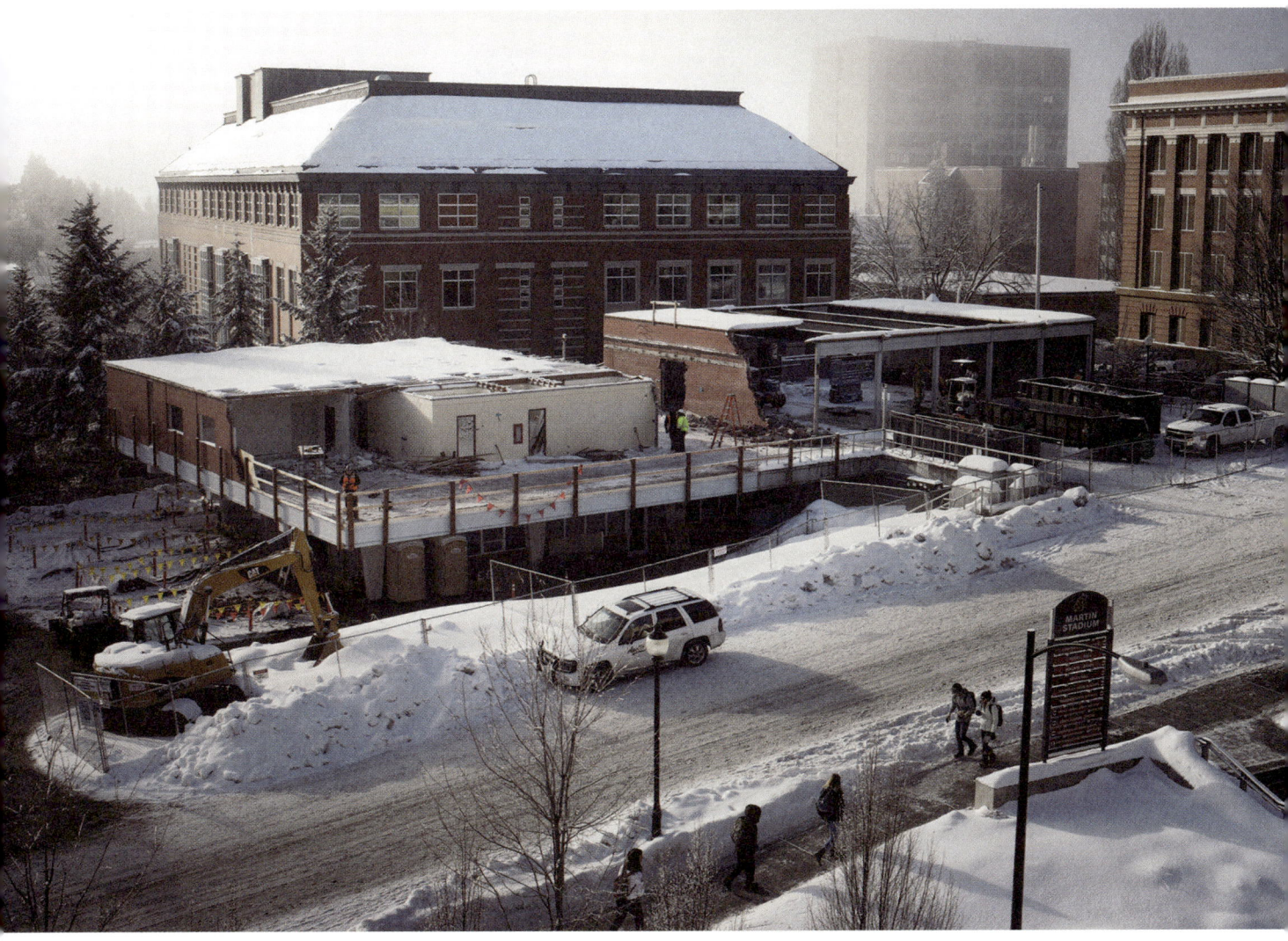

Taken from the fourth-floor camera at Martin Stadium in 2017, this image shows the partial deconstruction of the Public Safety Building on Terrell Mall, necessary to make way for the new museum

Photo: WSU Facilities Services

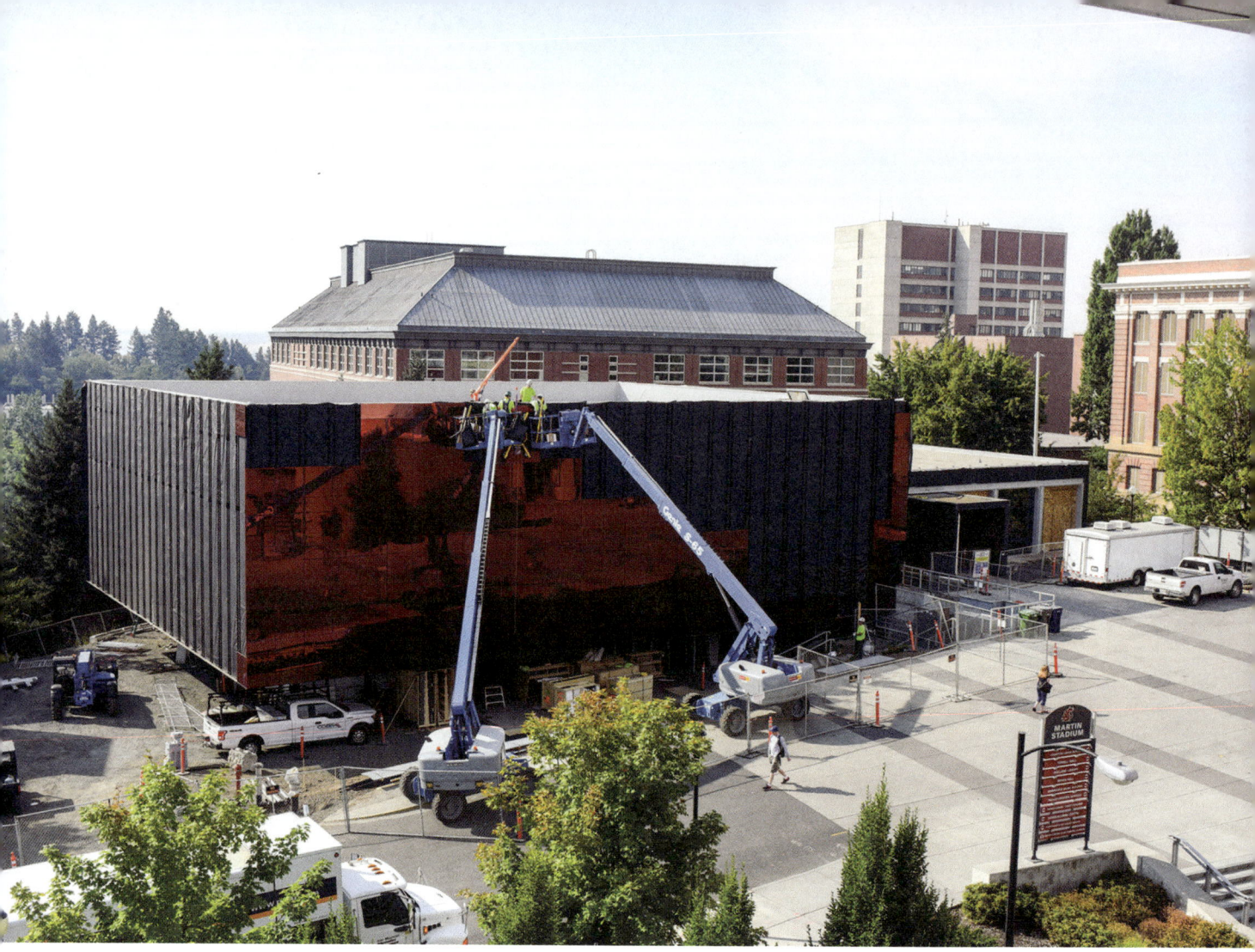

A construction image taken in 2017 from the fourth-floor camera at Martin Stadium, as installation of the mirrored cladding is underway

Photo: WSU Facilities Services

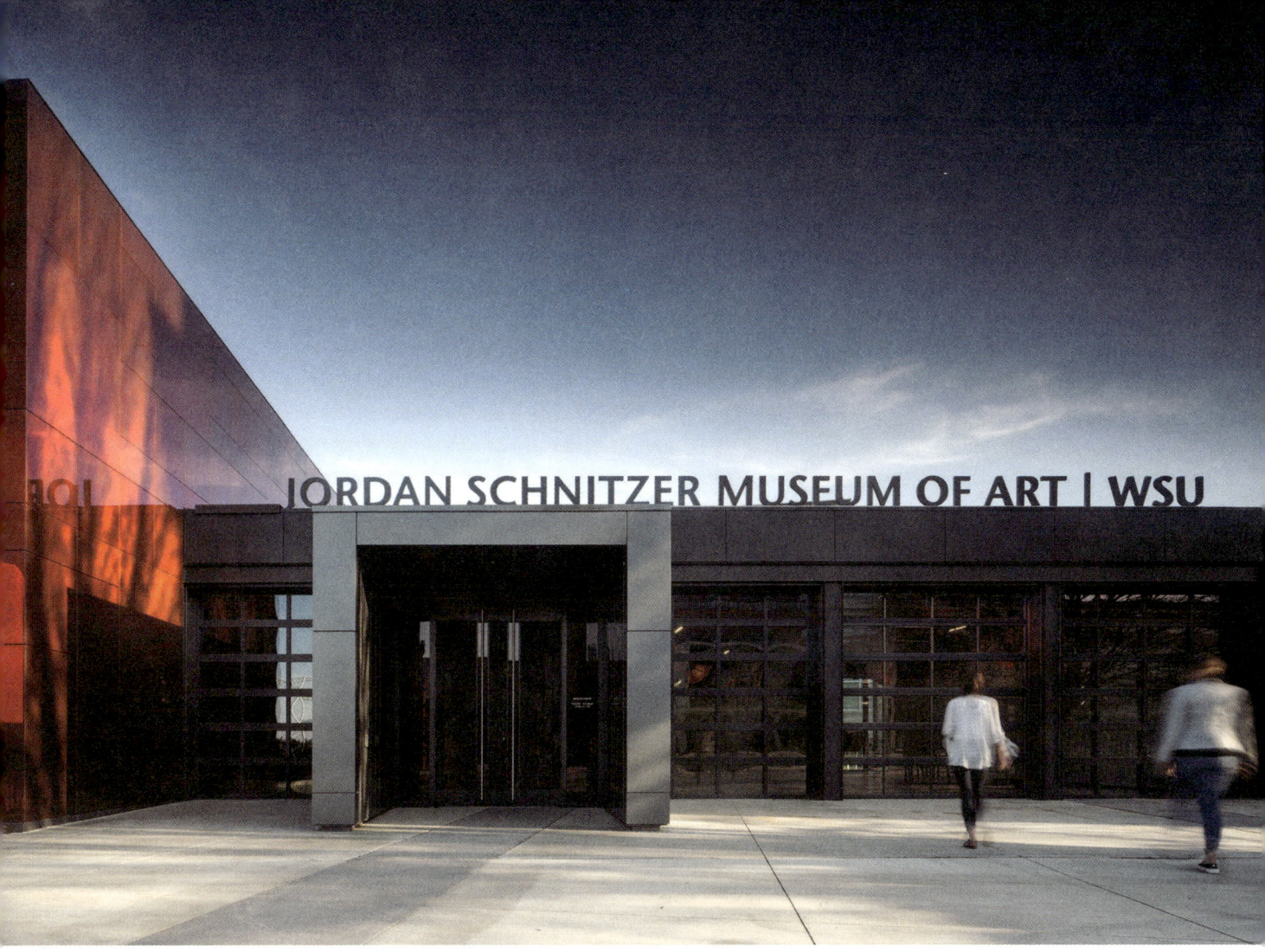

Visitors approach the Jordan Schnitzer Museum of Art WSU during the inaugural exhibitions in April 2018

Photo: @NicLehoux

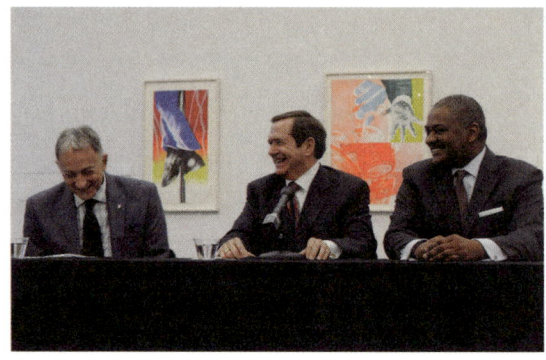

From left to right: Chris Bruce, Jordan Schnitzer, and WSU President Elson Floyd are shown at a 2013 press conference announcing Schnitzer's $5 million gift launching a $15 million campaign toward the new Jordan Schnitzer Museum of Art WSU

Photo: WSU Photo Services

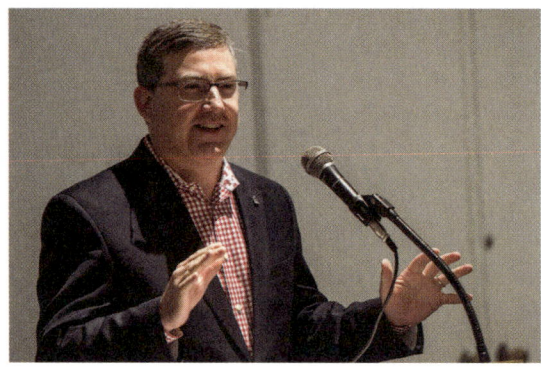

WSU President Kirk Schulz at a 2017 launch party marking the closure of the Museum of Art/WSU, and looking forward to the grand opening of the Jordan Schnitzer Museum of Art WSU

Photo: WSU Photo Services

awards. The collection grew.[2] The Buy-a-Bus program brought regional school groups to campus. All of which enhanced our visibility and credibility.

While these activities were going on, we assembled a fantastic Campaign Committee of influential individuals who believed that art mattered as an integral part of an educational and community experience.[3] Each made financial and emotional commitments to the idea of a new art museum building—of some undetermined scale, to be located somewhere on campus, and to be fully funded, somehow. Call it faith, aided by resolve.

Together, we persevered through three WSU presidents, four WSU Foundation executive officers, four Museum of Art development directors, three provosts, three football coaches, five basketball coaches, and, well, you get the picture. Eventually we'd have over 300 donors to the museum building—alumni, faculty, local residents, and Northwest art patrons, who committed everything from $1 to $5 million.

The "if" factor

Along the way, there were times when we had to reconsider our progress and re-set expectations. Without getting too deep in the weeds, here are a few examples.

In May 2007, Lane Rawlins retired, and Elson Floyd arrived as WSU's new president. This meant we needed to re-introduce the Building Campaign to our most essential

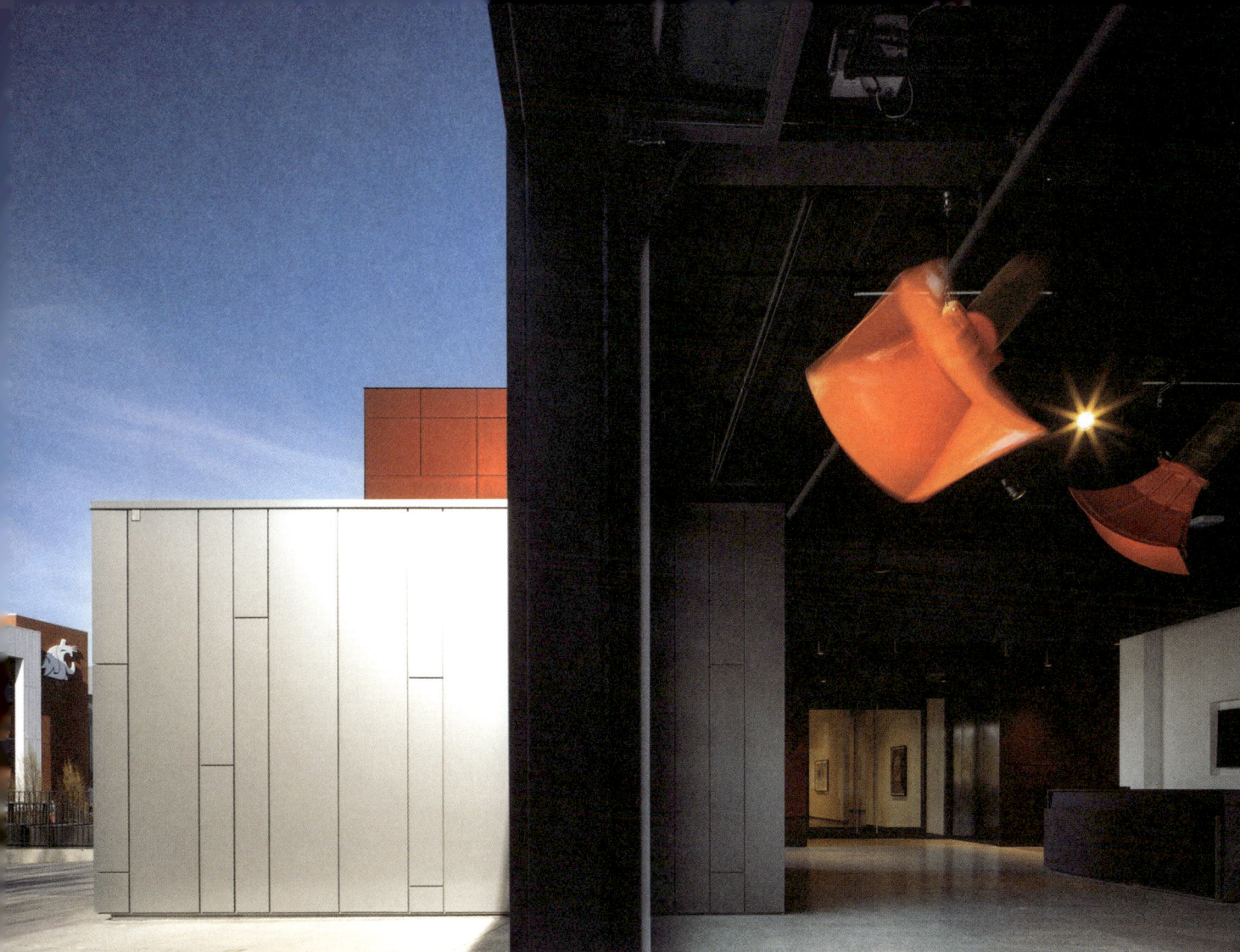

Looking into the Jordan Schnitzer Museum of Art WSU through the open doors of the Pavilion Gallery, highlighting the orange horns of Trimpin's sound sculpture *Ambiente432*, 2018

Photo: @NicLehoux

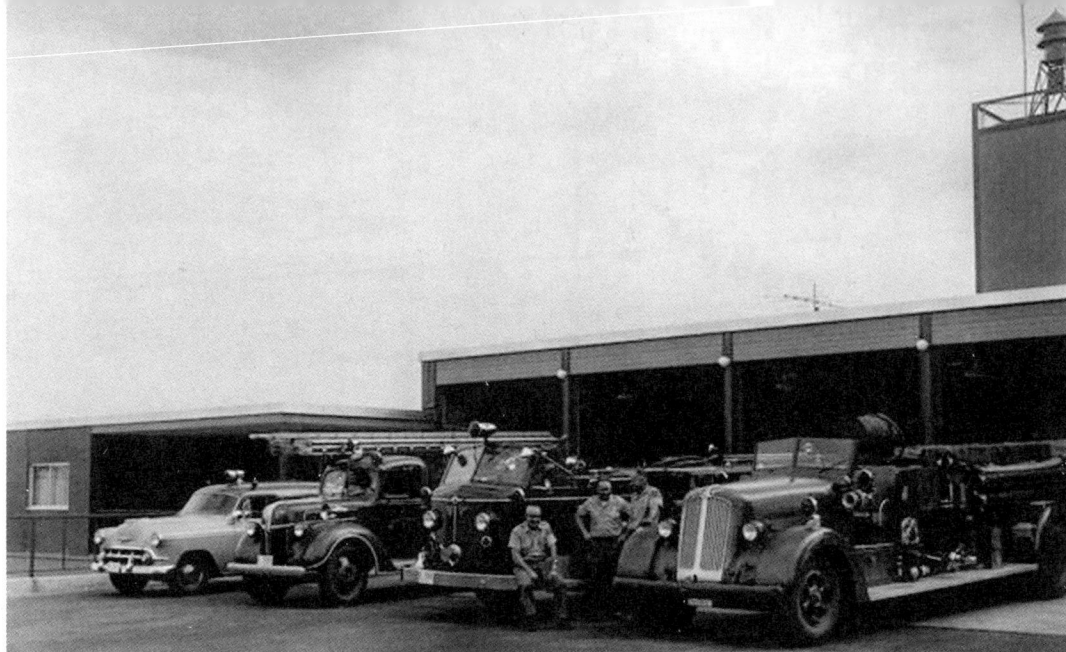

constituent. Our committee members were able to convince Elson of the merits of our cause, and he became a champion.

However, a year later the entire country became embroiled in the Great Recession, the worst financial crisis since the Great Depression. How do you ask people for donations when the global economy is on the brink? But the committee members stood strong, and, due to their continued support and advocacy, we managed to build interest.

At this time, we were essentially pitching an aspirational ideal that was haunted by the same old questions (What? Where? How much? When?). Incredibly, an answer appeared like a shining light on the hill: a prime site in the heart of campus was opening, as the fire department was moving from Terrell Mall to a new location. But was an art museum the one program that fit best within the university's master plan? Ultimately, we made the case that a venue that was free and open to all (our museum) was the perfect complement to other public spaces along the Mall like the student union, the stadium, and the library.

The site was ours—"if" we could pay for it. We commissioned drawings, which provided a vision that we could share, along with a clearer sense of scale and cost. The problem now (about year 10 of that initial "five-year plan") was that, even as generous as our funding commitments were, we were hovering at about half the needed $15 million. And yet, no one wanted to compromise the scope of our building.

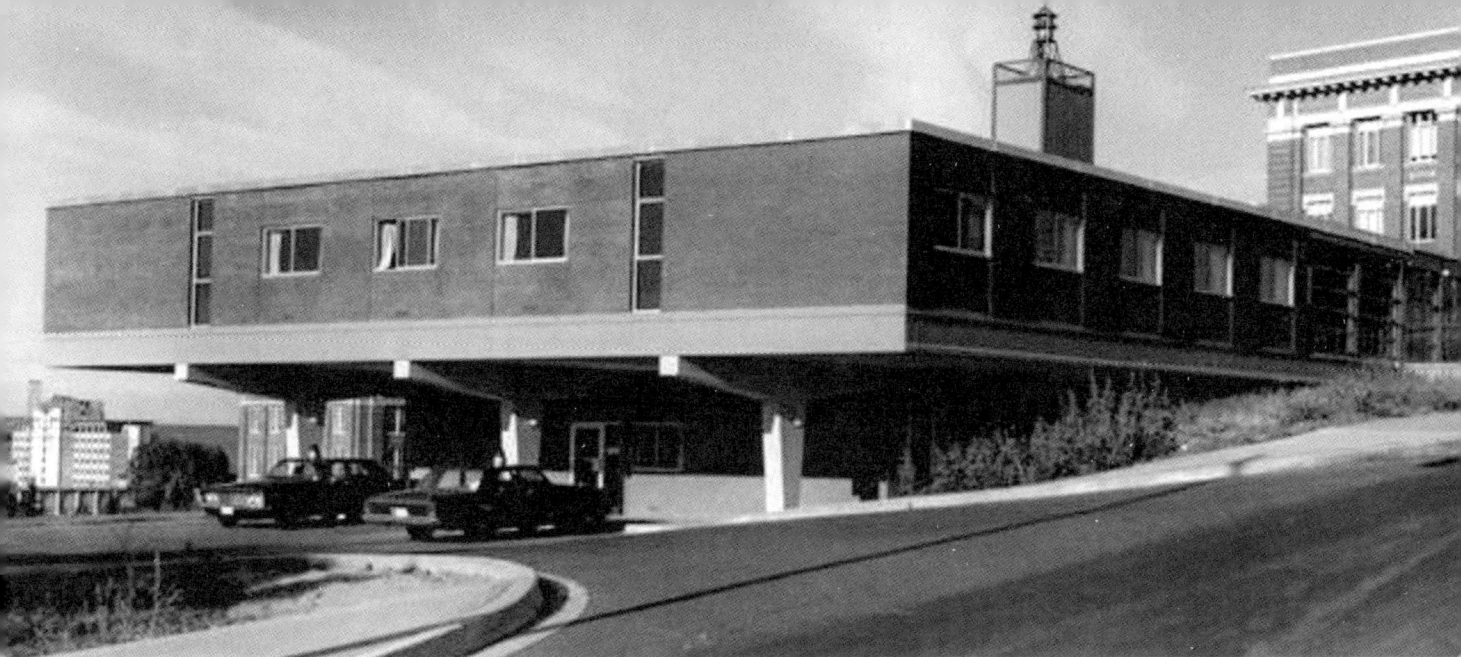

Above and left: The Public Safety Building as seen in 1963. Echoes of the building's history can be found in the current architecture, including the preserved floors showing fire truck parking spots, as well as newly fabricated garage doors

Photos: WSU Libraries' Manuscripts, Archives, and Special Collections

Where would the rest come from? Long story short, in 2013, Portland art patron Jordan D. Schnitzer emerged as an interested party. Being a real estate guy, Jordan understood the inherent value and opportunity of our central location, and he developed a fast appreciation of President Floyd's bold plans for the university. With Jordan's buy-in, Elson assured him that final funds would be there to see the building across the finish line. Jordan came through with a donation of $5 million, the largest gift to the arts in WSU's history.

Then, sadly, in June 2015, Elson passed away, which—aside from the great human loss—left a huge leadership void. For the museum, it opened the prospect of losing university funding. Here again, our committee members came to the rescue and, in one unambiguous voice, "strongly encouraged" the university's support to close the remaining gap in private funds.

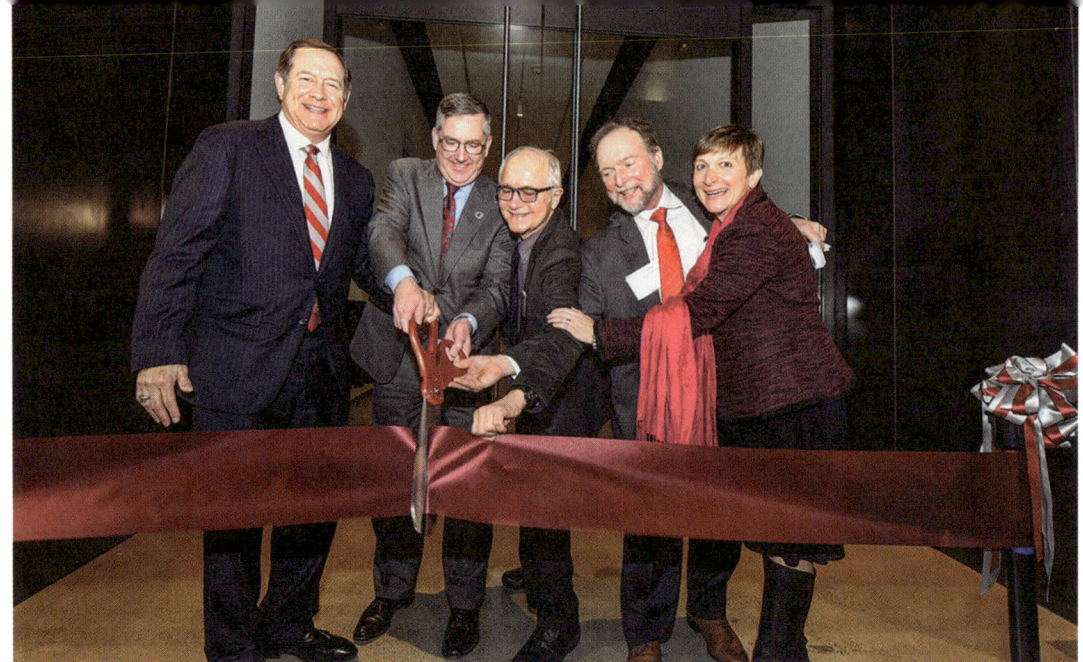

From left to right: Patron Jordan Schnitzer, WSU president Kirk Schulz, architect Jim Olson, WSU Regent Brett Blankenship, and interim director Anna-Maria Shannon at the April 6, 2018, inauguration of the Jordan Schnitzer Museum of Art WSU

Photo: WSU Photo Services

The "you" factor

Of course, everyone has their own idea of what an art museum should look like. To say "museum" is to call on notions of timelessness, reverence, and authority, a temple of permanence in a world of change. A place where, in Bob Dylan's words, "infinity goes up on trial."

We wanted something less self-important, more accessible. Architect Jim Olson's resolution was to clad the exterior in mirrored walls in which the surrounding area and activity would be reflected—an *immersive* presence, as opposed to an *imposing* edifice. It's an ostensibly simple solution that nevertheless stands out as an "art space"—clearly distinctive from its neighbors, elegantly unexpected, and ever-changing.

Think of the first time you saw it, say, just strolling along Terrell Mall. The genius of the building is that you saw yourself in it. You didn't know what you might get if you went inside, but it had included you and the world around you. Thus, you were already "part of the building" when you walked through the doors, and you encountered something you never imagined before. Something unexpected happened because you had seen yourself in a mirror-clad box, something that you may not even have understood. Art happened, right there, where a fire station once stood.

[1] Some of the core Museum of Art/WSU staff between 2003 and 2017 include Anna-Maria Shannon, Keith Wells, Zach Mazur, Debby Stinson, Tonya Murray, Ryan Hardesty, Boone Helm, Ann Saberi, Rob Snyder, Jill Aesoph, and Jeanne Fulfs.

[2] Notably, the Marian E. Smith Glass Collection and the Jim Dine Print Collection, which is the largest collection of this artist's prints outside of the Museum of Fine Arts, Boston.

[3] Campaign committee members include Melinda Beasley, Cleve Borth, Judith Borth, Jeannie Butler, Jack Creighton, Jan Creighton, Dan Harmon, Patricia Smith, Samuel Smith, and Howard S. Wright III.

MANY VOICES

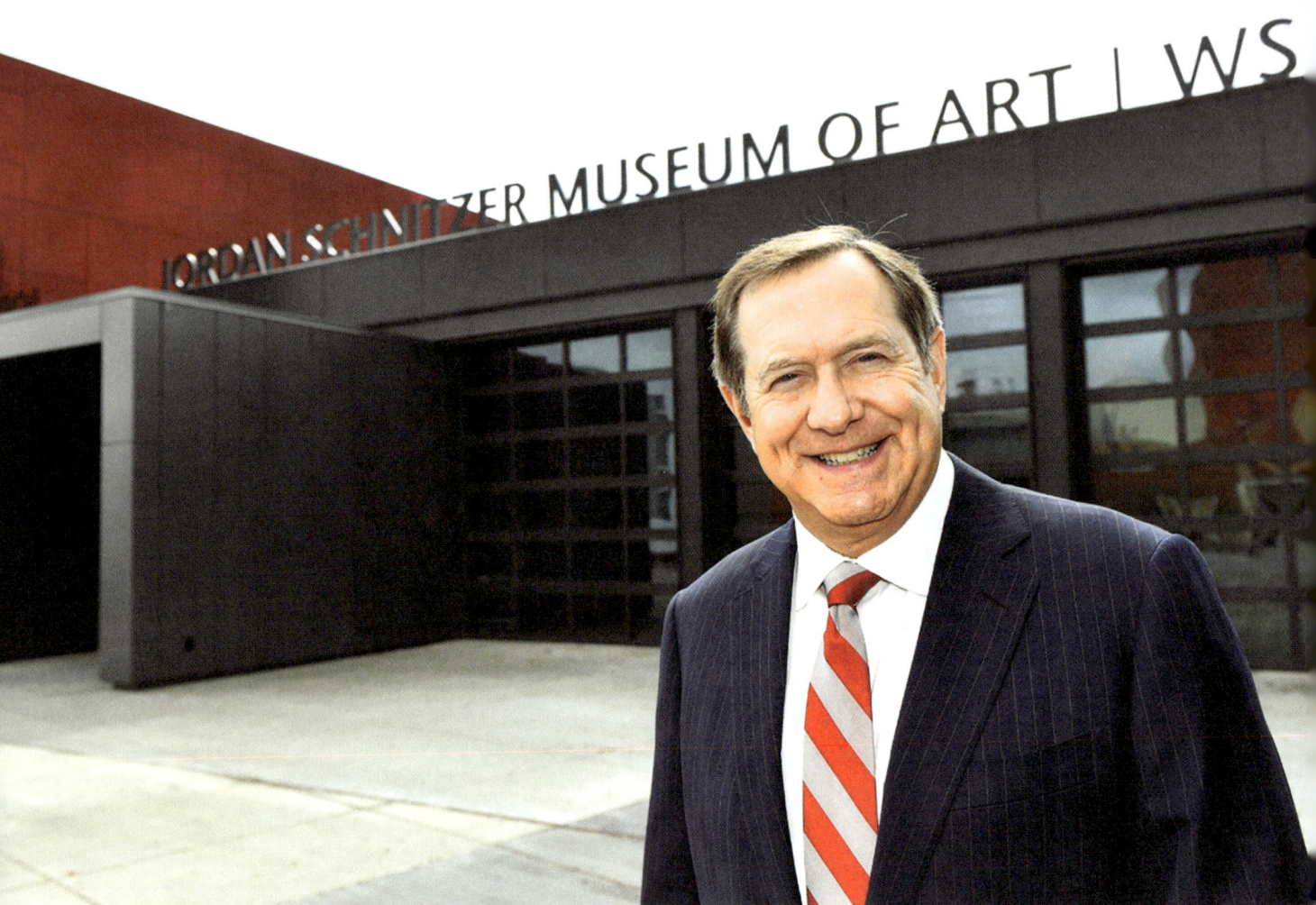

Jordan D. Schnitzer in front of the newly built Jordan Schnitzer Museum of Art WSU, 2018
Photo: WSU Photo Services

Jordan D. Schnitzer

Many people view museums as a place for some elitist few. I firmly believe that art is for everyone. I am trying to tear down those perceived walls. A university campus is just the place to start. The arts are the highest ideals of every society. They are the ultimate legacy we leave for future generations.

This new museum at WSU will reach out to every student on campus, every adult within hundreds of miles—providing activities that will enrich their hearts, minds, and souls.

—Jordan D. Schnitzer
    President,
    Jordan Schnitzer Family Foundation

Kirk Schulz

The arts are essential to creating interdisciplinary connections and making all of us better, more critically observant individuals. The Jordan Schnitzer Museum of Art WSU—placed in the heart of the Pullman campus—symbolizes the treasured role of the arts and our commitment to offering our students a transformative educational experience.

—Kirk Schulz
    President,
    Washington State University

Howard Wright

The Jordan Schnitzer Museum of Art WSU is a beacon in the region, a bright light on the horizon. It plays a critical role in fostering curiosity and critical thinking in the liberal arts world. I am so proud of WSU for inserting "A" in STEM, making it STEAM. So many in the community have embraced a museum that previously so few knew of. Thank you, and the community, for enabling it to play a critical role in the community and greater region!

—H.S. Wright III
    Chairman & Founder,
    Seattle Hospitality Group

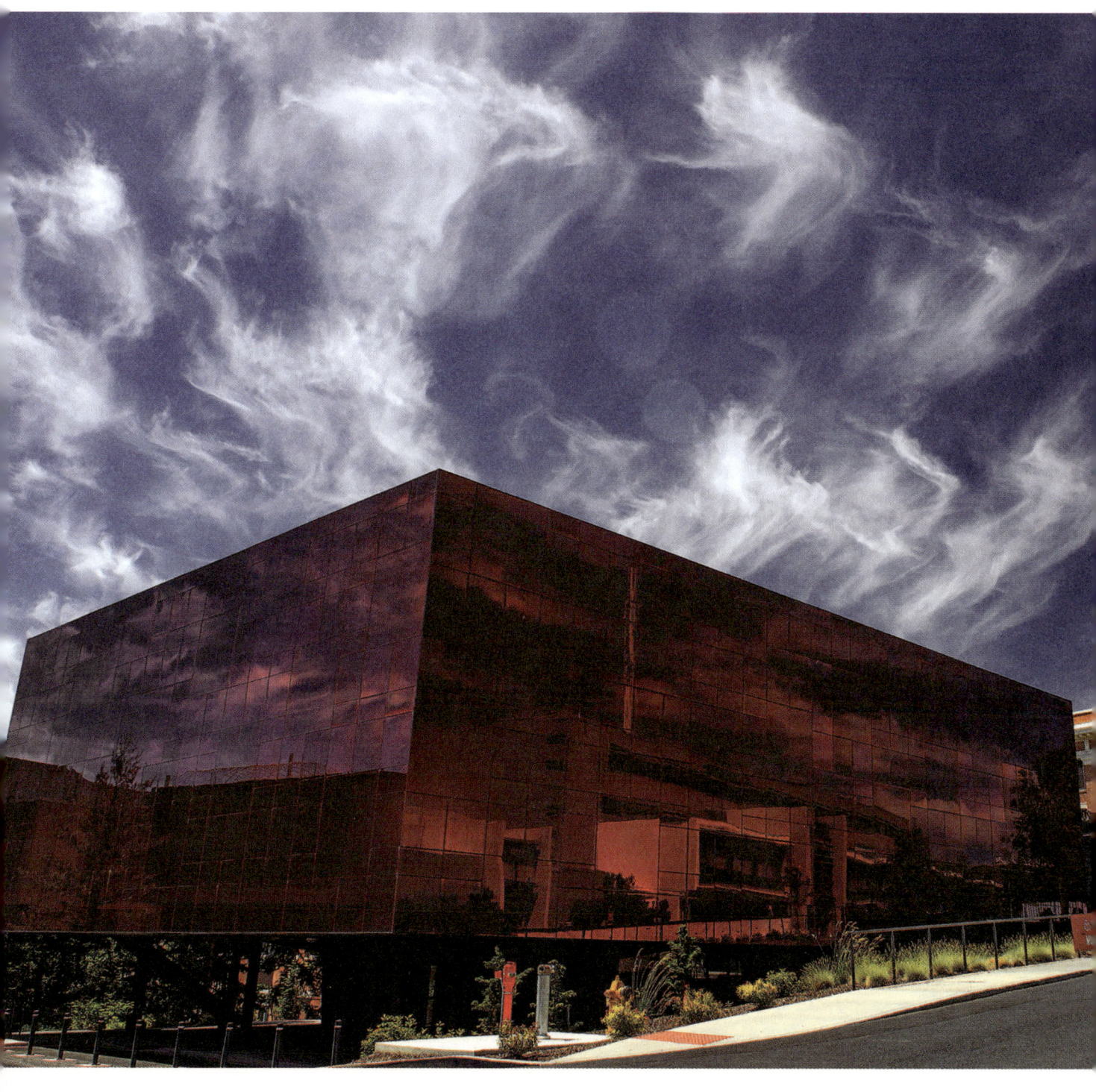

Elizabeth Chilton

The Jordan Schnitzer Museum of Art WSU is a cornerstone of the WSU Pullman campus and the greater regional community. Across all human societies, the arts serve to bring joy, but also to challenge, provoke, and heal—all critical to an educational institution. The arts can provide an all-important leveling and connecting mechanism for people of all backgrounds, cultures, and professional contexts. For the campus, the museum serves as a hub to bring the community together. One recent example is the exhibition opening for Jeffrey Gibson; Gibson is a queer Cherokee-Choctaw artist, who was recently selected as the first Indigenous artist to represent the United States with a solo exhibition at the 2024 Venice Biennale. As Ryan Hardesty put it, "So much of Gibson's art is about creating community," and the exhibit has allowed us to do just that. The museum hosted a guided panel discussion featuring Gibson alongside members of the Nimíipuu (Nez Perce) Tribe, as well as faculty and students, followed by a fabulous reception.

But this was just one of dozens of events that the museum hosts in any given year: they host numerous visits and provide free guided tours for regional K-12 students, community organizations, and students from other colleges and universities. This includes the "Buy-A-Bus program," which covers the reimbursement of travel to the museum for K-12 grade schools within a 100-mile radius.

Many of the museum's exhibitions feature local artists and/or subjects, including Juventino Aranda (Walla Walla), Keiko Hara (Walla Walla), and Irwin Nash (photographs of Yakima Valley migrant laborers from the 1960s–70s), to name a few recent examples. This connection to the state of Washington provides a grounding in the subjects most immediate and relatable to our faculty, staff, and students.

Most of all, the museum plays a major role in fostering cultural understanding and diversity. It does this not only through its exhibitions and programming, like those described above, but also by providing space for community events that promote inclusivity. For example, the museum recently hosted students from the Native Student Center as they created traditional ribbon skirts and shirts; they hosted students and teachers from the ROAR program (a program for students with intellectual and developmental disabilities), who participated in a guided walking meditation and chalk drawings; they hosted programming for the National Day of Racial Healing; and they hosted the Chicanx Latinx Student Center and muralist Joseph 'Nuke' Montalvo for a discussion about the history of Montalvo's murals on campus.

As we look to the future of WSU Pullman, the museum will continue to have a critical role as we work to promote a culture of belonging for all students, faculty, and staff. Located at the literal heart of campus, the museum is very much at the core of our mission as an institution: to help students become more aware, engaged, and creative; to contribute to the betterment of human existence through the creative expression of human experience; and to serve the needs of Washingtonians by sharing its expertise and helping residents integrate that knowledge into their daily lives.

—Elizabeth Chilton
  former Provost and
  Executive Vice President,
  Chancellor, WSU Pullman

Chancellor Elizabeth Chilton giving opening remarks for *Jeffrey Gibson: They Teach Love, From the Collections of Jordan D. Schnitzer and His Family Foundation*, 2023

Photo: Dal Perry

Zach Mazur

The Museum of Art/WSU was much more than a job for me; it was a place of immense growth with co-workers, mentors, and colleagues that I consider a second family. From fundraising and building a new museum space to speaking nationally on the importance of museums, together we gave purpose and pride to our work and challenged the status quo of what these spaces are and can become.

To this day, I regularly hear from students whose professional lives we helped shape, many of whom I now call colleagues and draw upon for expertise. The museum provided the support, mentorship, and freedom to be creative in my approaches to museum education, which has profoundly impacted both my personal and pedagogical endeavors. To my team who I miss dearly: I love you all and will always cherish our adventures and accomplishments!

—Zach Mazur
Preparator, 2006–2008, Assistant Curator, 2008–2013
Curator of Education & Collections, 2013–2018, Museum of Art/WSU

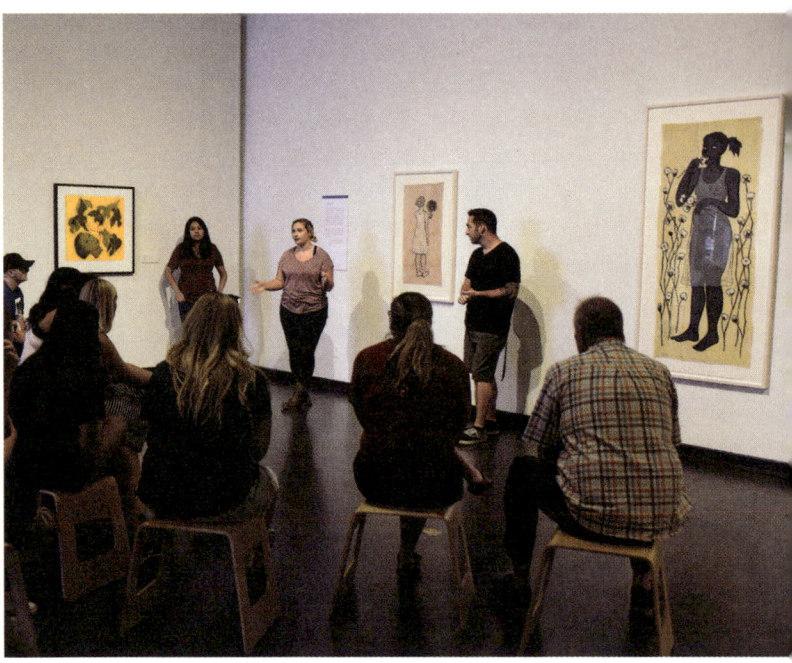

Zach Mazur (standing at right) and students giving a lesson during the exhibition *Contemporary Women Printmakers, From the Collections of Jordan D. Schnitzer and His Family Foundation*
August 22–November 17, 2017

Photo: Jordan Schnitzer Museum of Art WSU Archives

Jim Olson

To me, the museum is a crimson magnet for creativity. I dream that students will see themselves reflected in the building and realize that each of them is part of the power of art, and their imaginations will create the world of the future. May they always contemplate their own reflections in this building.

—Jim Olson
    Principal/Founder, Olson Kundig

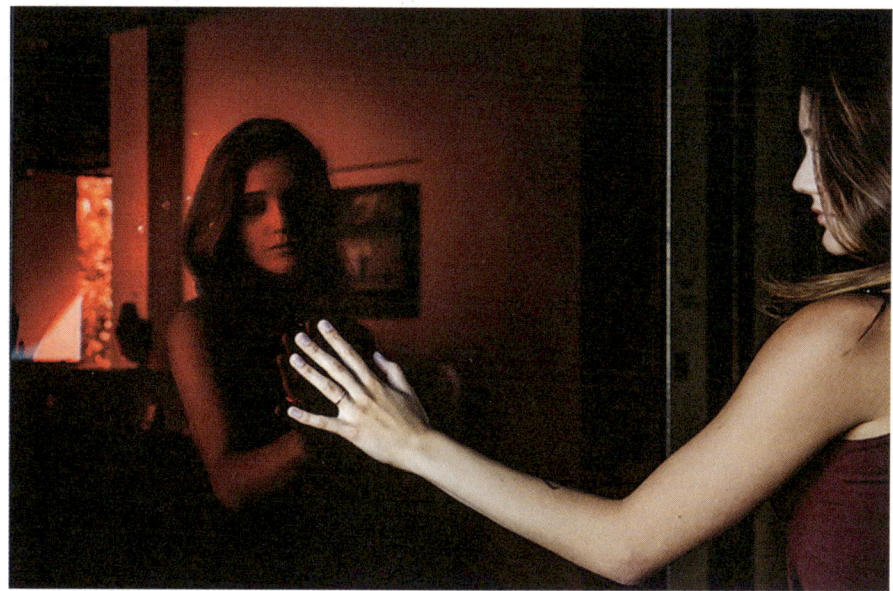

Photo: Kris Faulkner,
courtesy of Design West Architects

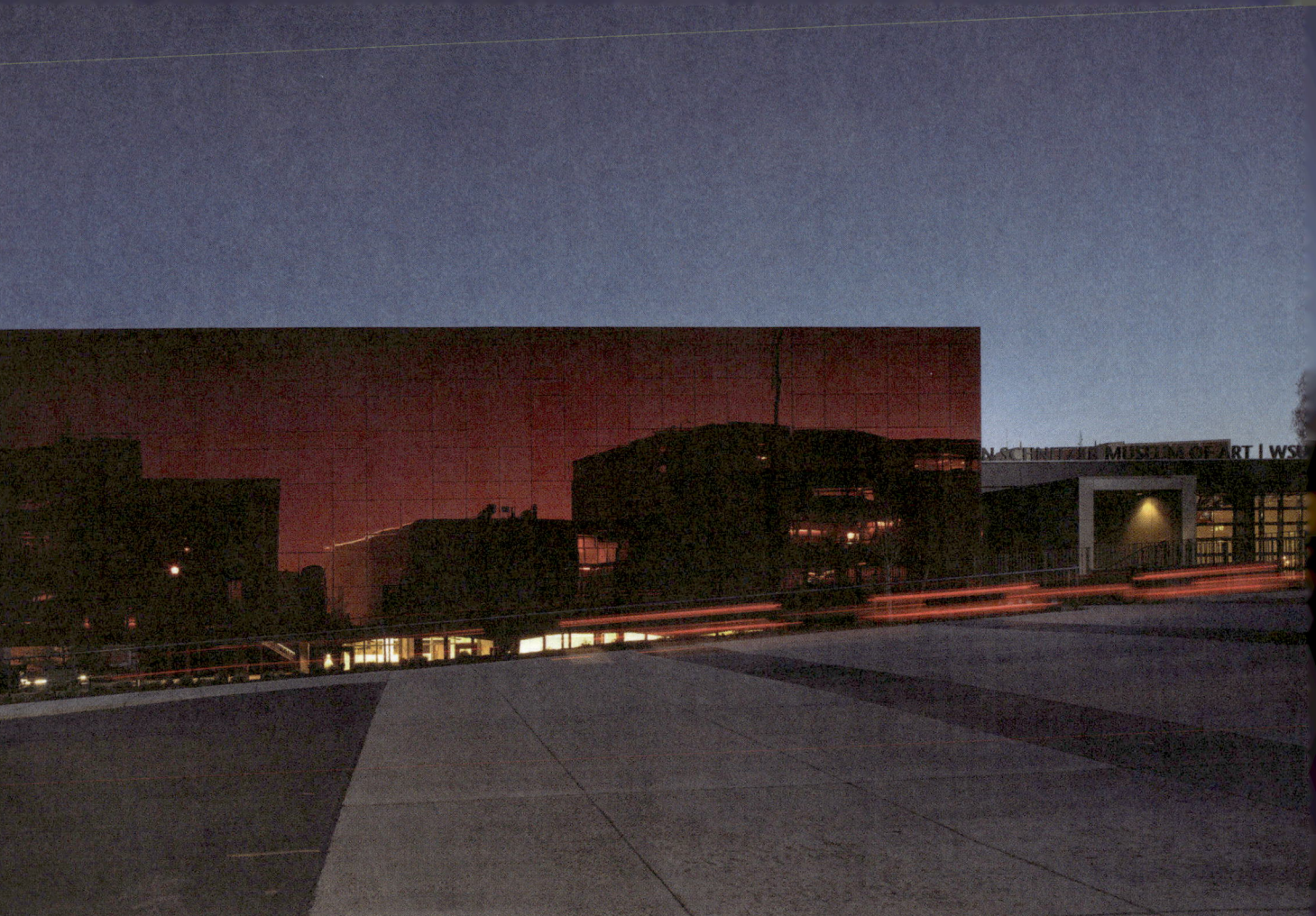

A time-lapse, early-evening shot, looking toward the Jordan Schnitzer Museum of Art WSU "Crimson Cube" from Martin Stadium, 2018

Photo: @NicLehoux

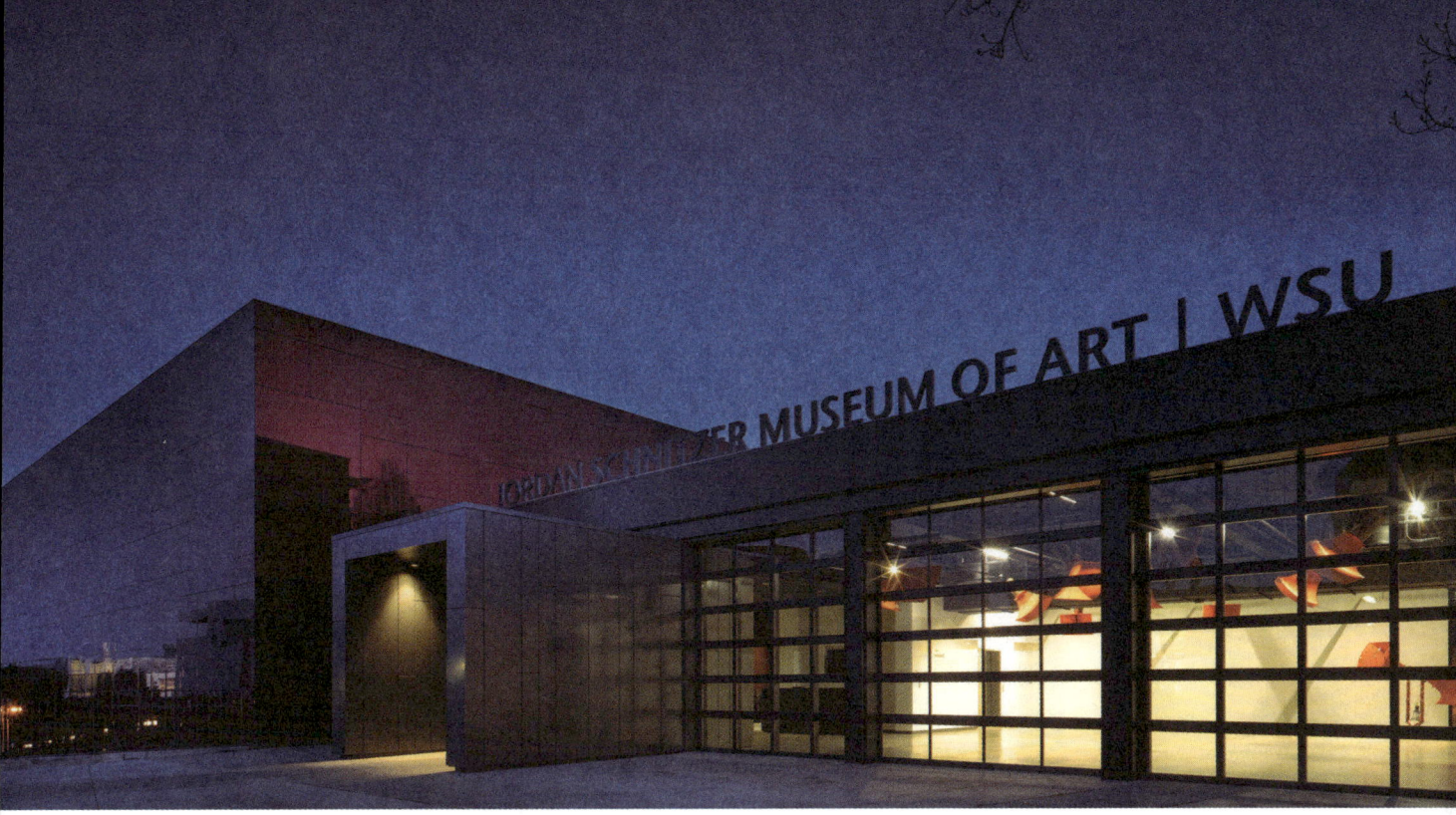

Early evening, looking into the warmly lit Pavilion Gallery of the newly-constructed
Jordan Schnitzer Museum of Art WSU, 2018

Photo: @NicLehoux

Greg Kucera

In 2016 Ryan Hardesty, as curator then, approached Larry Yocom and me about organizing an exhibition from our personal collection, aside from artists exhibited or inventory owned by my Seattle gallery. (The gallery had often loaned works to exhibitions at the museum.) We jumped at the chance—and not just because we could have our house walls repainted since much of the art would be removed from them.

The exhibition borrowed about 50 sculptures, paintings, prints and photographs from our home. It turned into a substantial overview of our collection's many diversions, with a nicely illustrated brochure and checklist. As part of the programming for that exhibition, I agreed to speak with WSU students about what it means to be not just a gallery owner but also a collector of art.

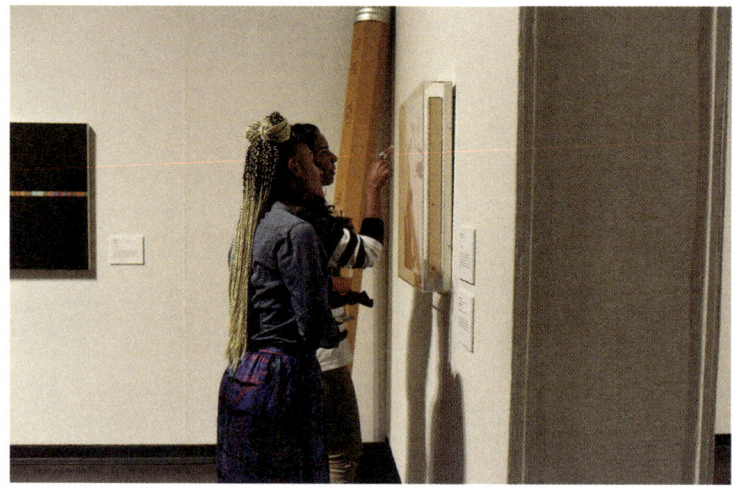

Visitors explore artworks from the exhibition *Curators' Choices: The Greg Kucera & Larry Yocom Collection*, 2016
Photo: Zach Mazur

The conversation with the students, along with a few faculty members, was one of the most engaging and thought-provoking discussions I have had about my roles in the art world. The students came prepared with interesting questions and concerns, many of which were focused on diversity and inclusion in our collection and in the gallery. I felt challenged to come up with equally good answers, and appreciated hearing their immediate thoughts on how diversity might influence both business and personal aspects of collecting. The fact that our collection included works by many artists from minority backgrounds facilitated these questions and grounded the answers.

We had collected without any particular direction, but always with a great deal of personal passion. Works by Asian American, Latinx, Black, and Indigenous artists were juxtaposed with those from majority populations, offering insights into the progression of civil rights.

Additionally, our collection contains many works by female artists. Viewing them in contrast to their male colleagues provided discussion about how much the art market (indeed, the world) has changed to accommodate the growing status of women artists. Works by both gay and non-gay artists provided a lively look at the gender and sexual content that is so much a part of contemporary art.

Works by a broad range of contemporary artists were informed by their historical predecessors, going back as early as the seventeenth century. For impulses unknown to us, we had collected a great number of works with religious content: Viewing these in contrast to so many secular artists also provided fascinating observations.

Hearing from the students in a free-ranging discussion about our collection in terms of art issues and contemporary politics—and their various intersections—was very meaningful for Larry and me.

—Greg Kucera
Greg Kucera Gallery, Seattle

Jeffry Mitchell

A Box-Shaped Heart.

In the center of Washington State University's campus sits a building, a mirrored box. It reflects the surrounding world in mirrored crimson: the stadium, the student union, parking lots, sky and weather, the rolling velvet hills of the Palouse, and all of us.

This is a very good building, uncategorizable and holding its mysteries until we enter and find a familiar, classical progression of spaces: a vestibule leading to a central hall, flanked by galleries, ending in a great room. It's not fancy but it is elegant in its proportions and has the feeling of a special place. These gracious volumes honor the makers, the scholars, the viewers, and the things and events that pass through.

The vitality of the place starts with director Ryan Hardesty and extends to the entire museum team. A gentle choreographer of artists and audience, Ryan's adept at orchestrating. He holds high ambitions, has a very good heart, is intelligent, and makes people feel at ease. For the inaugural show, Trimpin installed a body-ringing sound work in the vestibule, Marie Watt built a colossal wolf of fragrant cedar wood in the room across the hall, dizzying videos from the Bill and Ruth True collection ran in the room next to mine, and a blockbuster selection of artwork from the Schnitzer collection hung in the great room. I made a multi-part installation depicting the death of Buddha, comprised of ceramic figurines, fabric embroidery, elephant lanterns, prints, and paintings.

With synergistic power, Ryan pulled together such unlikey-to-hang-together work. His unexpected curation, and the whole experience, gave me such physical delight. Did you know he was in a punk band in his youth? Anyway, the building and what goes on there has an undeniable pulse. A good energy emanates from the combination of the place, the space, and the people. I'm not sure how that works but I'm grateful for it. It's a mystery. We love mysteries. Life is full of them.

—Jeffry Mitchell
  Artist

Visitors enjoy artworks from the exhibition *Jeffry Mitchell: The Death of Buddha*, 2018
Photo: @NicLehoux

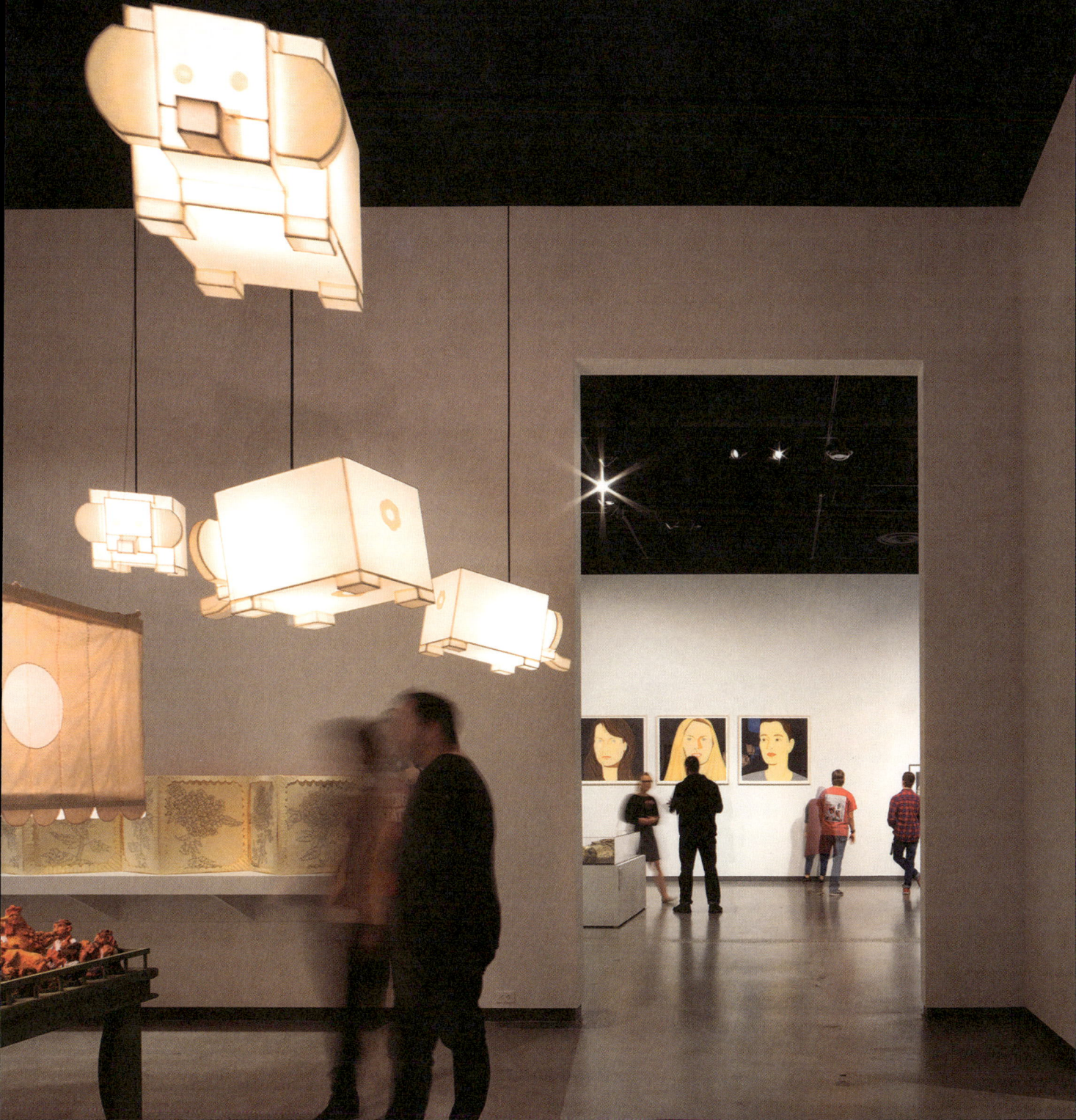

Marie Watt

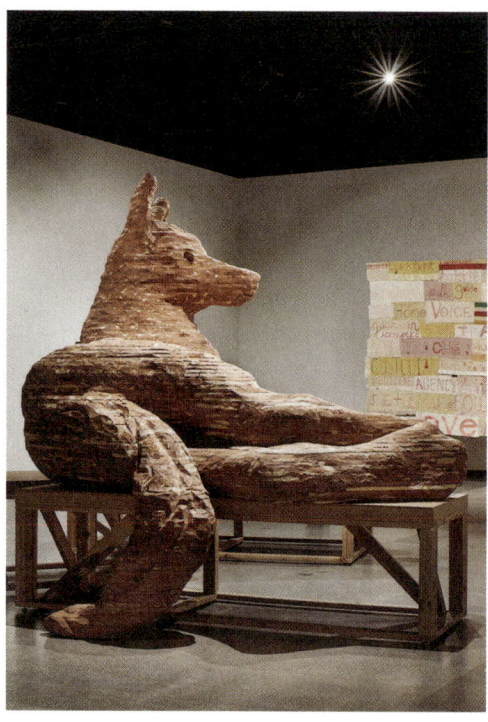

Marie Watt: Companion Species (Underbelly)
installed at the Jordan Schnitzer Museum of Art
WSU in 2018

Photo: Benjamin Benschneider / OTTO

At the invitation of Ryan Hardesty and the Jordan Schnitzer Museum of Art WSU, I had the great pleasure of creating one of my largest and most ambitious sculptures to date—a one-and-a-half-ton carved cedar canine, over 10 feet high and 15 feet long. Based on my ruminations about motherhood, the stories I grew up with, historical depictions like the Capitoline Wolf, and what it means to inhabit the earth as companion species, *Companion Species (Underbelly)* invited visitors to consider a Seneca and Indigenous teaching that our relationship with animals and the environment is one of reciprocity and interconnection rather than dominion. Visitors could smell the cedar aroma wafting from this monumental sculpture before they even reached the gallery. I enjoyed hearing people respond with wonder to the sculpture's scale as it exceeded the dimensions of all the doorways. As an artist it is thrilling to work with museums that both trust and empower the vision of the artist. This is one of the Jordan Schnitzer Museum of Art WSU's superpowers.

—Marie Watt (Seneca)
  Artist

Polly Apfelbaum

My exhibition *Frequently the Woods are Pink* opened at the Jordan Schnitzer Museum of Art WSU on August 27, 2019. It was the first survey show of my prints. I chose the title from an Emily Dickinson poem, which catalogues the seasons. For me, it was an opportunity to see and catalogue *my* seasons. I studied printmaking in art school and had returned to it seriously many years later, with my now 22-year-long collaboration with Durham Press. The show included pieces I worked on with the LeRoy Neiman Center, Tamarind Institute, and Dieu Donné as well. *Flower Garden*, *Love Flowers*, *Just Flowers*, *Love Alley*, *Persephone*, *Atomic Pinwheel*, *Atomic Mystic Aura*, *Atomic Mystic Particles*, *Flags of Revolt and Defiance*, *Love Park*, *Baroque Time Machine*, *Byzantine Rocker* & *Byzantine Roller*...

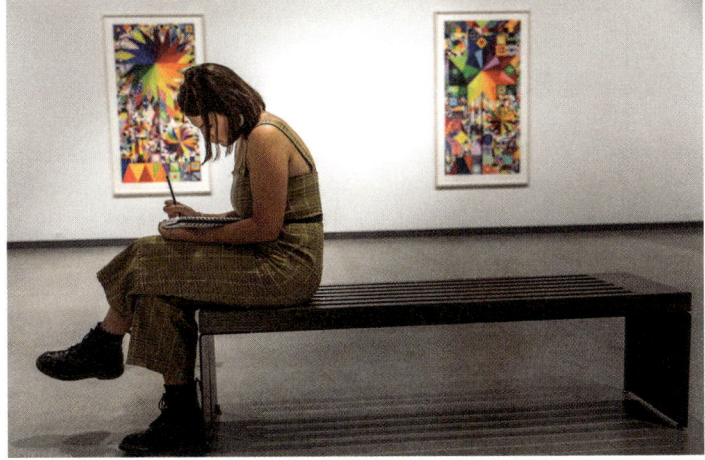

Frequently the Woods are Pink, thank you Jordan Schnitzer Museum of Art WSU for letting me time travel through my seasons of prints. Happy 50th! Keep on Rockin' & Rollin'!

—Polly Apfelbaum
 Artist

A student enjoys a quiet moment sketching at the exhibition *Polly Apfelbaum: Frequently the Woods are Pink, From the Collections of Jordan D. Schnitzer and His Family Foundation*, 2019

Photo: Kris Faulkner, courtesy of Design West Architects

Sister June T Sanders

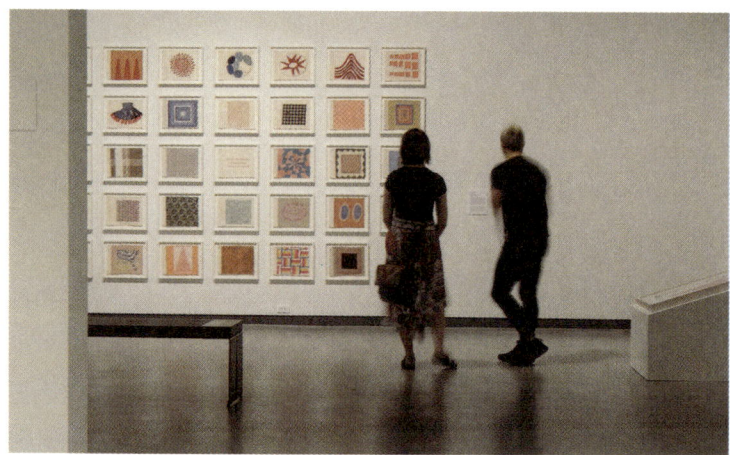

Visitors enjoy the exhibition *Louise Bourgeois: Ode to Forgetting, From the Collections of Jordan D. Schnitzer and His Family Foundation*, 2019

Photo: WSU Photo Services

To recall that forever-meandering summer—when a print by Louise Bourgeois made everything in the fields feel fresh, new. Her devout forms, rough lines, shapes revealing patterns and meaning in our own landscape. To commit to moments that I cannot write about, only view—when a piece has spent time with me, and I with it, in silence, until moved. Was it McDermitt? Mitchell? Hopkina? Feves? Poignancy and semblance. To believe in art's capacity for healing, contemplation, community, and growth. To believe that there is art happening anywhere, especially here. To believe that you are someone who sees art and is changed by it. To foster the opulence of a clear and true and pious experience. I am more now. Pliant. That is what the museum is to me.

—Sister June T Sanders
  Artist
  Director of Undergraduate Studies & Assistant Professor,
  Digital Technology & Culture Program, WSU Pullman

Kristin Becker

The museum is a remarkable place to teach and learn—about art, of course, but also about other areas of study, and about life itself. Semester after semester, year after year, the museum offers ever-changing opportunities to see the world through the eyes of artists. The ideas and inspirations that arise may intersect with any of the myriad disciplines that students explore at WSU. I am especially excited when educators from outside the arts bring their expertise to our exhibitions because it opens my eyes to connections I might not instinctively perceive with my training as an artist. Recently we have hosted Human Development professors leading classes about curiosity and mindfulness, pre-service math teachers developing activities in response to pattern and geometric form, and a plant scientist finding meaningful detail in what seemed to be the sketchiest of landscapes. Most importantly, I see the museum as a place where we learn about one another—our fellow students, our colleagues, the people we live with, and those visiting from afar.

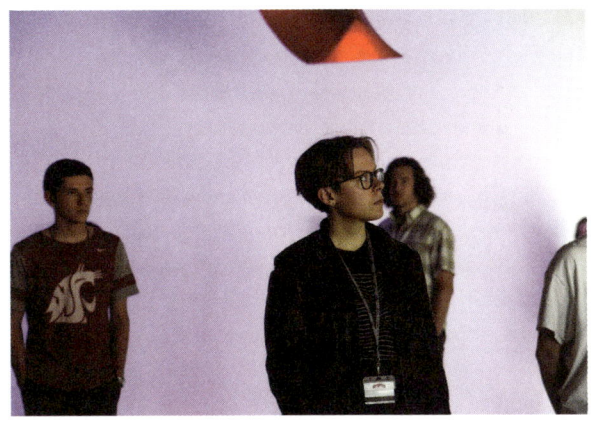

Art & Healing Walking Meditation with Nitivia Jones on September 1, 2022, for Kristin Becker's course, Honors 280: The Art Museum as Interdisciplinary Classroom

Photo: Jasper Willson

When we engage in discussions about art, whether we find the work thrilling, perplexing, or emotional, we gain insights into new perspectives—not just through the eyes of the artist, but through the eyes of our peers as well. In the museum, I hope we cultivate the ability to see and listen in diverse ways, and to many different people.

—Kristin Becker
Curator of Education & Programs
Jordan Schnitzer Museum
of Art WSU

Nick Nicolai

From January 17, 2023–March 11, 2023, the Jordan Schnitzer Museum of Art WSU hosted *Hostile Terrain 94 (HT94)*, a participatory art exhibition created by the Undocumented Migration Project (UMP) and directed by UCLA anthropologist Jason De León. Occurring in more than 130 cities around the globe, the installation intended to raise awareness about the realities of the US-Mexico border, focusing on the deaths that have occurred almost daily since 1994 as a direct result of the Border Patrol policy known as "Prevention Through Deterrence."

I became aware of the installation through the *WSU Insider*, then went to the art museum's website to read more. I attended a workshop in the Moscow community led by Kristin Becker, Curator of Education & Programs at the WSU Schnitzer Museum.

Becker shared an overview of the project, led us in conversation, and then invited us, if willing, to write out the names (when known) and other information (age, sex, cause of death, condition of body, location of recovery) on toe tags for each person. These tags would be pinned on the installation map in the exact location where those remains were found.

I took a tag and a piece of paper with the information to be written. As I read the information on the paper, I was moved, but was caught off guard when physically writing the information on the tag. I began to cry. When finished, I held the tag in my hands and asked the group if I could share the information out loud with them. They said yes. I read her name out loud and the information. The physical act of writing and giving voice to this person was overwhelming for me. I came intending to receive information; I did not expect it to be so personal and visceral.

Following the event, I shared with Kristin Becker that Andrea Sierra Meza, age 31, from Honduras, was now a part of my life and that every year on the anniversary day when her remains were found (12/27/2012), would be a day of remembrance. I would name her name in my family.

The details of the exhibit will most likely fade, but the ongoing migrant rights issues have a name for me: Andrea, she is *familia*.

Thank you, Jordan Schnitzer Museum of Art WSU.

—Nick Nicolai, Pullman Community Member

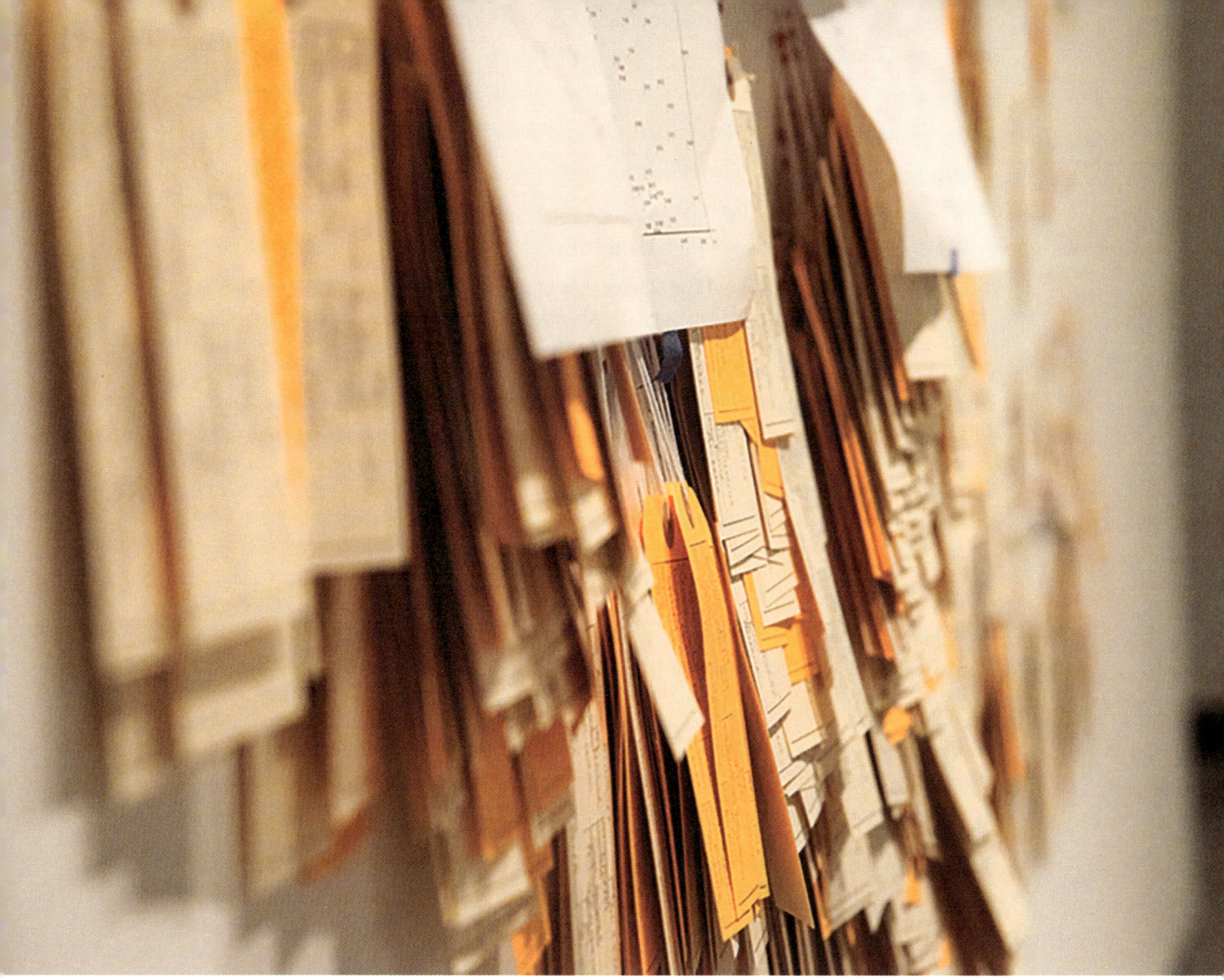

The participatory art exhibition *Hostile Terrain 94* was on view from January 17 through March 11, 2023

Photo: Jasper Willson

Arifa Raza

The Jordan Schnitzer Museum of Art WSU holds a unique space, not only for WSU but for the broader community. Transitioning from a border state to the Pacific Northwest, I initially felt distanced from societal matters affecting both me and my community. However, my engagement with the museum's *Hostile Terrain 94* exhibition proved transformative. By bringing together community members and academics, the exhibition facilitated conversations regarding the complexities of border-related issues through the lens of art. Through exhibits such as this one, the museum brings thought-provoking art that sparks introspection and dialogue—something everyone in our community benefits from.

—Arifa Raza, Assistant Professor,
    Department of Criminal Justice and Criminology, WSU Pullman

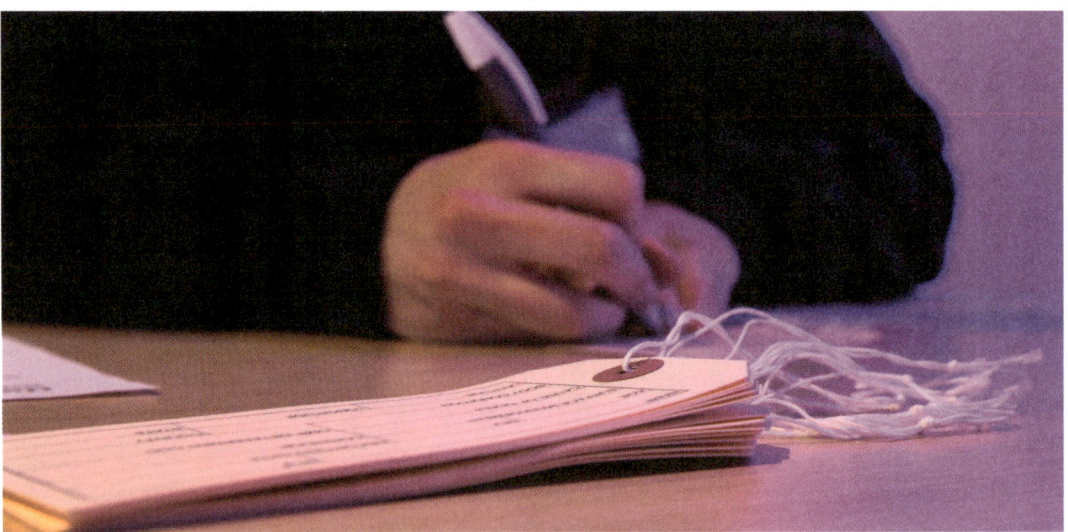

Workshop participant filling out toe tags for *Hostile Terrain 94*
directed by anthropologist Jason De León

Photo: Jasper Willson

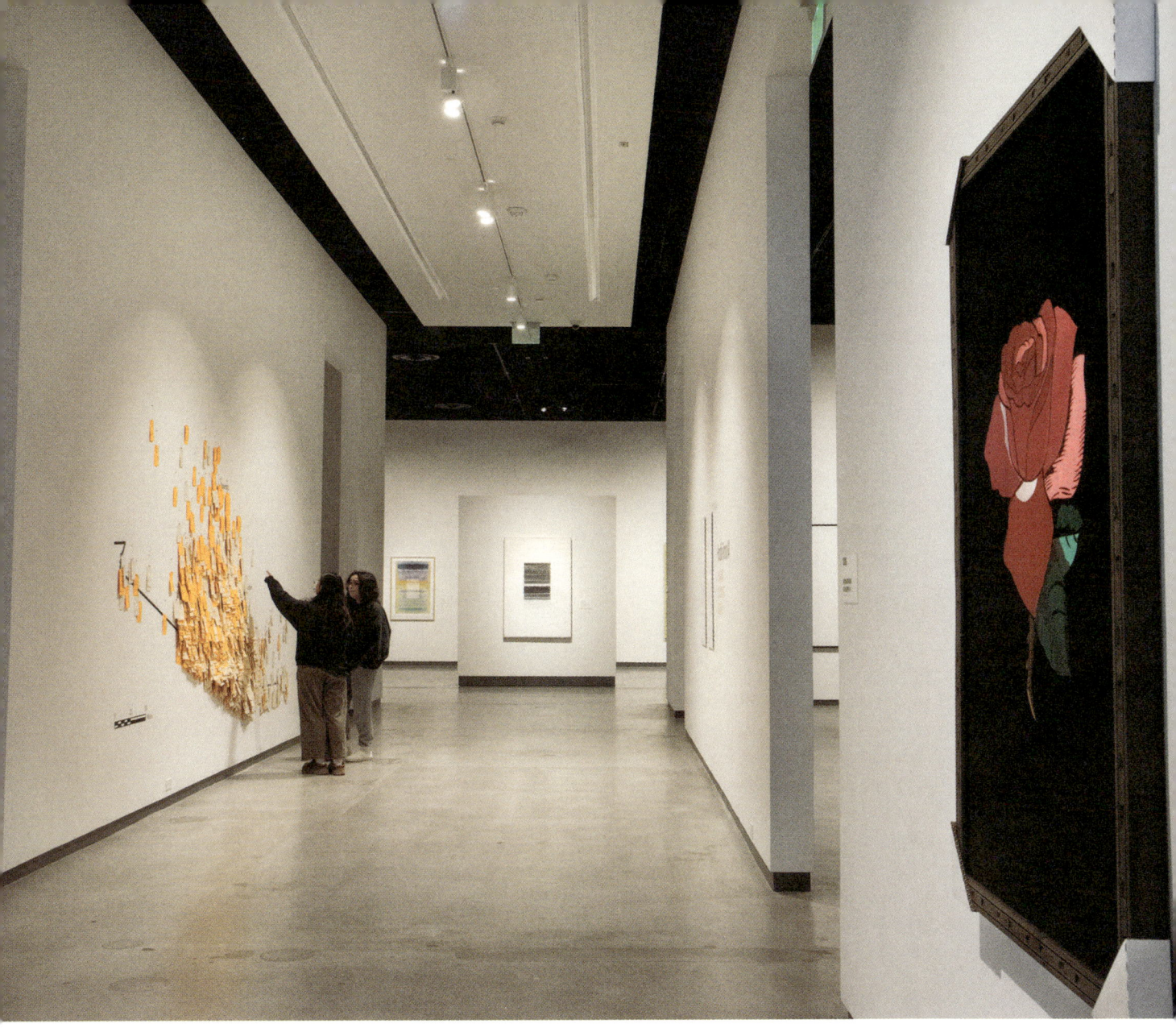

Museum visitors engage with the participatory art exhibition
Hostile Terrain 94 during its installation in 2023

Photo: WSU Photo Services

Trymaine Gaither

As a deeply engaged member of the Jordan Schnitzer Museum of Art WSU, I am honored to contribute to its 50th anniversary celebration. My journey with the museum has been profound, marked by meaningful collaborations and transformative experiences.

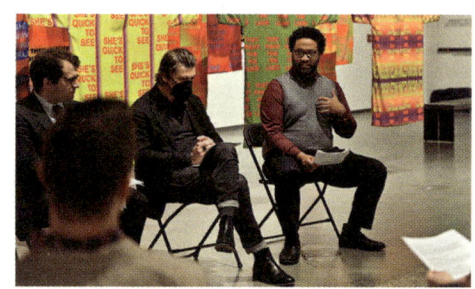

Trymaine Gaither speaking at a Creative Writing & Mindfulness Workshop for the National Day of Racial Healing on January 16, 2024

Photo: WSU Photo Services

One highlight was the partnership with the inaugural National Day of Racial Healing and the 2024 National Day of Racial Healing. The museum hosted "Writers Give Voice," a powerful reading and open-mic poetry event in the museum's Pavilion. These programs, in collaboration with WSU's English Department, featured WSU Campus Civic Poets and finalists, fostering healing dialogue through artistic expression.

Additionally, serving as a juror for the museum's $50,000 Black Lives Matter artist grant program was a profoundly impactful experience. Alongside fellow jurors, I helped select 20 artists whose work exemplified the spirit of racial justice and empowerment, a testament to the museum's commitment to social change through art.

As a mindfulness practitioner, I've found the museum to be an exceptional partner. Leading mindfulness programs in the galleries has solidified its role as a cultural and community center. These initiatives have not only strengthened my connection to the museum but also highlighted its role as a catalyst for societal transformation.

Looking ahead, I envision the museum continuing to be a beacon of creativity and inclusivity, inspiring generations to come. My contemplations on its legacy underscore its enduring influence and indispensable role within our community.

—Trymaine Gaither
    Special Assistant to the Provost for Inclusive Excellence, WSU

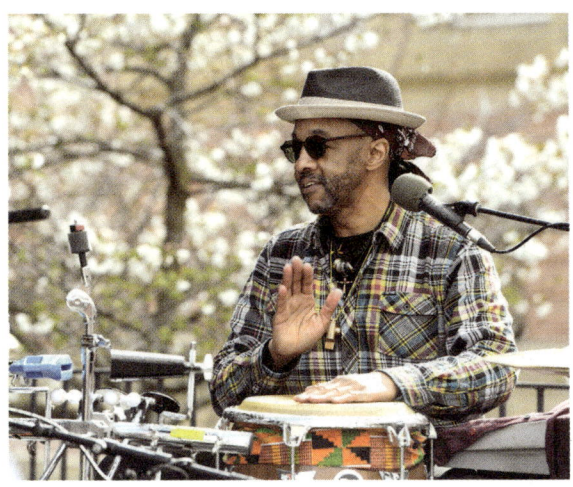

Darryl Singleton performing with his group Raza NorthWest at *Indie Folk: Sounds from the Northwest Concert* on April 29, 2022

Photo: WSU Photo Services

Darryl M. Singleton

I consider the Jordan Schnitzer Museum of Art WSU as synonymous with my time at WSU. It is the first place that "Crimson Ties," WSU's world music ensemble, performed, and it remains our favorite campus venue. The variety of cultural influences embraced and celebrated at the museum align organically with our *raison d'être*. The artistic equity and expression of the museum exhibitions also parallels my own creative motivations. Indigenous and diasporic communities regularly are central to who I am as an artist and are foundational to the communities I hope to help build and reach with my music.

—Darryl M. Singleton ("Doc D")
    Assistant Professor of Black American
    Music, Social Justice, and
    Jazz Percussion
    School of Music, WSU Pullman

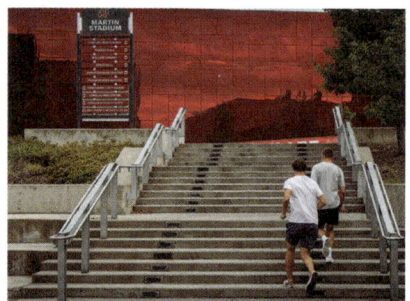
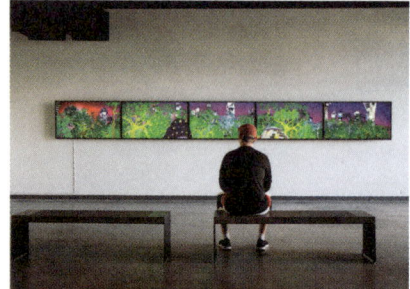
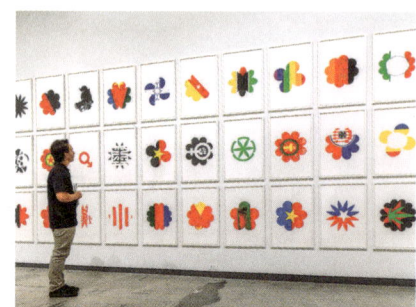
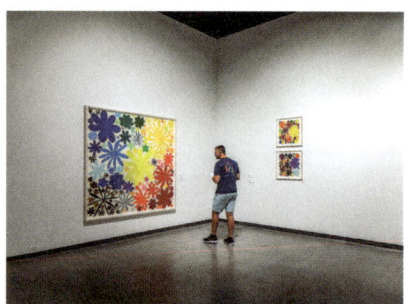
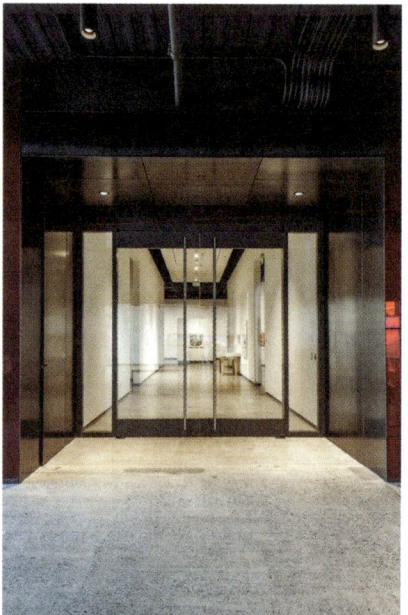
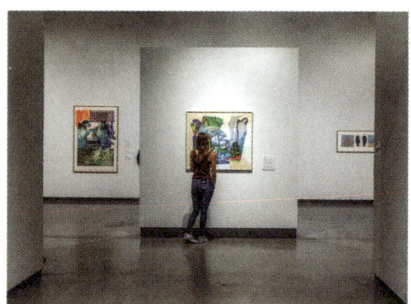
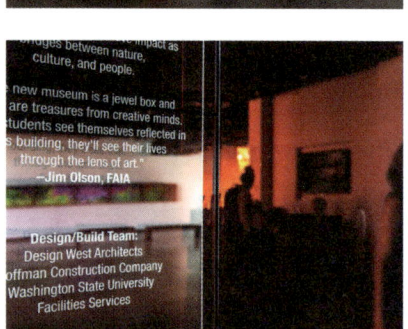
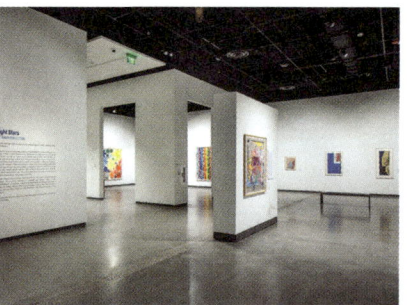

facing page | Squeak Meisel, *The Persistence of Memory*, 2024 |

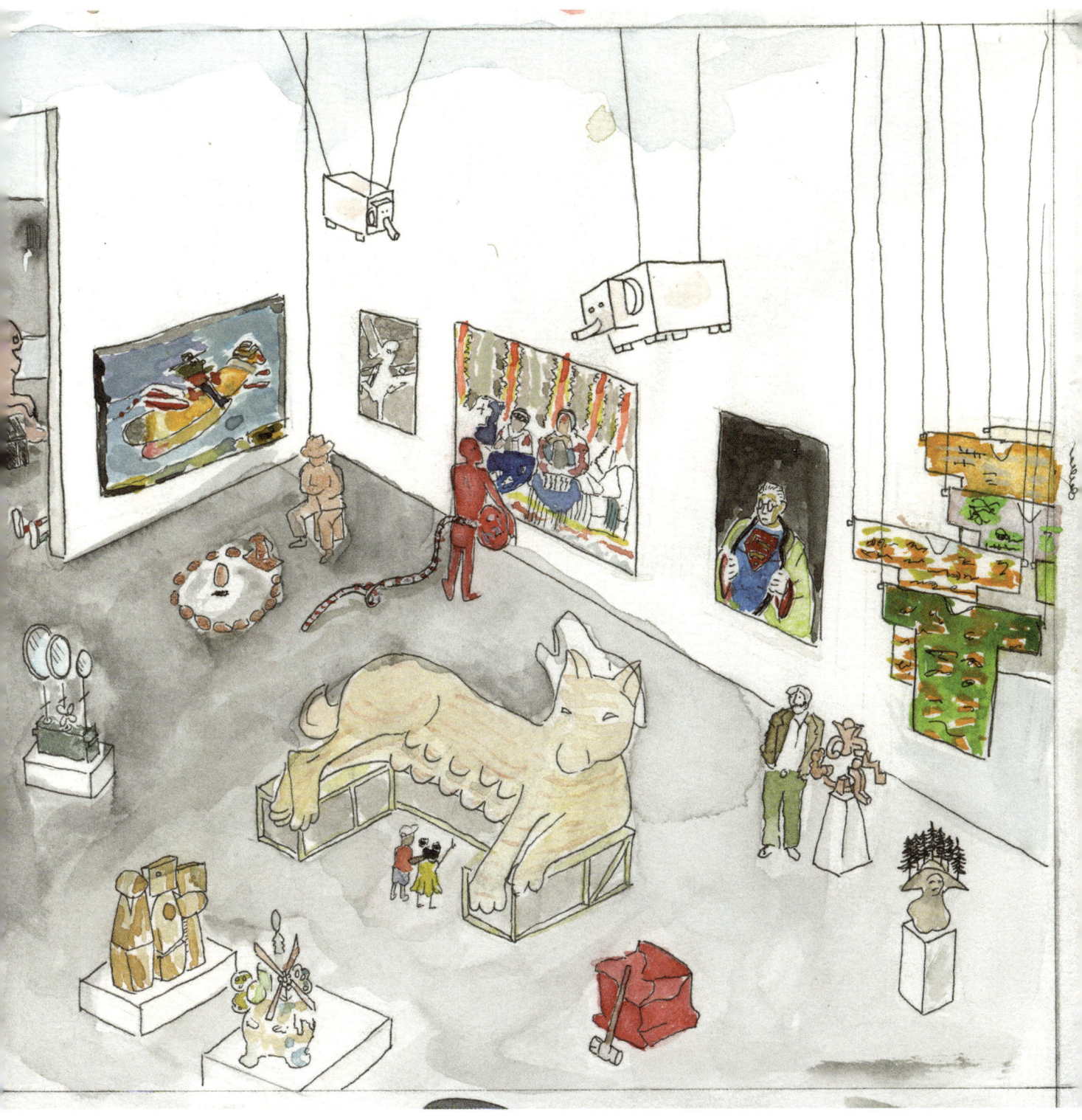

OUTRO

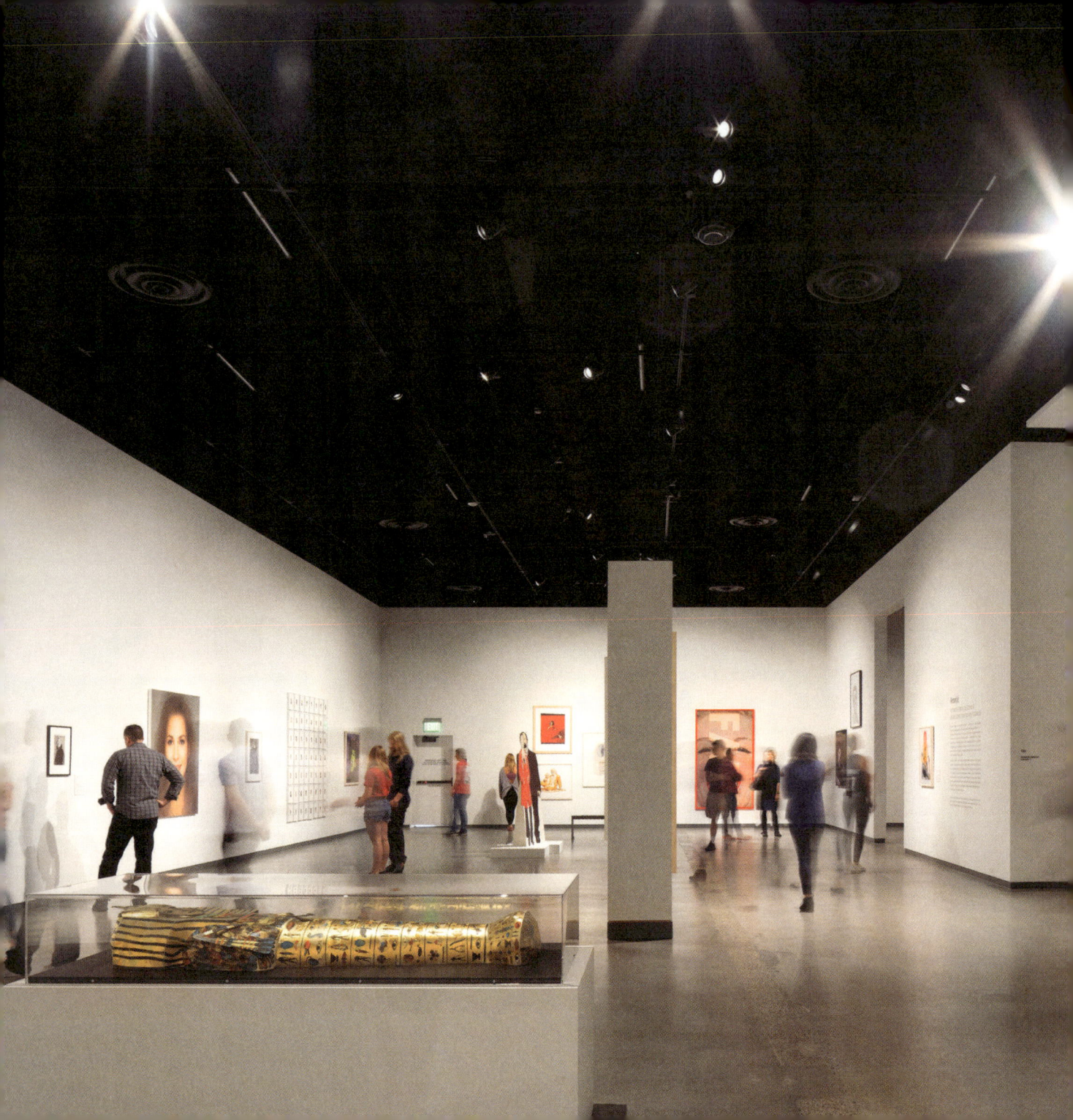

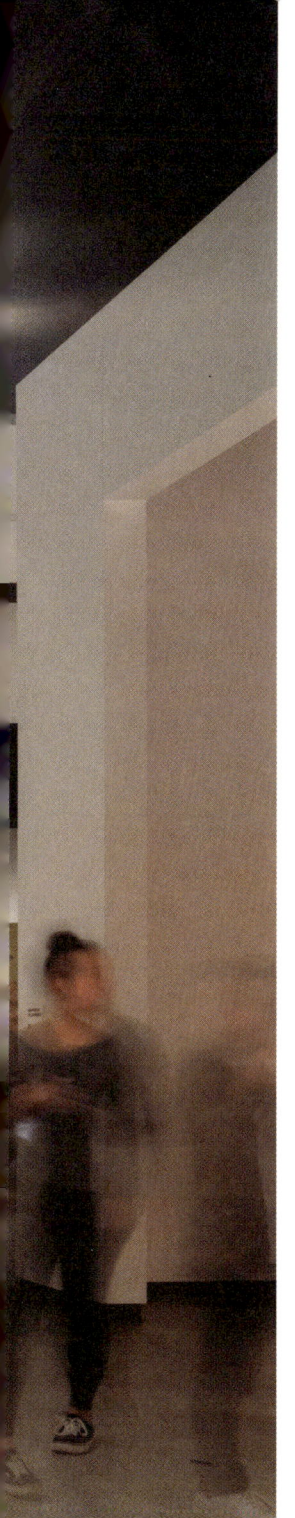
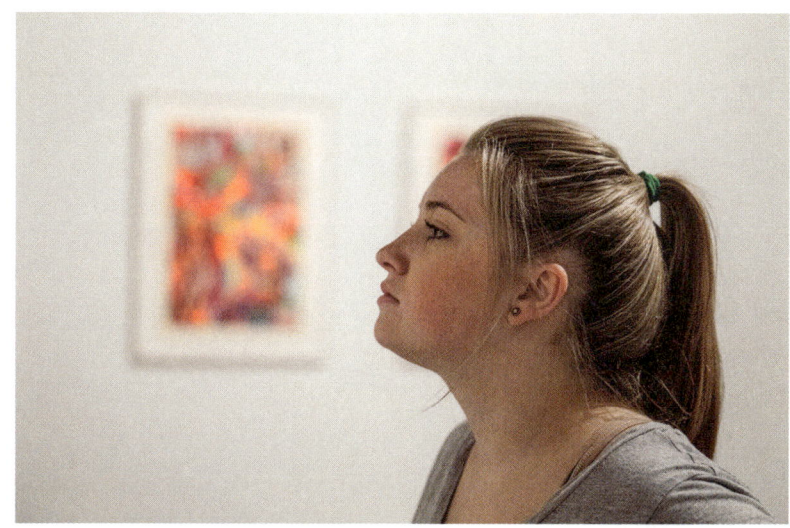
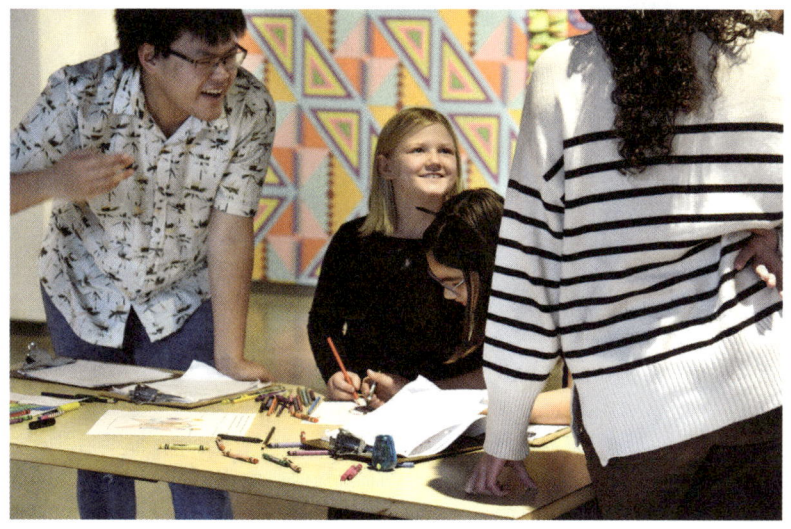

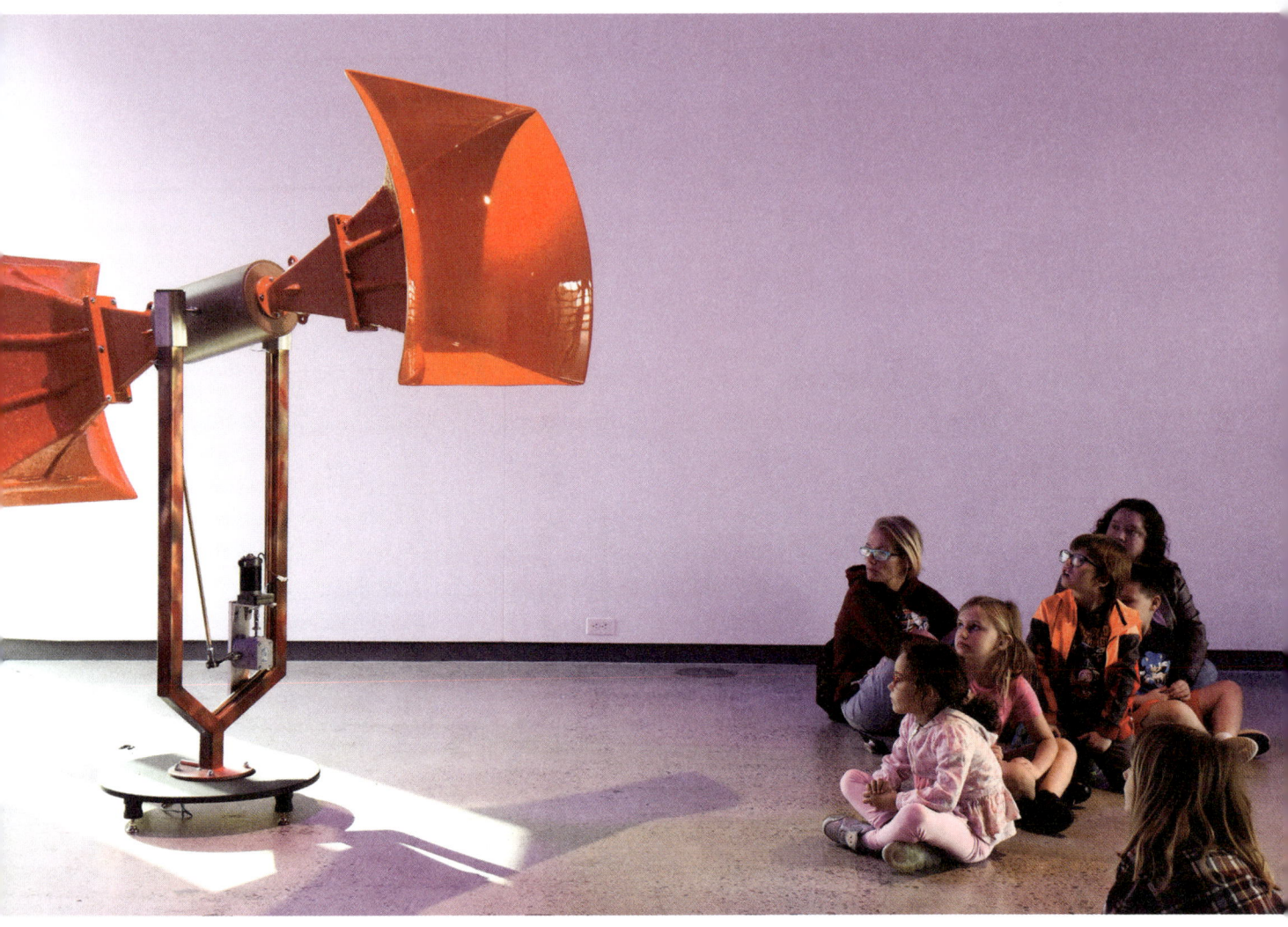

Above and right: A second-grade class from Lena Whitmore Elementary School, Moscow, ID, visiting on September 16, 2022

Photos: Kristin Becker

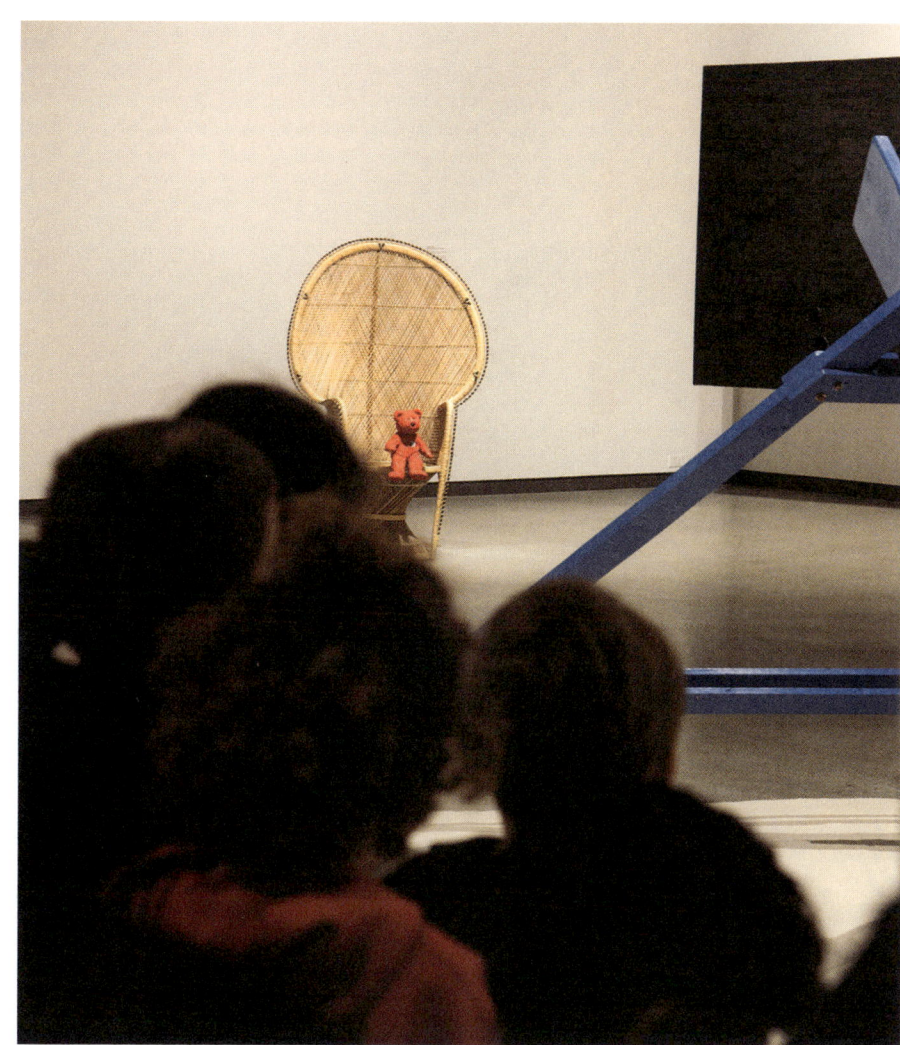

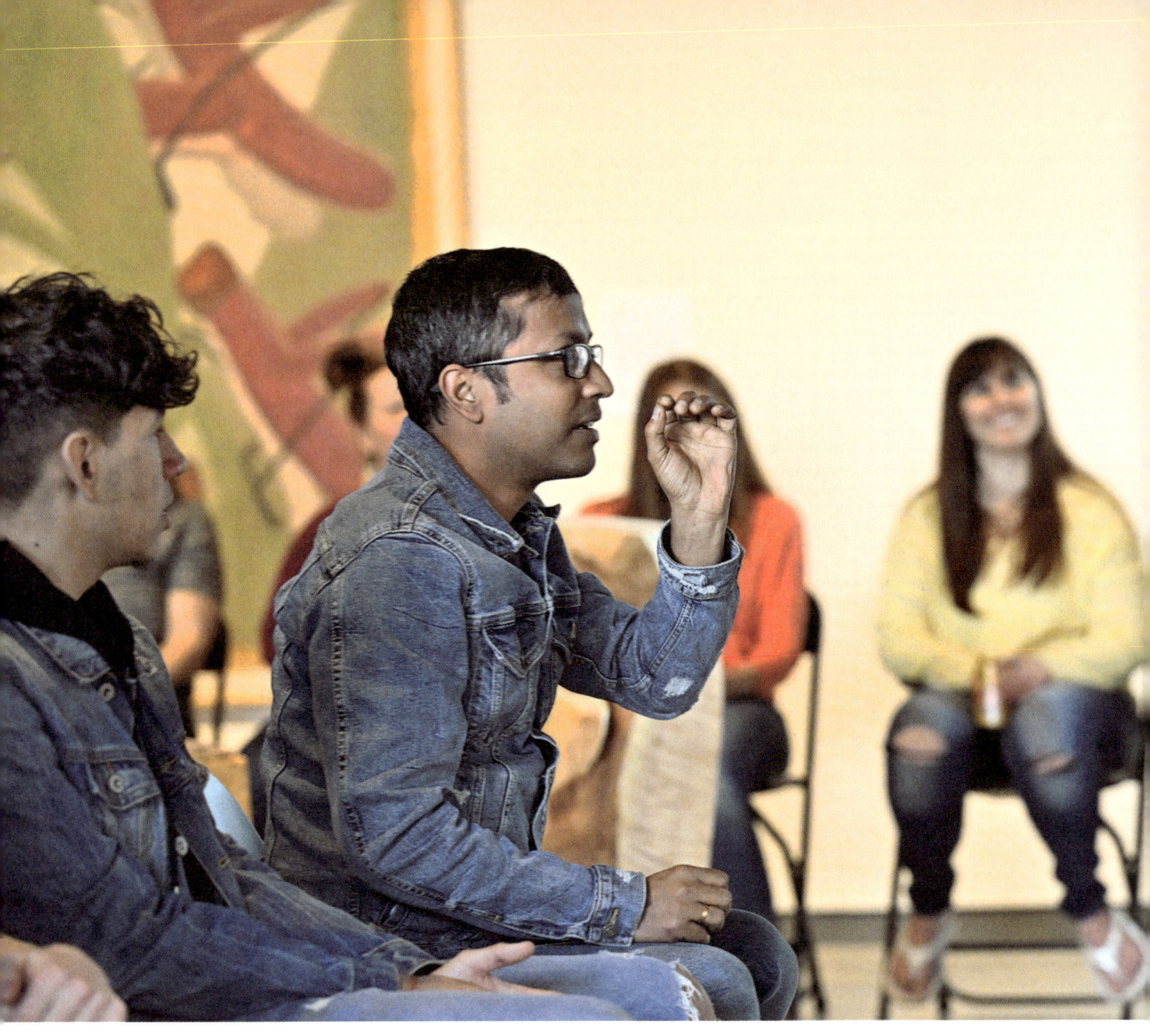

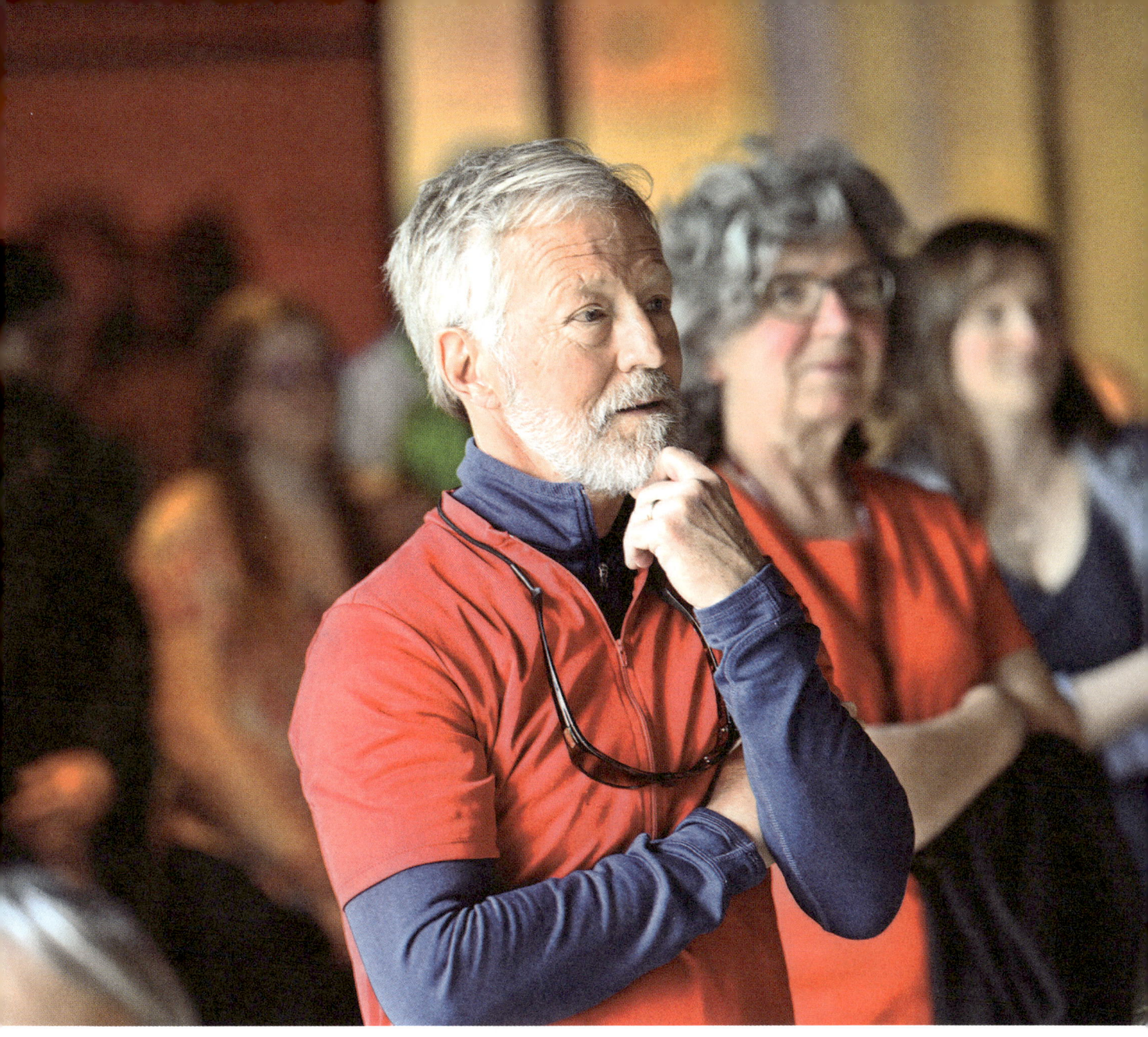

Left and above: Engaged visitors at an April 22, 2022, program for the exhibition
Indie Folk: New Art and Sounds from the Pacific Northwest

Photos: WSU Photo Services

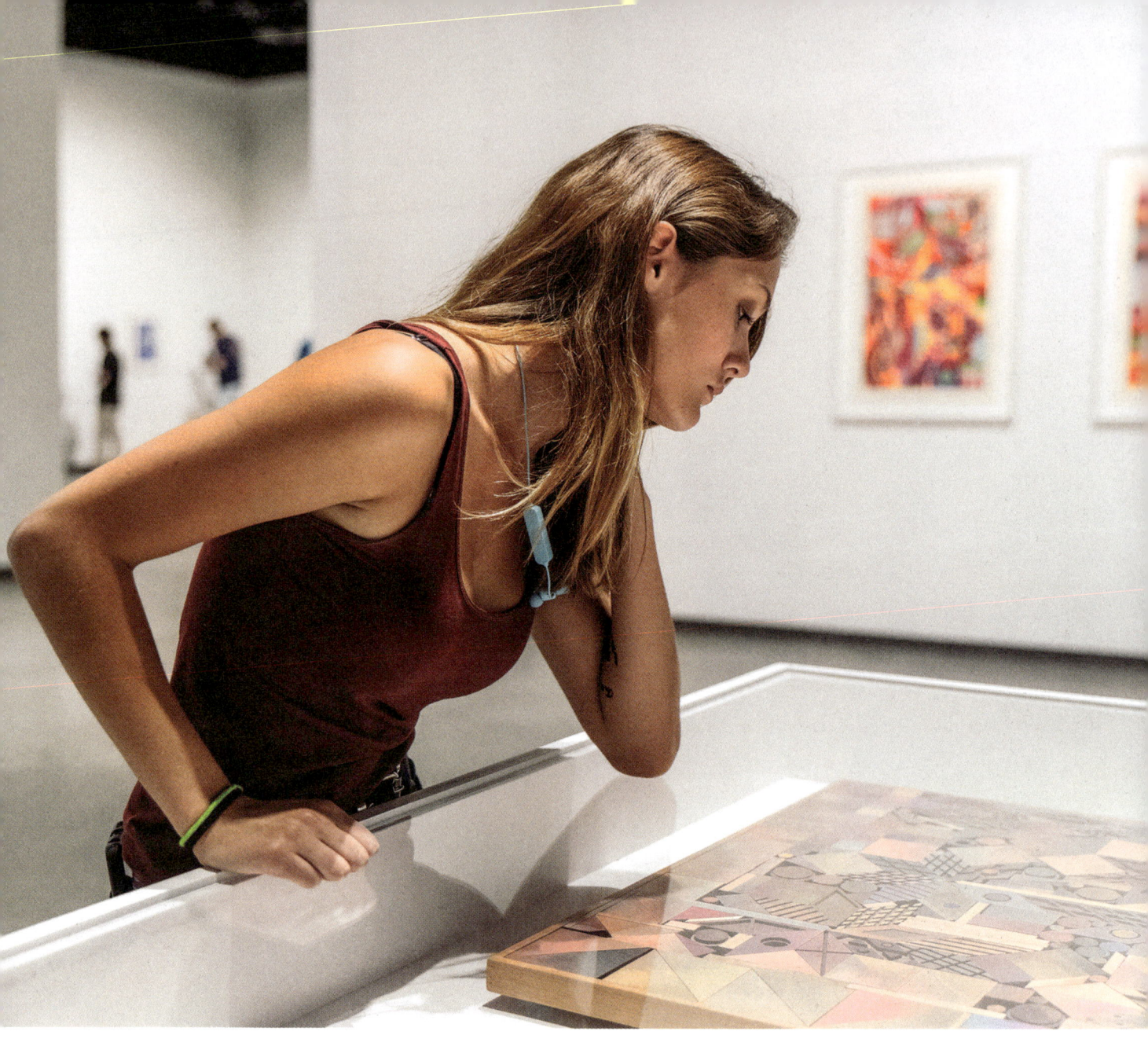

A student visiting *Polly Apfelbaum:*
Frequently the Woods are Pink, Prints From the Collections of Jordan D. Schnitzer and His Family Foundation,
August 27, 2019–March 14, 2020

Photo: Kris Faulkner, courtesy of Design West Architects

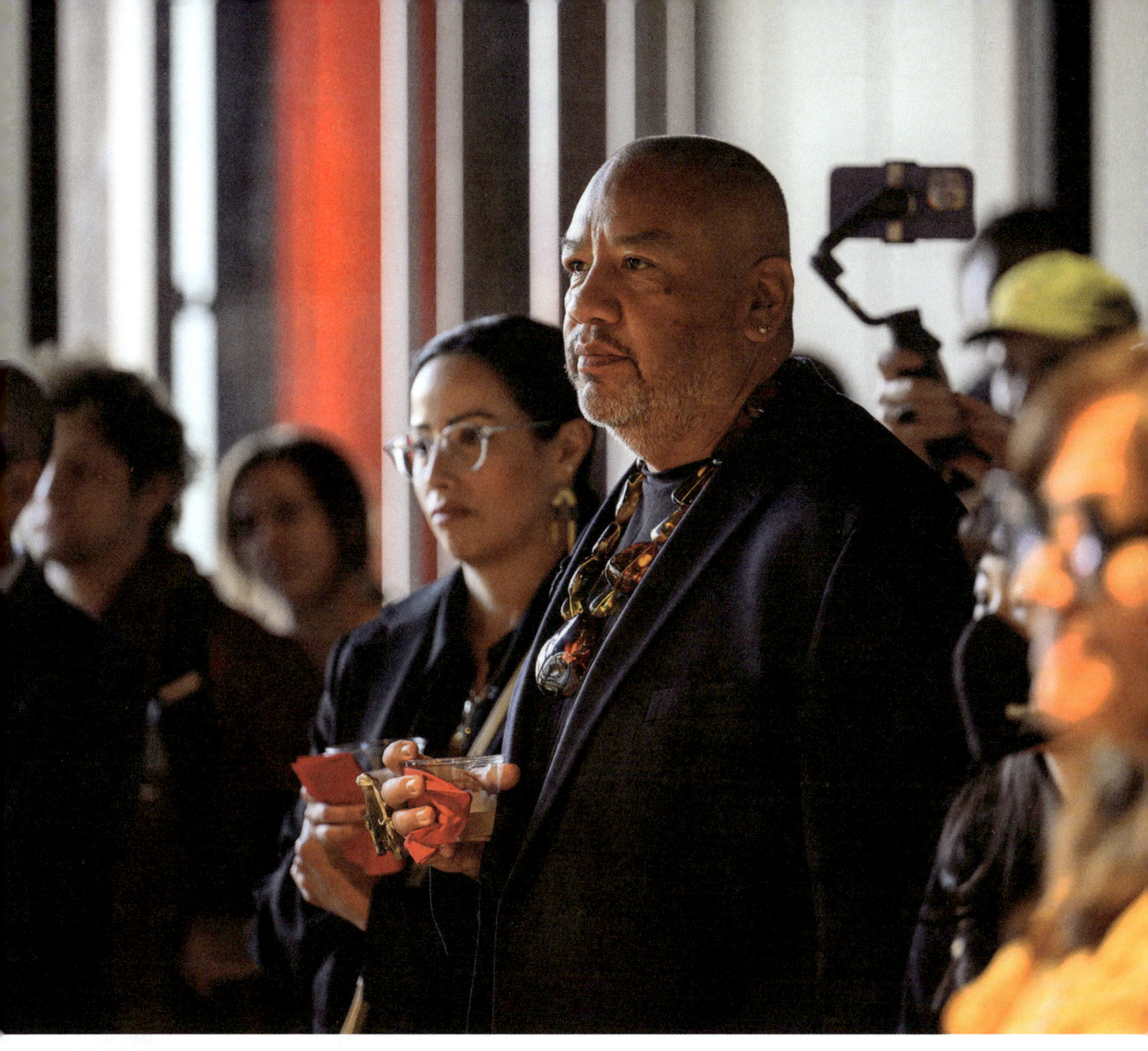

Wendy Red Star (left) and Jeffrey Gibson (right) at the reception for
Jeffrey Gibson: They Teach Love, From the Collections of Jordan D. Schnitzer and His Family Foundation
on September 19, 2023

Photo: WSU Photo Services

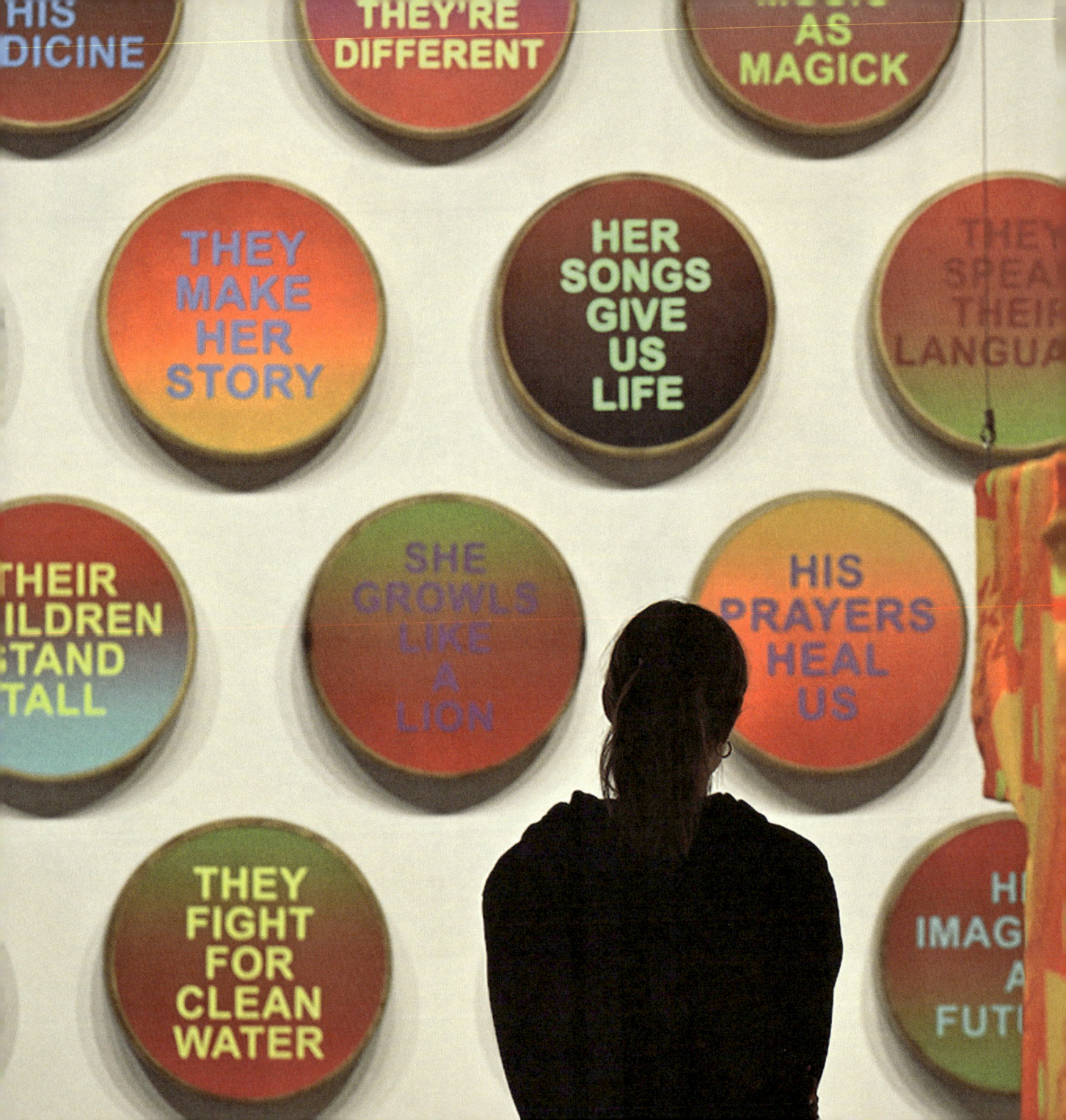

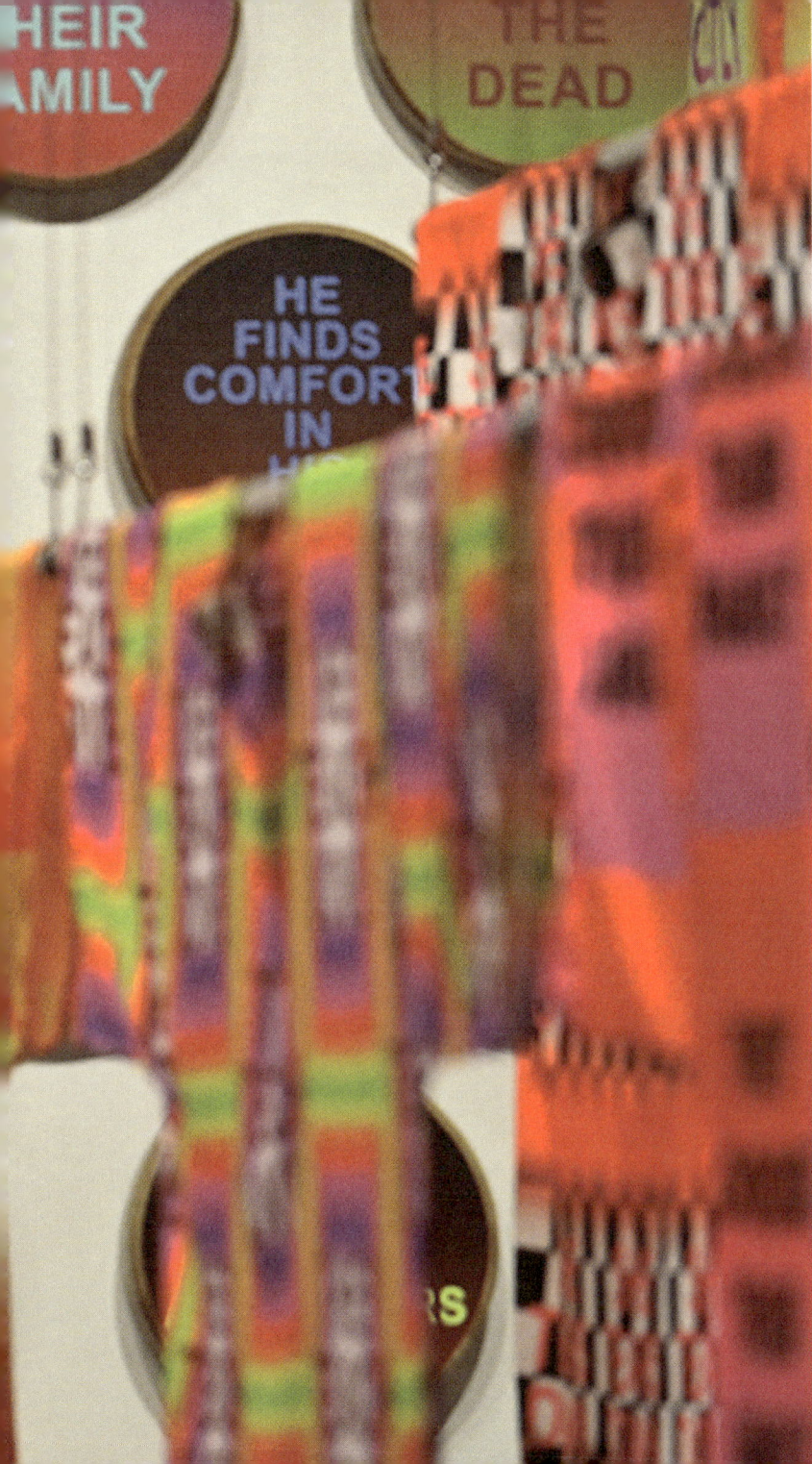

A student visiting *Jeffrey Gibson: They Teach Love, From the Collections of Jordan D. Schnitzer and His Family Foundation*, August 22, 2023–March 9, 2024

Photo: WSU Photo Services

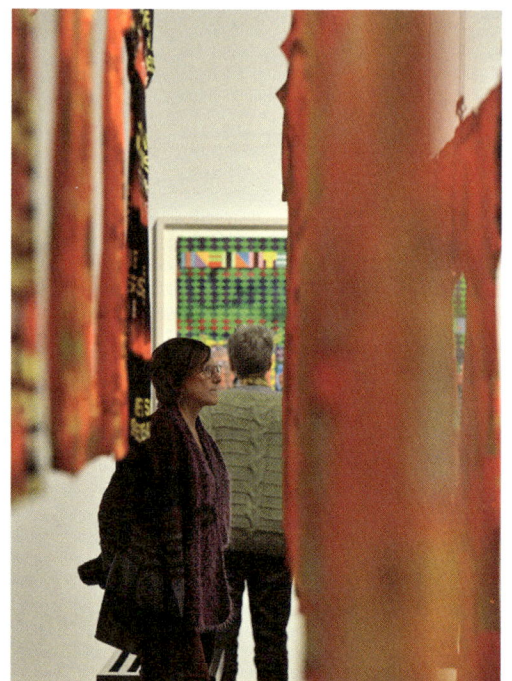
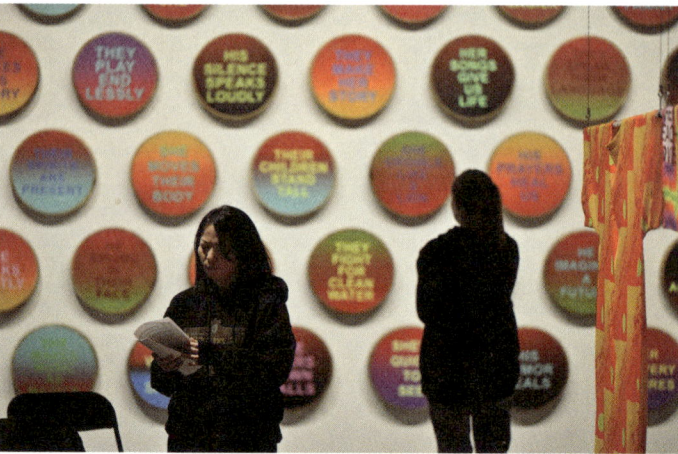
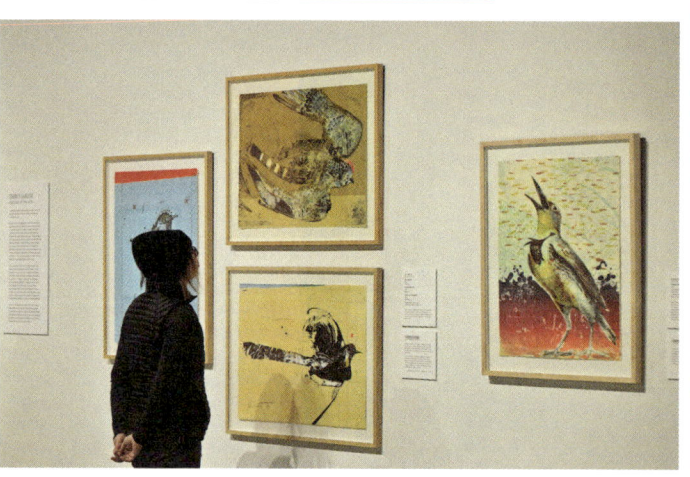
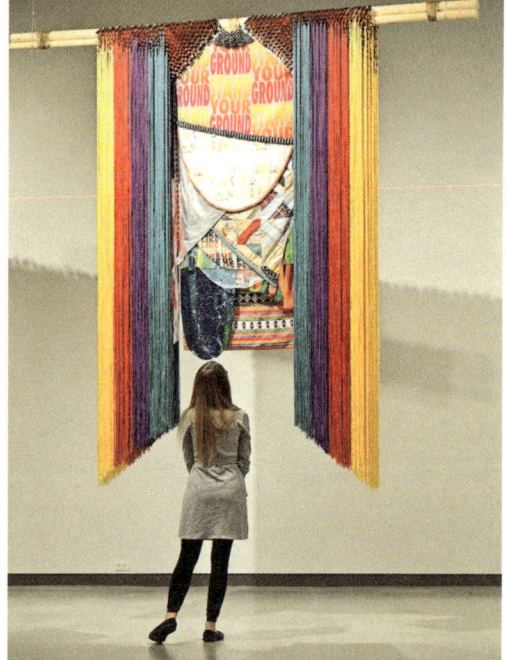

Visitors to the museum reception for the National Day of Racial Healing on January 16, 2024

Photos: WSU Photo Service

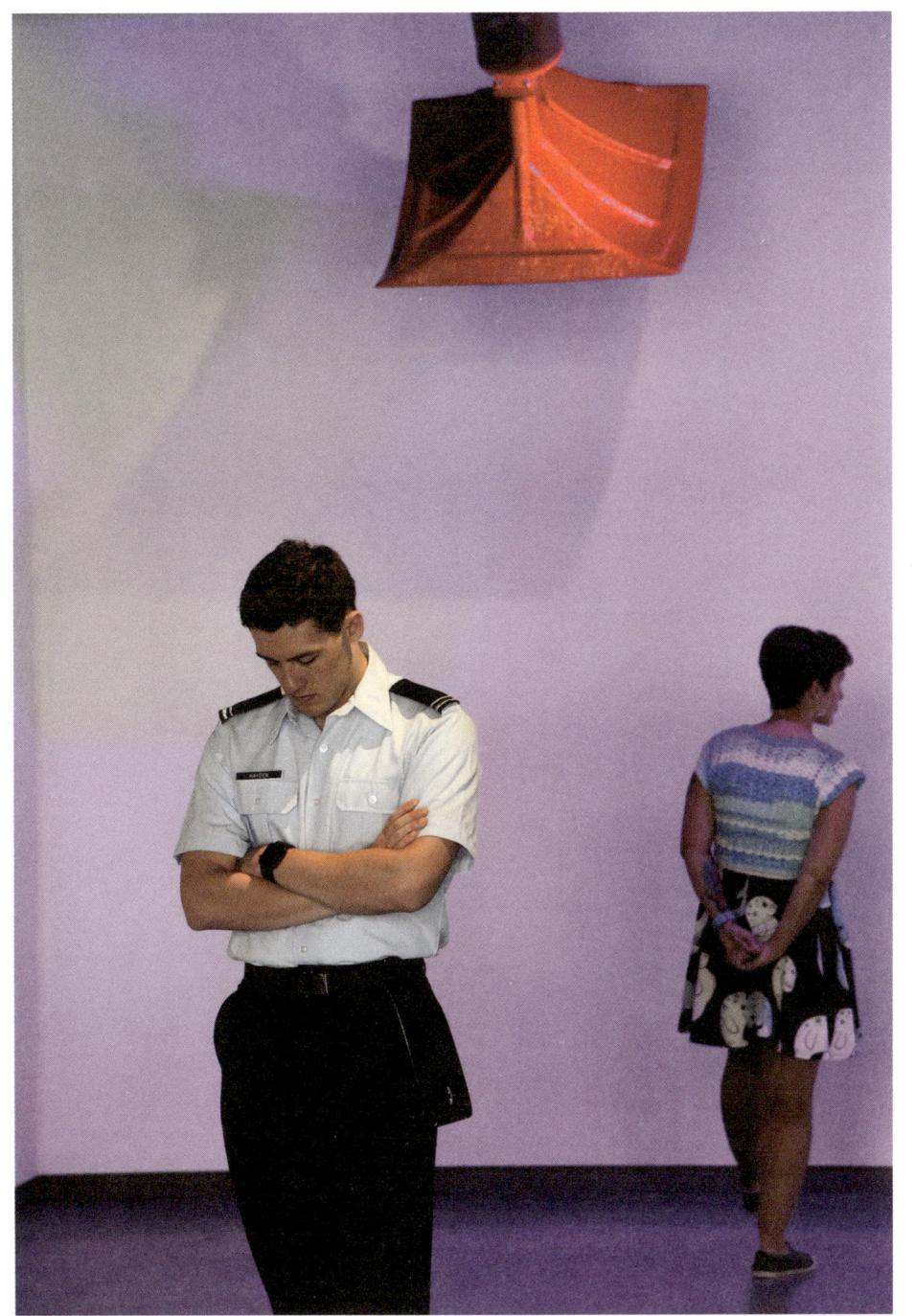

Art and Healing Walking
Meditation on
September 1, 2022

Photo: Jasper Willson

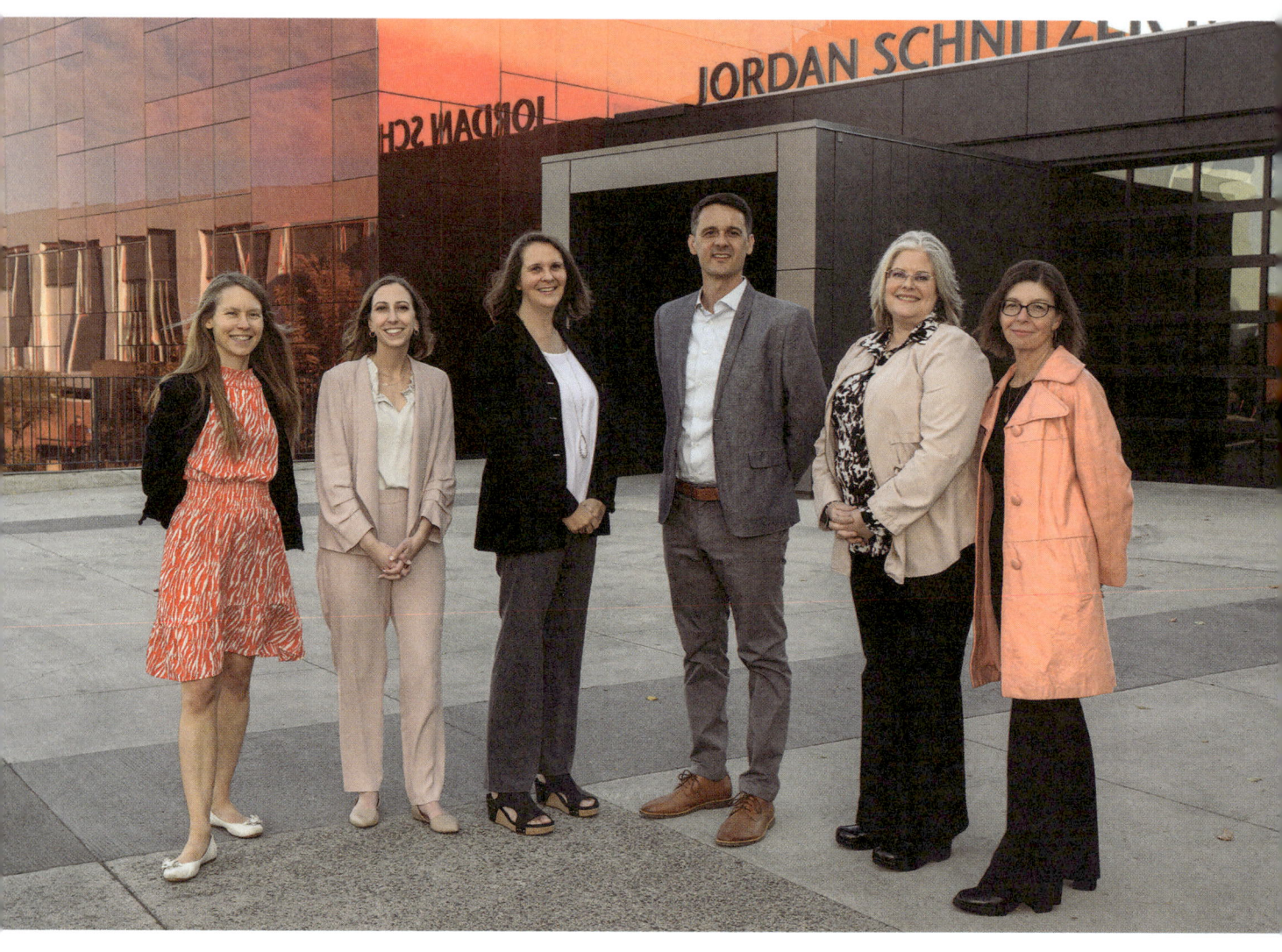

Museum staff in 2024, from left to right:
Kristin Becker, Kira MacPherson, Debby Stinson, Ryan Hardesty, Karey Strong, and Ann Saberi
Photo: WSU Photo Services

APPENDICES

Ryan Hardesty	Executive Director, Curator of Exhibitions & Collections
Karey Strong	Deputy Director of Finance & Administration, Associate Director
Debby Stinson	Marketing & PR Manager
Ann Saberi	Collection Manager
Kristin Becker	Curator of Education & Programs
Kira MacPherson	Director of Development

LIST OF DIRECTORS

Harvey West	1973–1976 and 1977–1978 Director
Bruce Guenther	1976–77 Acting Director, 1978–1979 Director
Terry Toedtemeier	1979–1980 Acting Director
Sanford Shaman	1980–1984 Director
Patricia Watkinson	1984–1985 Acting Director, 1985–1998 Director
Martha Mullen	1998 Acting Director
Dyana Curreri-Ermatinger	1998–2001 Director
Ross Coates	2001–2003 Interim director
Chris Bruce	2003–2016 Director
Anna-Maria Shannon	2016–2018 Interim director
Robin Held	2018–2020 Director
Ryan Hardesty	2020–present Director

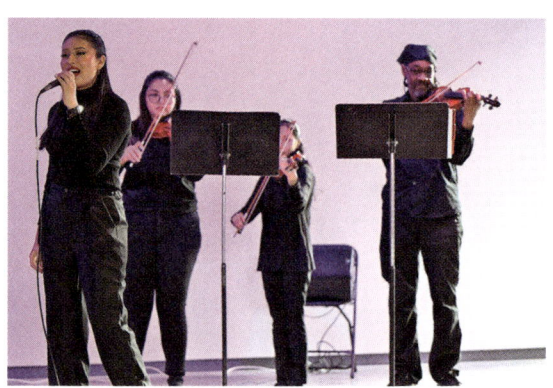

WSU School of Music student ensemble Mariachi Leones del Monte performing during the *Hostile Terrain 94* closing reception on March 2, 2023

Photo: WSU Photo Services

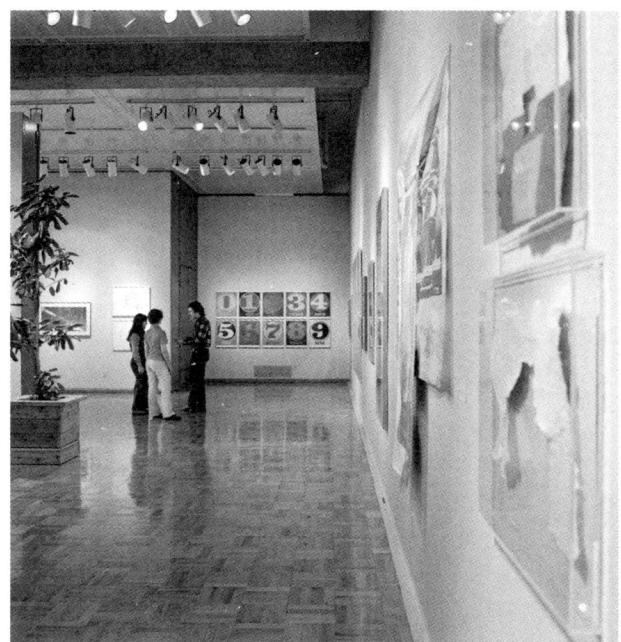

American Printmaking 1960–1975: A Major Survey
Exhibition of Directions in American Printmaking,
November 1–November 22, 1975

Photo: WSU Libraries' Manuscripts, Archives, and
Special Collections

1974 |

Fine Arts Faculty Exhibition
September 12–October 6, 1974

Recent Acquisitions, Ancient Art
Greco-Roman Artifacts–Getty Museum
October 9–October 30, 1974

Francisco Goya–Los Disparates
October 9–October 30, 1974

Honoré Daumier–Histoire Ancienne
October 9–October 30, 1974

Ancient Northwest Indian Tools and
Their Modern Counterparts
October 9–October 30, 1974

American Abstraction, 1960-1974:
Select Paintings and Sculptures
from the Bagley and Virginia Wright Collection
November 1–November 22, 1974

Retrospective: Paintings by Andrew Hofmeister
December 2–December 20, 1974

1975 |

Graduate Review
    January 8–January 18, 1975

MFA Thesis Exhibition
    January 20–January 25, 1975

*Alden Mason Abstract Paintings and
Eleanor Dickinson Figure Drawings*
    February 9–March 2, 1975

*Washington State University Museum of Art
Permanent Collection*
    March 3–March 9, 1975

The Chair
    March 12–April 4, 1975

Northwest Painters Invitational
    April 14–May 4, 1975

MFA Thesis Exhibition
    May 5–May 11, 1975

MFA Thesis Exhibition
    May 12–May 18, 1975

BFA Review
    May 19–June 1, 1975

Jack Lenor Larsen Textiles
    June 2–July 31, 1975

MFA Thesis Exhibition
    July 22–31, 1975

Fine Arts Faculty Exhibition
    September 15–October 5, 1975

Northwest Sculpture
    October 8–October 29, 1975

*American Printmaking 1960–1975:
A Major Survey Exhibition of Directions
in American Printmaking*
    November 1–November 22, 1975

George A. Laisner: A Retrospective Exhibition
    December 1–December 20, 1975

1976 |

Graduate Review
    January 7–January 18, 1976

MFA Thesis Exhibition
    January 20–January 28, 1976

Rodin: The Maryhill Collection
    February 4–February 29, 1976

Greek and Roman Antiquities from
the Getty Museum
    February 4–February 29, 1976

Honoré Daumier Lithographs
    February 4–February 29, 1976

Johna Cronk
    March 4–March 28, 1976

Kathleen Gemberling Adkison
    March 4–March 28, 1976

Judy Chicago: Recent Works in Porcelain
    April 12–May 2, 1976

Recent Acquisitions to the
WSU Permanent Collection
    April 12–May 2, 1976

BFA Review
    May 4–June 4, 1976

Summer Selections–W.S.A.S. Exhibition
    June 21–July 30, 1976

Fine Arts Faculty Exhibition
    September 13–September 30, 1976

A Temporary Possession: The Human Image in
20th Century Photography
    October 3–October 26, 1976

6 from California
    October 29–November 20, 1976

Wendell Brazeau 1910–1974
Retrospective Exhibition
    November 29–December 18, 1976

1977 |

Graduate Review
    January 4–January 28, 1977

Amistad II: A Survey of Afro American Art
    February 3–February 23, 1977

Works on Paper; American Art 1945-1975:
The Washington Art Consortium Collection
    February 28–April 1, 1977

Goya: Los Disparates
    April 11–May 1, 1977

Robert Smithson: Cayuga Salt Mine Project
    April 11–May 1, 1977

People of the Cedar
    April 11–May 1, 1977

MFA Thesis Exhibition I
    May 4–May 10, 1977

MFA Thesis Exhibition II
    May 12–May 18, 1977

BFA Exhibit
    May 20–June 4, 1977

Bicentennial Portfolio:
Marsha Burns Photographs, Michael Burns
Photographs, Meyer Shapiro Portfolio
    June 20–July 29, 1977

Fine Arts Faculty Exhibition
    September 12–October 2, 1977

Two Decades, 1957–1977: American Sculpture
from Northwest Collections
    October 7–November 18, 1977

Margaret Tomkins: 1943 to Present
    November 28–December 16, 1977

1978 |

MFA Thesis Exhibition
    January 3–January 29, 1978

Ritual and Change: Arts of the Sepik River, New Guinea
    February 2–February 26, 1978

John Yeon: Buildings and Landscapes
    February 2–February 26, 1978

Artist and Place: American Landscape Painting 1860–1914
    March 2–April 27, 1978

Graduate Review
    May 3–May 9, 1978

Graduate Review
    May 12–May 19, 1978

BFA Exhibition
    May 23–June 3, 1978

Ross Coates: Paintings and Drawings, 1975–1978
    June 19–July 30, 1978

Wilhelm Hester: Northwest Maritime Photographer, 1870–1947
    June 19–July 30, 1978

Fine Arts Faculty Exhibition
    September 18–October 8, 1978

Diverse Directions: The Fiber Arts
    October 13–November 17, 1978

The Fred Harvey Company Fine Arts Collection of American Indian Artifacts: An American Indian Show
    November 27–December 21, 1978

1979 |

Graduate Review
    January 8–January 21, 1979

MFA Thesis Exhibition
    January 25–February 1, 1979

Mel Katz: Works 1971–1978
    February 5–March 2, 1979

*A Partial View: Young Photographers
in the Northwest*
    March 6–April 5, 1979

Americans in Glass
    April 16–May 6, 1979

MFA Thesis Exhibition I
    May 10–May 16, 1979

MFA Thesis Exhibition II
    May 19–May 24, 1979

BFA Exhibition
    May 31–June 9, 1979

*Historic Visions: Early Photography
as Document*
    June 18–August 2, 1979

Richard Smith Recent Work 1972–1977
    September 17–October 14, 1979

*Drawings 1900–1945: A Survey of
American Works*
    October 19–November 15, 1979

Fine Arts Faculty Exhibition
    November 28–December 20, 1979

1980 |

Graduate Review
    January 9–January 31, 1980

Imperial Robes from the Ch'ing Dynasty
    February 7–March 2, 1980

*Canaletto Etchings and
WSU Permanent Collection*
    March 6–April 3, 1980

Spectrum: New Directions in Color Photography
    April 14–May 4, 1980

MFA Thesis Exhibition I
    May 8–May 13, 1980

MFA Thesis Exhibition II
    May 16–May 21, 1980

BFA Exhibition
    May 24–June 7, 1980

*The Contemporary American Potter:
New Vessels*
    October 20–November 19, 1980

Earthworks: Land Reclamation as Sculpture
    June 16–July 31, 1980

The Darius Kinsey Collection
    June 16–July 31, 1980

Form and Figure
    September 16–October 12, 1980

Fine Arts Faculty Exhibition 1980
    December 1–18, 1980

1981 |

Graduate Review
    January 7–January 28, 1981

Swords of the Samurai: Japanese Arms and Armor from Northwest Collections
    February 6–March 3, 1981

Perspectives on Landscape: Contemporary British Photographers
    March 9–April 1, 1981

Contemporary Metals: Focus On Idea
    April 13–May 3, 1981

MFA Thesis Exhibition I
    May 7–May 12, 1981

MFA Thesis Exhibition II
    May 15–May 20, 1981

BFA Exhibition
    May 26–June 5, 1981

Permanent Collection: Portraits & Figures
    June 22–July 30, 1981

Arts of Kenya
    September 14–October 11, 1981

British Prints: Highlights of Four Decades 1940–1981
    October 16–November 15, 1981

Fine Arts Faculty Exhibition
    November 30–December 18, 1981

1982 |

Graduate Review
    January 11–January 31, 1982

American Photographs: 1970–1980
    February 15–March 14, 1982

Gaston Lachaise: Sculpture and Drawings
    March 22–April 18, 1982

MFA Thesis Exhibition I
    April 26–May 2, 1982

MFA Thesis Exhibition II
    May 7–14, 1982

BFA Exhibition
    May 24–June 4, 1982

Land and Sea: From the Holland and Orton Collection
    June 21–July 28, 1982

Recent Acquisitions from the WSU Permanent Collection
    September 20–October 10, 1982

Fine Arts Faculty Exhibition
    October 18–November 7, 1982

Noritake Art Deco Porcelains: Collection of Howard Kottler
    November 13–December 17, 1982

1983 |

Graduate Review
 January 10–30, 1983

*Expressionism: German Expressionist Prints
from the Museum of Modern Art, New York*
 February 14–March 13, 1983

Arts of Indonesia: From Local Collections
 February 14–March 13, 1983

*Living with the Volcano:
Artists of Mount St. Helens*
 March 21–April 17, 1983

MFA Thesis Exhibition I
 April 25–May 1, 1983

MFA Thesis Exhibition II
 May 6–May 15, 1983

BFA Exhibition
 May 23–June 3, 1983

Toward an American Art
 June 20–July 13, 1983

Fine Arts Faculty Exhibition
 September 27–October 30, 1983

*Contemporary Trompe L'œil Painting
and Sculpture*
 November 7–December 15, 1983

1984 |

Philip Pearlstein: Painting to Watercolors
 January 10–February 12, 1984

Exploring Society Photographically
 February 21–March 11, 1984

*Theodore Wores: An American Artist
and His Contemporaries*
 March 19–April 11, 1984

MFA Thesis Exhibition I
 April 18–April 29, 1984

MFA Thesis Exhibition II
 May 3–May 13, 1984

BFA Exhibition
 May 22–June 1, 1984

*The Textile Paradigm: Contemporary Art
Fabric of the Netherlands*
 September 4–September 30, 1984

Fine Arts Faculty Exhibition
 October 9–October 28, 1984

Fabric Traditions of Indonesia
 November 6–December 16, 1984

1985 |

Graduate Review
    January 15–January 27, 1985

Disarming Images: Art For Nuclear Disarmament
    February 5–March 3, 1985

Nine by Three: Artists Choose Artists
    March 18–April 7, 1985

Fine Arts Faculty Exhibition I
    April 15–April 24, 1985

Fine Arts Faculty Exhibition II
    May 2–May 12, 1985

*Wild Beauty: Photography of the
Columbia River Gorge, 1865–1915*
    September 4–October 6, 1985

*Gaylen Hansen: The Paintings of a
Decade 1975–1985*
    October 15–November 17, 1985

Fine Arts Faculty Exhibition
    December 3–December 20, 1985

1986 |

Graduate Review
    January 21–February 2, 1986

*The Collector: E.O. Holland and the Washington
State University Permanent Collection*
    February 11–March 2, 1986

*Northwest Images: Lucinda Parker
and Michael Spafford*
    March 18–April 6, 1986

MFA Thesis Exhibition I
    April 15–April 23, 1986

MFA Thesis Exhibition II
    May 1–May 9, 1986

Works on Paper: American Art 1945–1975
    September 2–September 27, 1986

Outside Japan
    October 4–October 26, 1986

Fine Arts Faculty Exhibition
    November 4–November 20, 1986

Diane Arbus/Larry Clark
    December 3–December 19, 1986

1987 |

Graduate Review
  January 20–February 2, 1987

*Northwest Images: Kenneth Callahan
and Keith Monaghan*
  February 10–March 6, 1987

The Found Image in Contemporary Prints
  March 24–April 12, 1987

MFA Thesis Exhibition
  April 21–May 10, 1987

Modern Myths: Classical Renewal
  September 5–September 27, 1987

Fine Arts Faculty Exhibition
  October 6–October 25, 1987

The Master Weavers
  November 3–December 13, 1987

Robert Holmes: Photographs of India
  November 3–December 13, 1987

1988 |

Former Fine Arts Faculty Exhibition
  January 12–January 31, 1988

*New Traditions: Thirteen Hispanic
Photographers*
  February 9–March 6, 1988

Northwest Focus: Patrick Siler
  March 22–April 10, 1988

Northwest Expressionism
  March 22–April 10, 1988

MFA Thesis Exhibition
  April 16–May 8, 1988

Fine Arts Faculty Exhibition
  September 6–September 25, 1988

Facts of the Imagination
  October 4–October 30, 1988

Milton Avery: Progressive Images
  November 8–December 16, 1988

1989 |

Seasons of Life Museum Series—Impressions of a New Civilization: The Lincoln Kirstein Collection of Japanese Prints, 1860–1912
January 19–February 26, 1989

Seasons of Life Museum Series—Where Two Worlds Meet: Masami Teraoka and Roger Shimomura
January 19–February 26, 1989

Washington to Washington: Women in Art Today
March 7–March 30, 1989

MFA Thesis Exhibition
April 7–April 16, 1989

Graduate Review
April 22–May 6, 1989

From the Palouse: A Centennial Exhibit
September 4–October 1, 1989

Fine Arts Faculty Exhibition
October 10–November 5, 1989

The Art of Satire: Goya/Daumier/Hogarth
November 14–December 22, 1989

1990 |

Richard Misrach: Photographs of the American Desert
January 16–February 11, 1990

Child to Child: American-Soviet Children's Art Exchange and Children of the Palouse
February 17–March 18, 1990

MFA Thesis Exhibition
April 3–April 22, 1990

Graduate Review
May 1–May 12, 1990

American Realist Art: The Washington State University Permanent Collection
May 29–July 8, 1990

Fine Arts Faculty Exhibition
September 4–September 23, 1990

Marilyn Lysohir: The Dark Side of Dazzle and *Cheryl Laemmle: Recent Painting*
September 29–October 28, 1990

Shadowy Evidence: The Photographs of Edward S. Curtis and His Contemporaries
November 6–December 21, 1990

1991 |

Arnulf Rainer: Drawing on Death
January 15–February 10, 1991

Northwest Focus: Andrew L. Hofmeister and
Northwest Focus: Incisive Expressions
February 19–March 17, 1991

MFA Thesis Exhibition I
March 26–April 7, 1991

MFA Thesis Exhibition II
April 13–April 26, 1991

Graduates Review
May 1–May 11, 1991

British Printmakers and Some Literary Sources
and *Contemporary English Crafts*
May 28–July 7, 1991

Northwest Focus: Frank Munns and
Sue Coe: Porkopolis
September 3–September 29, 1991

From the Woods: Washington Wood Artists
October 5–November 10, 1991

Fine Arts Faculty Exhibition
November 19–December 20, 1991

1992 |

A Different War: Vietnam in Art
January 14–February 23, 1992

Gardens: Real and Imagined
March 3–April 11, 1992

MFA Thesis Exhibition I
April 17–April 25, 1992

MFA Thesis Exhibition II
April 30–May 9, 1992

Salon for Now
June 2–July 31, 1992

Casting Light: Acknowledging the Shadow
September 1–September 27, 1992

*World of Music: The Jack and
Dorinda Schuman Collection*
October 6–November 1, 1992

The Definitive Contemporary American Quilt
and two segments of the *NAMES Project
AIDS Memorial Quilt*
November 7–December 16, 1992 and
December 1–December 16, 1992

1993 |

Fine Arts Faculty Exhibition
　　January 20–February 7, 1993

Artists Who Teach and Jon Aesoph
　　February 23–March 28, 1993

MFA Thesis Exhibition I
　　April 6–April 18, 1993

MFA Thesis Exhibition II
　　April 27–May 8, 1993

*Northwest Artists from the
Permanent Collection*
　　May 25–August 1, 1993

Fine Arts Faculty Exhibition
　　August 31–September 26, 1993

*The Art of Architecture: Works by
Laureates of the Pritzker Architecture Prize*
　　October 5–October 31, 1993

Seriality in 20th Century Prints
　　November 9–December 16, 1993

1994 |

Eikoh Hosoe: META
　　January 11–February 20, 1994

Naive Paintings from the National Gallery of Art
　　March 1–March 27, 1994

MFA Thesis Exhibition
　　April 5–May 7, 1994

Heritage: Women Artists
　　May 24–July 14, 1994

Fine Arts Faculty Exhibition
　　September 6–September 25, 1994

*Tales and Traditions: Storytelling in
Twentieth-Century American Craft*
　　October 4–November 19, 1994

Curator's Choice
　　December 1, 1994–January 22, 1995

1995 |

*Our Land/Ourselves: American Indian
Contemporary Artists*
January 31–March 17, 1995

*The Feddersen Collection of Contemporary
Native American Art*
January 28–February 25, 1995

George Trakas/Catherine Howett–Open Studio
March 27–April 2, 1995

MFA Thesis Exhibition
April 11–May 13, 1995

The Elwood Collection
May 30–July 30, 1995

Clearly Art: Pilchuck's Glass Legacy
September 5–October 15, 1995

Robert Helm, 1981–1993
October 31–December 19, 1995

1996 |

Fine Arts Faculty Exhibition
January 23–February 18, 1996

Northwest Focus: William T. McDermitt and
Rock/Fracture/Chasm: Terry Toedtemeier
February 26–March 31, 1996

MFA Thesis Exhibition
April 9–May 11, 1996

Fine Arts Faculty Exhibition
September 3–September 29, 1996

*A Song to the Creator: Traditional Arts of Native
American Women of the Plateau*
October 14–December 15, 1996

1997 |

Fay Jones: A 20 Year Retrospective
  January 14–February 23, 1997

The Electronic Muse: Artists in the Information Age
  March 4–March 30, 1997

MFA Thesis Exhibition
  April 8–May 10, 1997

A University Collects
  May 19–June 1, 1997

Two in Montana: Deborah Butterfield and John Buck
  June 10–August 3, 1997

Fine Arts Faculty Exhibition
  September 2–September 28, 1997

Petland
  October 7–November 16, 1997

American Photographs, 1970–1980
  December 1, 1997–February 1, 1998

1998 |

Inescapable Histories: Mel Chin
  February 10–March 29, 1998

MFA Thesis Exhibition
  April 7–May 9, 1998

The Jewelry of Ken Cory: Play Disguised
  May 26–July 26, 1998

Gods, Lovers and Heroes: Classical Myths from the WSU Permanent Collection
  May 26–July 26, 1998

Fine Arts Faculty Exhibition
  August 31–September 27, 1998

From the Background to the Foreground: The Photo Backdrop and Cultural Expression
  October 12–November 22, 1998

Books and Pages: Ron Kitaj and Eduardo Paolozzi
  December 7–December 18, 1998

1999 |

Collaborations: William Allan, Robert Hudson, William Wiley
January 12–February 21, 1999

Art as Environ: The Contemporary Installation
March 2–March 28, 1999

MFA Thesis Exhibition
April 5–May 8, 1999

From Benton to Bartlett: Recent Acquisitions
May 26–August 1, 1999

Bearing Witness: Contemporary Works by African American Women Artists Celebrating Book Arts!
October 19–November 24, 1999

Fine Arts Faculty Exhibition
October 26–December 17, 1999

2000 |

At 60: Norman Lundin Landscapes and Still Lifes
January 19–March 26, 2000

MFA Thesis Exhibition
April 4–May 6, 2000

Permanent Collection Documentation Project
June 5–June 30, 2000

The American Vision: A Collection Survey
August 14–October 15, 2000

Morris Graves: Instruments for a New Navigation
September 11–October 15, 2000

Fine Arts Faculty Exhibition
October 23–December 15, 2000

2001 |

The Thread that Binds: Marita Dingus,
Mar Goman, and Joan Schulze
     January 8–February 4, 2001

Large Drawings: Works from the Arkansas Arts
Center Foundation Collection
     February 12–April 1, 2001

MFA Thesis Exhibition
     April 9–May 12, 2001

From the Vault: Work from the Museum of Art
Permanent Collection
     June 11–July 29, 2001

The Raw and the Cooked: A Cabinet of
Curiosities from the Collections of
Washington State University
     September 4–October 14, 2001

Fine Arts Faculty Exhibition
     October 29–December 16, 2001

2002 |

Optical Reaction | The Art of Julian Stanczak:
A Fifty-Year Retrospective
     January 14–February 24, 2002

An Elegant Light: Work from the European
Collection of the Maryhill Museum
     March 4–April 6, 2002

When Two Bulls Fight, The Leg of the
Calf is Broken
     March 4–April 6, 2002

MFA Thesis Exhibition
     April 12–May 11, 2002

Salon for Now...and Again
     June 9–August 3, 2002

Challenge VI- Roots: Insights & Inspirations in
Contemporary Turned Objects
     September 3–October 20, 2002

Pressure Points: Recent Prints from the
Collections of Jordan D. Schnitzer and the
Schnitzer Foundation
     November 1–December 14, 2002

2003 |

*Washington State University Fine Arts
Faculty Exhibition*
    January 17–February 16, 2003

*Extended Connections: Robt. R. Ecker &
Ruben Trejo*
    February 28–April 4, 2003

MFA Thesis Exhibition
    April 11–May 10, 2003

The Changing Shape of Landscape
    June 6–July 26, 2003

*Art in 2 Worlds: The Native American
Fine Art Invitational*
    September 2–October 19, 2003

Richard Weisman's Andy Warhols
    October 22–October 26, 2003

Fine Arts Faculty Exhibition
    October 31–December 13, 2003

2004 |

*3 Degrees of Cool: Works from the Virginia and
Bagley Wright Collection*
    January 6–February 29, 2004

Piranesi: The Grandeur of Ancient Rome
    March 9–April 11, 2004

Afghanistan: Land of Light and Shadow
    March 9–April 11, 2004

MFA Thesis Exhibition
    April 16–May 16, 2004

Richard C. Elliot & Recent Acquisitions
    May 23–July 25, 2004

Jim Dine Sculpture
    August 20–October 17, 2004

Sculpture from the Walla Walla Foundry
    August 20–October 31, 2004

Patrick Siler
    October 25–December 19, 2004

2005 |

Picturing Difference: Gender and Representation in Contemporary Photography
    January 7–February 13, 2005

Focus NW: Joey Kirkpatrick and Flora Mace
    February 22–April 3, 2005

MFA Thesis Exhibition
    April 8–May 8, 2005

Curator's Choices
    May 23–July 24, 2005

Fine Arts Faculty Exhibition
    August 17–September 17, 2005

Roy Lichtenstein Prints 1956–1997
    September 24–December 16, 2005

2006 |

Countdown to Eternity
    January 9–February 12, 2006

Focus NW: Trimpin-Soundworks
    February 17–April 9, 2006

MFA Thesis Exhibition
    April 14–May 7, 2006

Focus NW: Curators Choice
    May 22–July 23, 2006

Focus NW: Francis Ho
    August 28–September 24, 2006

Art & Context: The 1950s and 60s
    September 29–December 15, 2006

2007 |

Video and Photography from Western Bridge
    January 5–February 11, 2007

*Focus NW | Gaylen Hansen:
Three Decades of Painting*
    February 16–April 8, 2007

MFA Thesis Exhibition
    April 13–May 5, 2007

Fine Arts Faculty Exhibition
    August 17–September 22, 2007

A Brief History of Photography
    September 28–December 15, 2007

2008 |

Sherry Markovitz Retrospective
    February 22–April 12, 2008

MFA Thesis Exhibition
    April–May 3, 2008

Curator's Choice
    Summer 2008

Fine Arts Faculty Focus: Sandra Deutchman
    August 28–September 27, 2008

Wrapped in Tradition: The Chihuly Collection of Native American Trade Blankets
    October 3–December 19, 2008

2009 |

Chris Jordan: Running the Numbers
    January 14–April 4, 2009

MFA Thesis Exhibition
    April 10–May 9, 2009

Curator's Choice: Selected Works from the Permanent Collection
    May 18–July 2, 2009

Fine Arts Faculty Exhibition
    August 27–September 26, 2009

This Land is Your Land, This Land is My Land, Issues of Eminent Domain Photography by Don Normark
    October 2–December 19, 2009

2010 |

Pause: Art + Architecture
    January 14–April 3, 2010

MFA Thesis Exhibition
    April 9–May 8, 2010

World of Mateo: Matthew Leiker
    May 18–July 2, 2010

Fine Arts Faculty Focus: Ross Coates
    August 26–September 25, 2010

Contemporary Australian Aboriginal Art, From the Collection of Margaret Levi and Robert Kaplan
    October 1–December 11, 2010

2011 |

Claudia Fitch: Works 1987–2010
    January 13–April 2, 2011

MFA Thesis Exhibition
    April 8–May 7, 2011

Curator's Choice: Works from the Permanent Collection, Image Empire
    May 19–July 1, 2011

Fine Arts Faculty Exhibition
    August 25–September 24, 2011

Jim Olson: Architecture for Art
    September 30–December 10, 2011

2012 |

From the Vault: Recent Acquisitions, Warhol and the Safeco Collection
    January 9–March 31, 2012

MFA Thesis Exhibition
    April 6–May 5, 2012

Curator's Choice: Patrick Siler Mural
    May 17–July 20, 2012

Fine Arts Faculty Focus: Jo Hockenhull
    August 20–September 22, 2012

The Artist's Hand: American Works on Paper 1945–1975
    September 28–December 15, 2012

2013 |

Ceramics From the Kolva-Sullivan Collection
January 8–March 30, 2013

MFA Thesis Exhibition
April 5–May 4, 2013

Curator's Choice Exhibition | Making Faces: Portraits from the Permanent Collection
May 16–July 19, 2013

Fine Arts Faculty Exhibition
August 12–September 14, 2013

Made in U.S.A.: Rosenquist/Ruscha, Prints From the Collections of Jordan D. Schnitzer and His Family Foundation
September 20–December 14, 2013

2014 |

CREATE: Art by Artists Outside the Mainstream
January 23–April 5, 2014

MFA Thesis Exhibition
April 11–May 10, 2014

Curator's Choice: Behind the Scenes
May 20–July 3, 2014

Fine Arts Faculty Focus: Ann Christenson
August 18–September 13, 2014

Roger Shimomura: An American Knockoff
September 19–December 13, 2014

2015 |

Corbis and Vivian Maier: Through the Lens, an American Century
January 12–April 3, 2015

MFA Thesis Exhibition
April 10–May 9, 2015

Curator's Choice: LEGACY
May 19–July 2, 2015

Fine Arts Faculty Exhibition
August 24–September 26, 2015

Jim Dine: A Life in Printmaking
October 2–December 12, 2015

2016 |

Curators' Choices: The Greg Kucera & Larry Yocom Collection
January 14–March 25, 2016

MFA Thesis Exhibition
April 4–May 7, 2016

Curators' Choice: From the Collection, New Acquisitions
May 17–July 1, 2016

Fine Arts Faculty Focus: Chris Watts
August 22–September 17, 2016

Northwest Alternative Comics Exhibition
September 26–December 17, 2016

2017 |

Rick Bartow: Things You Know But Cannot Explain
    January 24–March 11, 2017

MFA Thesis Exhibition
    April 4–May 6, 2017

Points of Interest: Ruth Boden, Kevin Haas, Taiji Miyasaka, and Linda Russo
    May 16–June 30, 2017

Contemporary Women Printmakers
    August 22–November 17, 2017

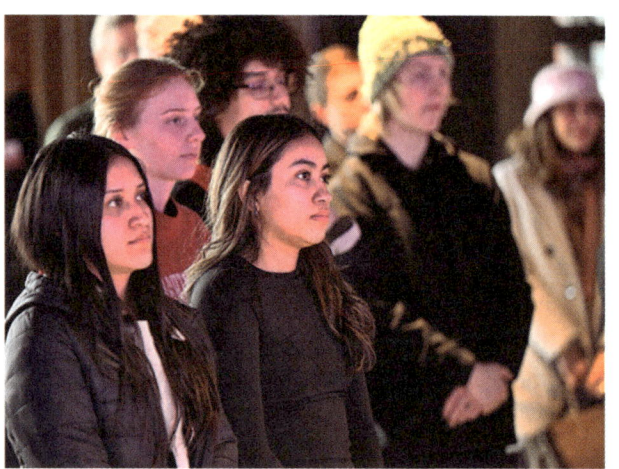

2018 |

Trimpin: Ambiente432
    April 6, 2018

Hearts: Selections from the Jim Dine Collection
    April 6–June 30, 2018

Video from the True Collection
    April 6–October 6, 2018

Jeffry Mitchell: The Death of Buddha
    April 6–August 4, 2018

Marie Watt: Companion Species (Underbelly)
    April 6–September 1, 2018

Person(a): Portraiture, From the Collections of Jordan D. Schnitzer and His Family Foundation
    April 6–August 4, 2018

MFA Thesis Exhibition
    April 3–May 5, 2018

Crow's Shadow: Institute of the Arts at 25
    September 18–December 22, 2018

Memento: Selected Works from the Elwood Collections
    September 18, 2018–August 10, 2019

2019 |

Michael Schultheis: Venn Pirouettes
January 15–June 29, 2019

MFA Thesis Exhibition
April 2–May 4, 2019

Fine Arts Faculty Exhibition Self*ish: Doug Gast, Joe Hedges, and Io Palmer
August 21–October 6, 2019

Kate Gilmore: In Your Way
October 16–December 22, 2018

Social Space: From the Collections of Jordan D. Schnitzer and His Family Foundation
January 15–March 9, 2019

Louise Bourgeois: Ode to Forgetting, From the Collections of Jordan D. Schnitzer and His Family Foundation
May 21–August 10, 2019

Closer to You: Performance Films from On the Boards
May 21–August 10, 2019

Night Stars: The Aiken Collection
July 23, 2019–May 2, 2020

Chiho Aoshima: City Glow
August 20–December 14, 2019

Polly Apfelbaum: Frequently the Woods are Pink, From the Collections of Jordan D. Schnitzer and His Family Foundation
August 27, 2019–March 14, 2020

2020 |

MFA Thesis Exhibition
March 31–May 9, 2020

Etsuko Ichikawa: Broken Poems of Fireflies
May 26, 2020–March 20, 2021

Follow the Sun: The Holland and Orton Collections
May 26, 2020–February 12, 2021

Betty Feves: The Earth Itself
May 26, 2020–February 12, 2021

2021 |

World Without Reason: Goya's Los Disparates
April 6–August 7, 2021

Follow the River: Portraits of the Columbia Plateau
March 9–August 7, 2021

Under the Same Sun and Moon: New Acquisitions from the Collection
March 9–August 7, 2021

MFA Thesis Exhibition
April 6–May 8, 2021

Black Lives Matter Artist Grant Exhibition
September 7–December 18, 2021

Art & Healing: Works by Jim Dine and Corita Kent
May 7–August 7, 2021

Mirror, Mirror: The Prints of Alison Saar From the Collections of Jordan D. Schnitzer and His Family Foundation
September 7, 2021–March 12, 2022

2022 |

Indie Folk: New Art and Sounds from the Pacific Northwest
January 18–May 21, 2022

Keiko Hara: Four Decades of Paintings and Prints
May 24, 2022–June 30, 2023

Our Stories, Our Lives: Irwin Nash Photographs of Yakima Valley Migrant Labor
May 24, 2022–March 11, 2023

MFA Thesis Exhibition
March 29–May 7, 2022

Sky Hopinka: Lore
June 7–August 6, 2022

Juventino Aranda: Esperé Mucho Tiempo Pa Ver
August 23, 2022–March 11, 2023

2023 |

Hostile Terrain 94
January 17–March 11, 2023

What Was Always Yours and Never Lost
May 16–June 30, 2023

MFA Thesis Exhibition
March 28–May 6, 2023

Jeffrey Gibson: They Teach Love, From the Collections of Jordan D. Schnitzer and His Family Foundation
August 22, 2023–March 9, 2024

Here in a Homemade Forest: Common Reading Connections
August 22, 2023–March 2, 2024

2024 |

MFA Thesis Exhibition
March 26–June 29, 2024

Beyond Hope: Kienholz and the Inland Northwest
March 26–June 29, 2024

Subversive Intent: Selections from the Collection
March 26–June 29, 2024

Your Collection: Celebrating 50 Years
August 20–December 13, 2024

The Art of Food, From the Collections of Jordan D. Schnitzer and His Family Foundation
August 20, 2024–March 8, 2025

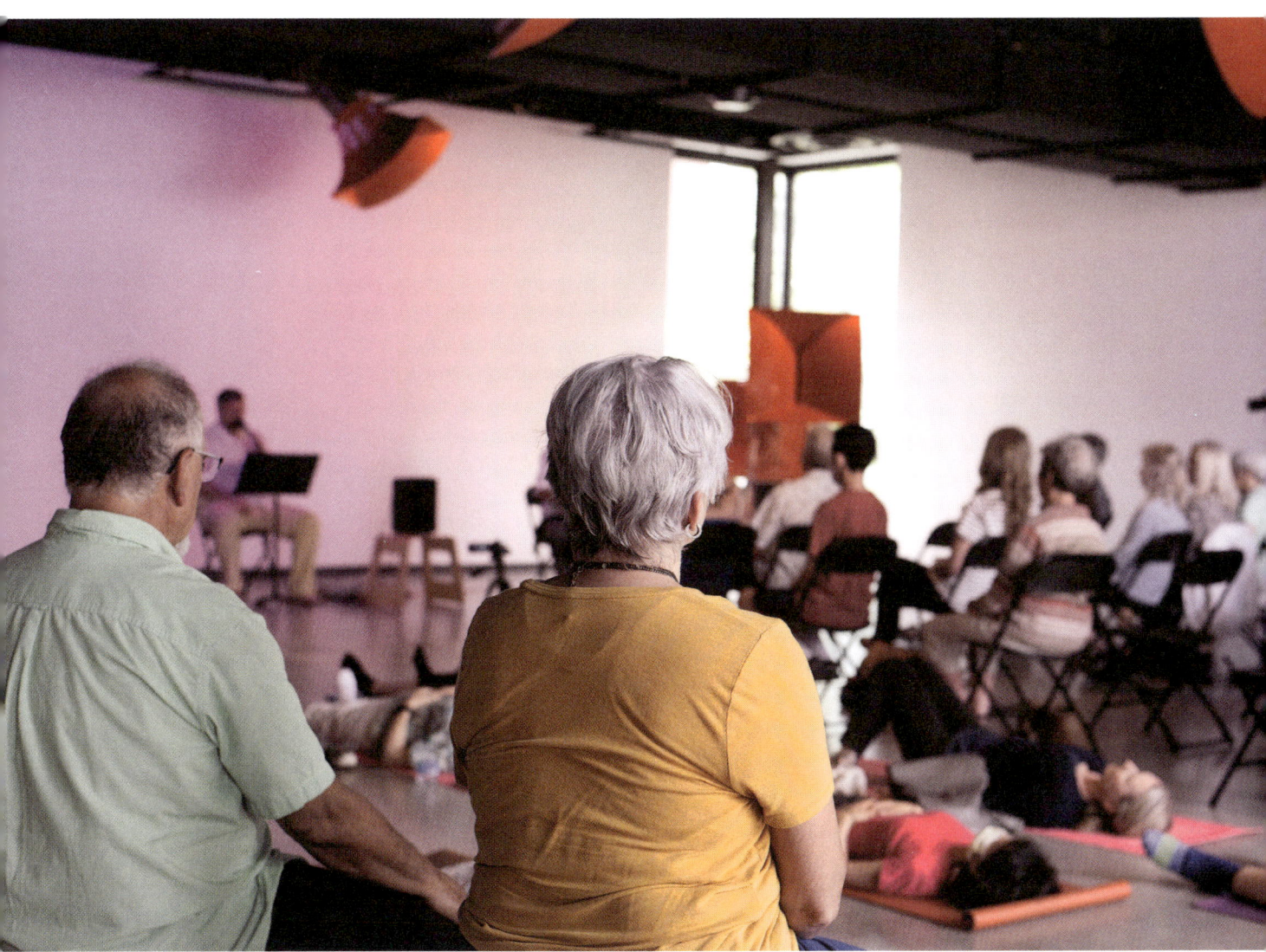

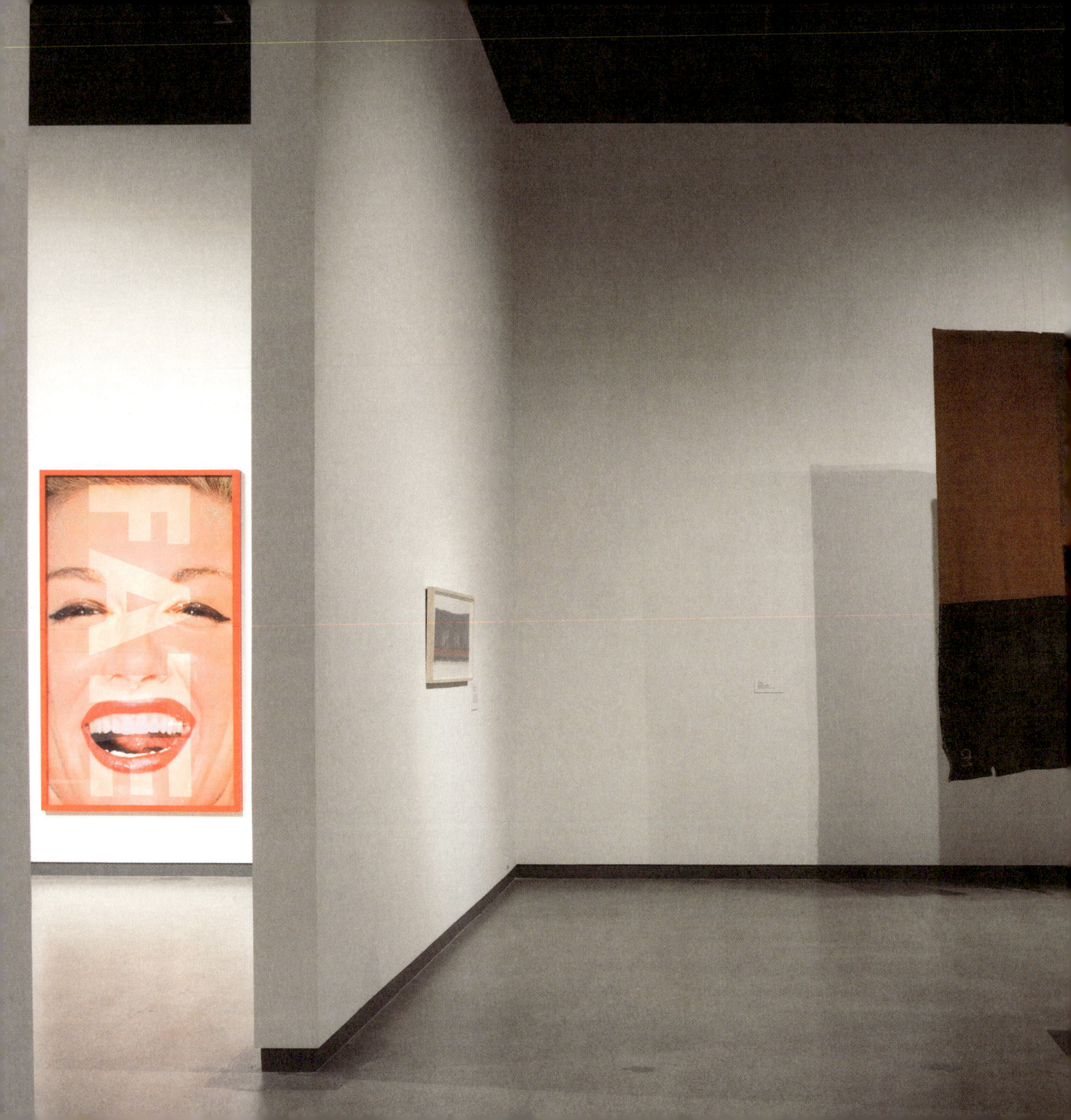

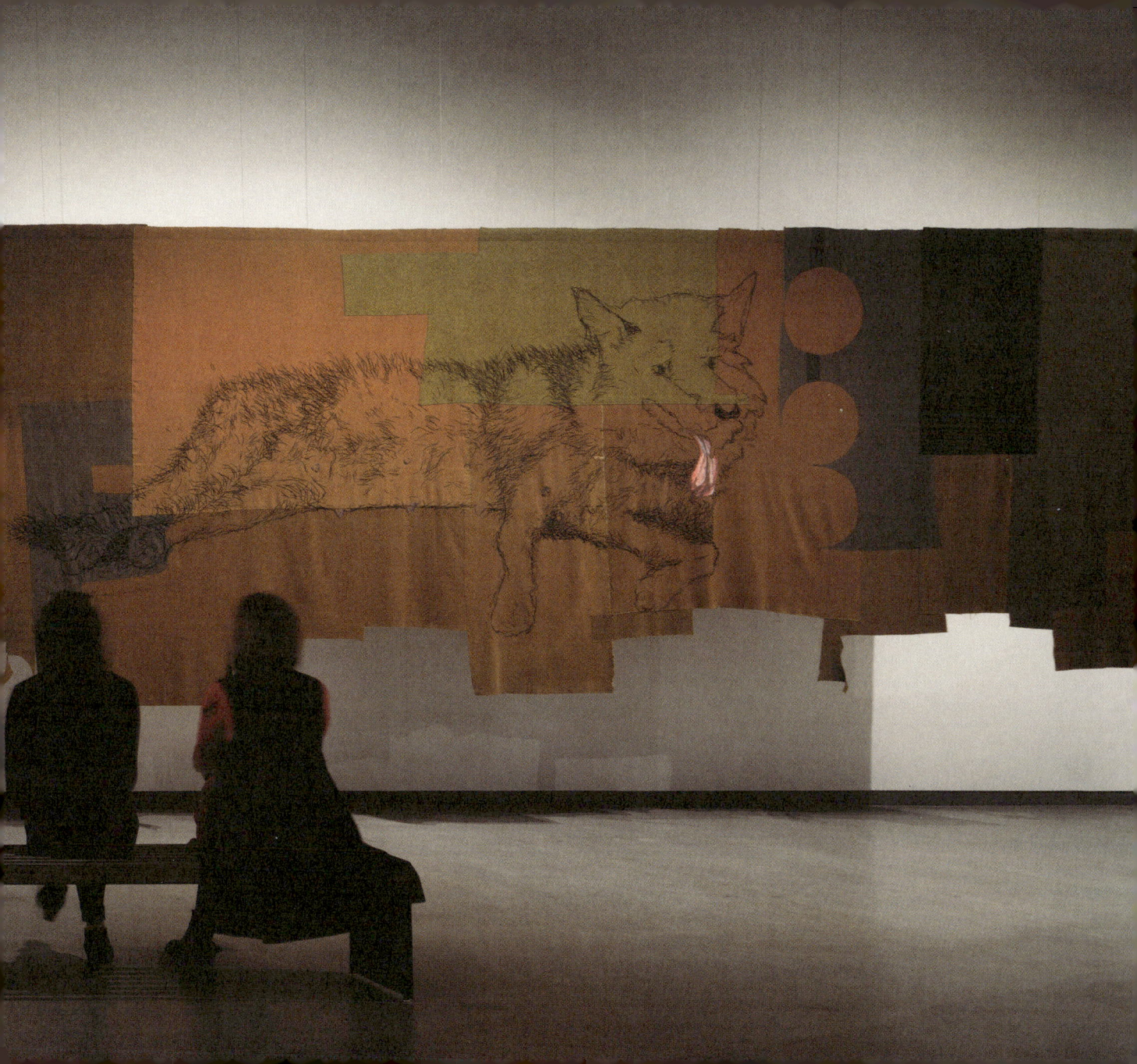

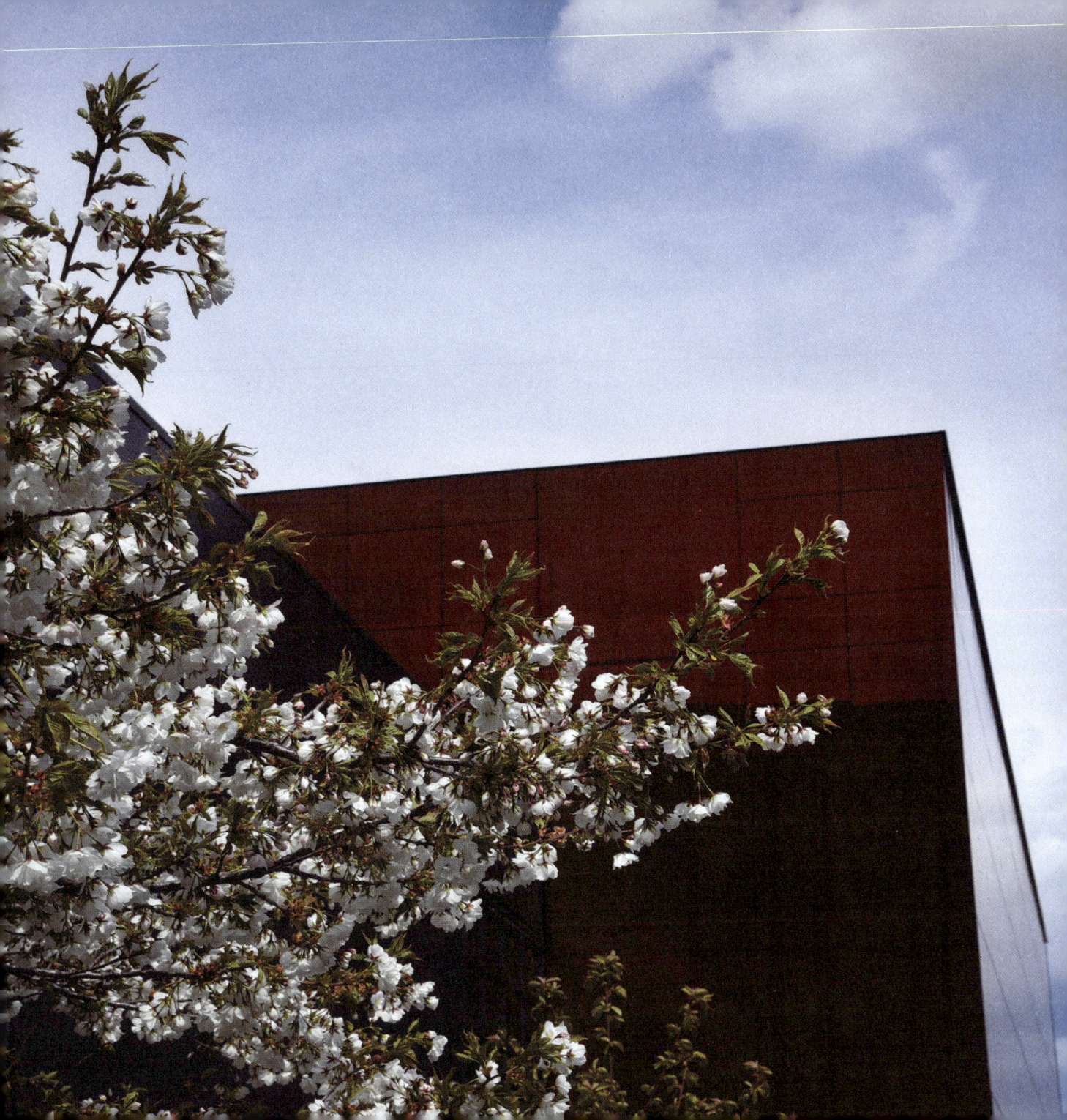

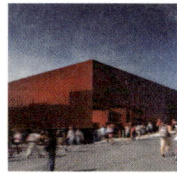

Page 66–67
Photo: @NicLehoux

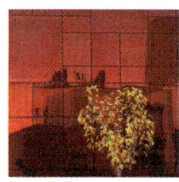

Page 98–99
Photo: WSU Photo Services

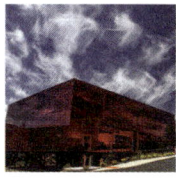

Page 119
Photo: WSU Photo Services

facing page | Double Japanese Yoshino cherry trees bloom outside the Jordan Schnitzer Museum of Art WSU. Koichiro Iwasaki donated twenty-six trees "to symbolize a permanent and true friendship between WSU and Japan," on March 14, 2002

Photo: Debby Stinson

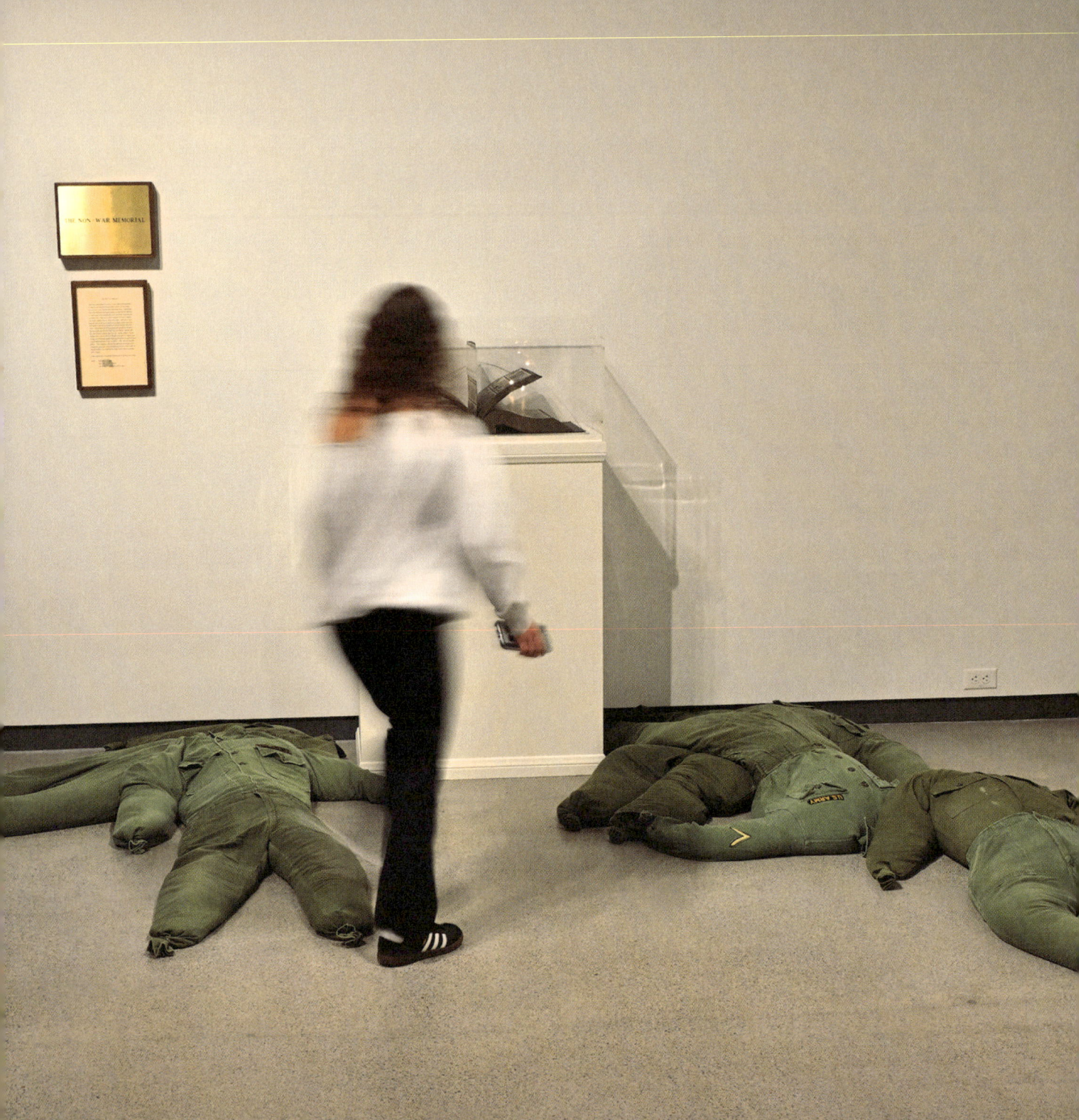

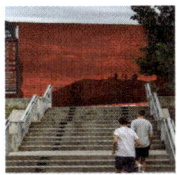

Page 140
Photo: Kris Faulkner,
courtesy of
Design West Architects

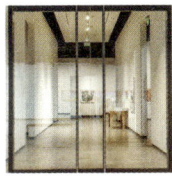

Page 140
Photo: Kris Faulkner,
courtesy of
Design West Architects

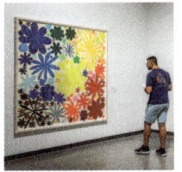

Page 140
Photo: Kris Faulkner,
courtesy of
Design West Architects

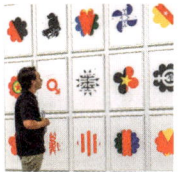

Page 140
Photo: Kris Faulkner,
courtesy of
Design West Architects

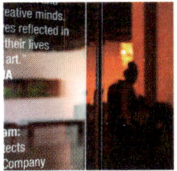

Page 140
Photo: Kris Faulkner,
courtesy of
Design West Architects

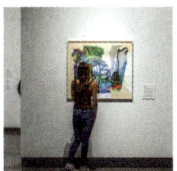

Page 140
Photo: Kris Faulkner,
courtesy of
Design West Architects

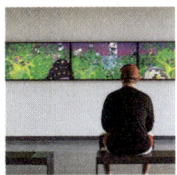

Page 140
Photo: Kris Faulkner,
courtesy of
Design West Architects

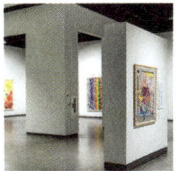

Page 140
Photo: Kris Faulkner,
courtesy of
Design West Architects

facing page | A visitor with *Beyond Hope: Kienholz and the Inland Northwest*, 2024
Photo: WSU Photo Services

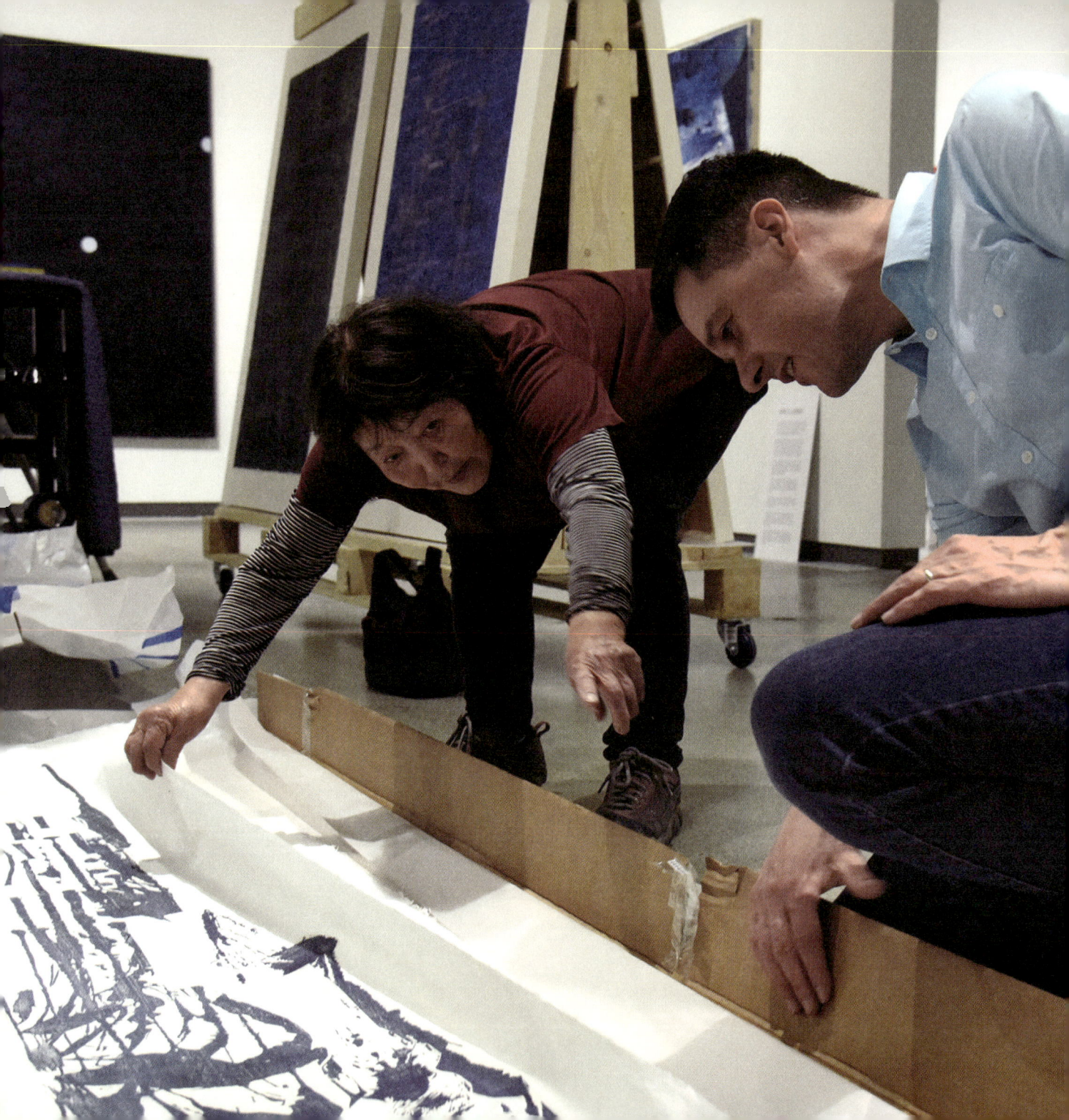

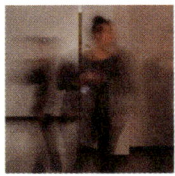

Page 144
Photo: @NicLehoux

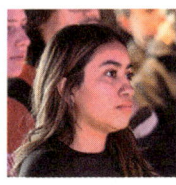

Page 180
Photo: WSU Photo Services

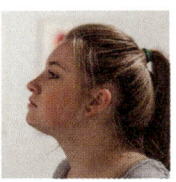

Page 145
Photo: Kris Faulkner,
courtesy of
Design West Architects

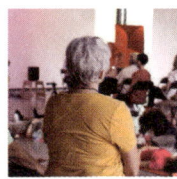

Page 183
Photo: Kristin Becker

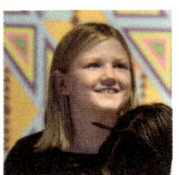

Page 145
Photo: Kristin Becker

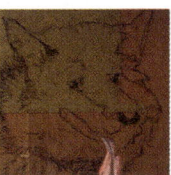

Page 184–185
Photo: @NicLehoux

facing page | Artist Keiko Hara and Ryan Hardesty
during the installation of *Keiko Hara: Four Decades
of Paintings and Prints*, 2022

Photo: Kristin Becker

following page | Photo: Kris Faulkner, courtesy of
Design West Architects, 2019

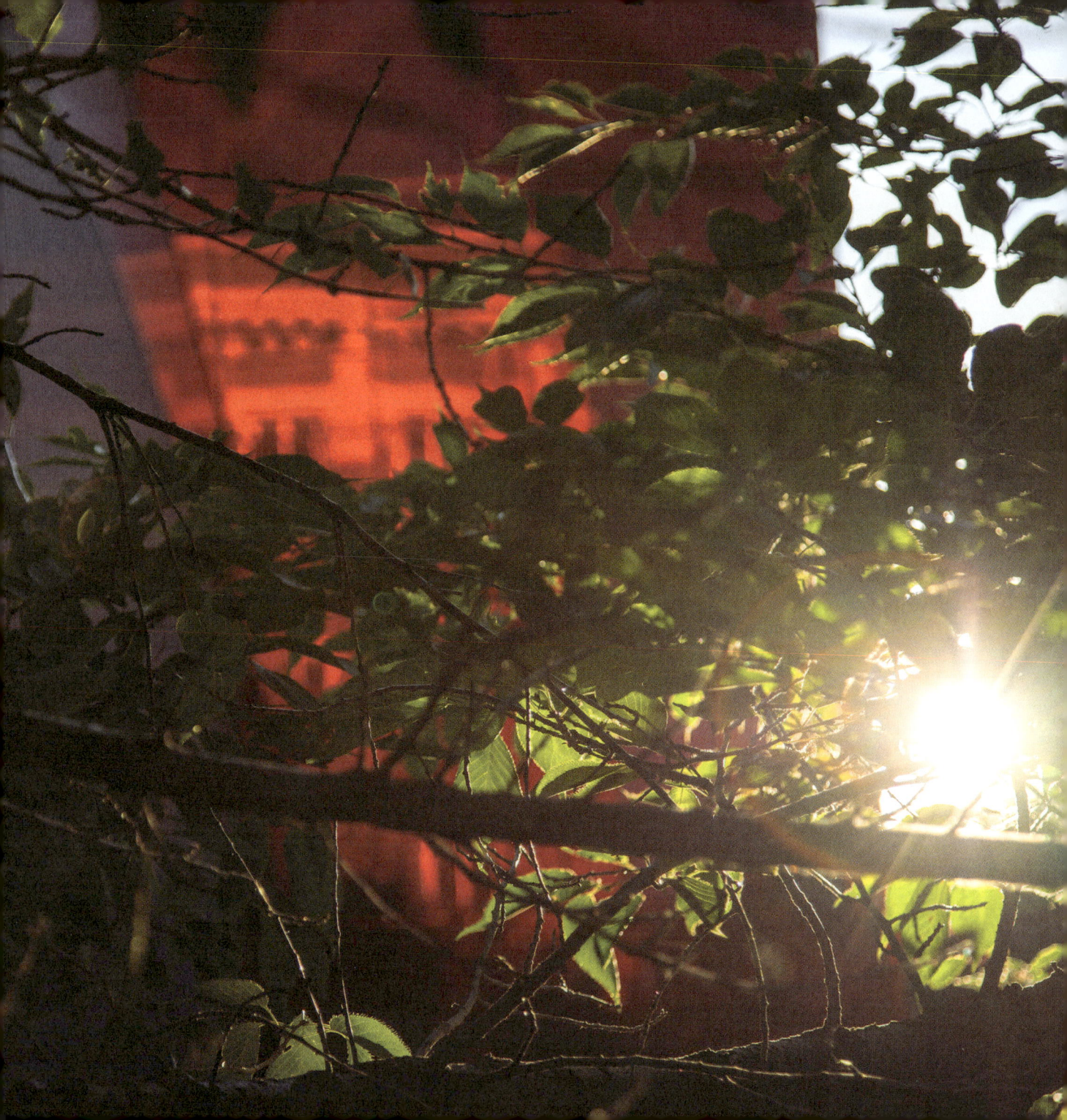